TEN
PRAYERS
THAT
CHANGED
the WORLD

TEN PRAYERS THAT CHANGED *the* WORLD

Extraordinary Stories *of* Faith
That Shaped *the* Course *of* History

JEAN-PIERRE ISBOUTS

NATIONAL GEOGRAPHIC

Washington, D.C.

Published by National Geographic Partners, LLC

Library of Congress Cataloging-in-Publication Data
Names: Isbouts, Jean-Pierre.
Title: Ten prayers that changed the world : extraordinary stories of faith
    that shaped the course of history / Jean-Pierre Isbouts.
Description: 1st [edition]. | Washington, DC : National Geographic Books,
    2016. | Includes bibliographical references and index.
Identifiers: LCCN 2015033586 | ISBN 9781426216442 (hardcover : alk. paper)
Subjects: LCSH: Prayers. | Prayers--History. | History--Religious
    aspects--Christianity. | History--Religious aspects.
Classification: LCC BV245 .I83 2016 | DDC 242/.8--dc23
LC record available at http://lccn.loc.gov/2015033586

Since 1888, the National Geographic Society has funded more than 12,000 research, exploration, and preservation projects around the world. National Geographic Partners distributes a portion of the funds it receives from your purchase to National Geographic Society to support programs including the conservation of animals and their habitats.

National Geographic Partners, LLC
1145 17th Street NW
Washington, DC 20036-4688 USA

Become a member of National Geographic and activate your benefits today at natgeo.com/jointoday.

For information about special discounts for bulk purchases, please contact National Geographic Books Special Sales: ngspecsales@ngs.org

For rights or permissions inquiries, please contact National Geographic Books Subsidiary Rights: ngbookrights@ngs.org

Interior design: Melissa Farris/Nicole Miller

Printed in the United States of America

16/QGF-CML/1

To Cathie,
my muse, my strongest critic,
and my best friend

CONTENTS

AUTHOR'S NOTE

Although I have dramatized the following ten stories to some extent, the dialogue is based on historical sources that are documented at the back of this book. At the end of each chapter I also examine the story from the critical perspective of a historian, to see what verifiable impact each prayer or "whisper from God" had on the course of history.

Jerusalem is holy to three of the world's great religions: Judaism, Christianity, and Islam.

INTRODUCTION

Is there someone in heaven who governs what happens on Earth? Since the dawn of time, men and women have asked this simple but fairly fundamental question. And if the answer is yes, then the next question is, What is this divine presence like? Does it take an active interest in human affairs? Does it even *speak* to us?

In prehistoric times, this was not a matter of idle speculation. A typical community lived or died by the outcome of its harvest, the fall of rain, or the health and fertility of its herd. That is why the earliest gods were all creatures of agriculture: Baal, the lord of rain and dew; Enki, the god of freshwater; Inanna, the goddess of fertility and love. People thought that when the rains stopped and the land lay dry, the reason was that Inanna, later known as Ishtar, had had a marital spat with her husband, Baal, and refused to share his bed. This belief, which originated among the irrigated fields of Mesopotamia, would continue for more than a thousand years, well into the time of ancient Israel. For example, many Hebrew farmers would first worship Yahweh and then steal away to the shrines of Ishtar and Baal lest some harm come to their crops.

But is it true that the Divine truly takes an active interest in humankind? To this day, it continues to be an important question. Hebrew Scripture (what Christians call the "Old Testament") has a clear answer on the subject:

All of the Torah, the Five Books of Moses, is predicated on the belief that God is actively engaged with his people, for he rescued them from the clutches of Pharaoh and led them to the safety of the Promised Land.

It wasn't until some two and a half millennia later, during the period we now call the Enlightenment, that many thinkers—including Thomas Jefferson, among others—began to question the idea that God was interested in life on Earth. Why would he do so, they asked, if he gave us free will? Would it not be more plausible to think that while God may have created the heavens and the Earth, he would rather leave us to our own devices to figure out how to live a moral life on our own accord? How else, they argued, could one explain the existence of war, pestilence, drought, and famine? Would a merciful God deliberately inflict such horrors on his own creation?

Of course, the philosophers of the Enlightenment had a special motive for arriving at such ideas. Many of them had witnessed the devastation wrought by the Thirty Years' War, which left almost a third of Europe in ruins. More to the point, the motive for this terrible war was Christianity itself: the religious conflict between Catholic and Protestant states. How was it possible, philosophers such as Voltaire asked, that such death and destruction could be sown in the name of Christ, the Prince of Peace?

In our modern day, the question is no less pertinent than it was then. Although some 70 percent of Americans identify themselves as Christians, that number is now far lower in Europe, where two world wars caused the death of more than 40 million people. Is it still possible, in the face of such a staggering toll, to believe in the grace of a divine agency? Is it still possible to believe in a merciful God when violent extremists such as ISIS and Boko Haram delight in decapitating innocent people for the glory of his name? Have we progressed at all from the days of the Crusades, or the Thirty Years' War?

This book is in some ways an effort to respond to that question. For all of its technological prowess, our world is as volatile as it was at any time in the past, as recent global events have shown, and so the question of what role spirituality can still play in our lives is no less urgent today. What I hope to illustrate with the ten short stories that make up this book is that God, whomever we hold that to be, still has one channel, one powerful conduit with which to intervene in our lives: *ourselves*.

The Greek philosopher Plato once said that each of us, regardless of race, speech, or social status, carries a spark of the Divine—a beacon through which God can speak to us and we can speak to him. Plato formulated this idea almost four centuries before anyone would ever hear of Jesus, but in some ways, he articulated something that the rabbi from Nazareth would continue and develop further: the idea that God does not dwell in the clouds or on a heavenly throne but in ourselves. All we need to figure out is the right bandwidth by which to reach him. Some call that spirituality; others call it prayer.

I think of it as whispers of God—whispers that have an incredible power to stir our mind, urge us to action, and make us do things we didn't think we were capable of. We sometimes refer to such moments as "flashes of inspiration," a word rooted in the Latin *inspirare*, which means "breathing into" someone. Literally, it means that someone whispered in our ear. The Greeks thought that such whispers came from their gods, such as Apollo, Athena, or the Muses. In Hebrew Scripture, the prophets call it the voice of God. Christians believe such moments come from the Holy Spirit.

Whatever we call such whispers, what matters is that they can lift us from our material consciousness into the limitless domain of the spiritual—into *spirituality*. What does that term mean, exactly? No one has ever come up with a good definition, but what we do know is that spirituality is the one thing that Jews, Christians and Muslims, Hindus and Buddhists, Native Americans and Aboriginals, Sufis and Sikhs, Baha'is and Shintoists, have in common. So clearly these people must be on to something.

My premise in writing this book is to see to what extent these prayers, these spiritual conversations with the Divine, helped shape the course of history in a positive way. That's how I arrived at the ten stories in this book.

At this point I should add that I'm not a priest or a theologian. I'm a historian. What really interests me is how some perfectly ordinary men and women can sometimes do extraordinary things simply by virtue of their inspiration, their strength, and their iron determination. In historical scholarship, that's a pretty novel way of looking at things. We've always thought that history is shaped by kings and queens, by powerful leaders and rulers, individuals set far above our station. But that's not always true.

Indeed, the people you are about to meet come from all walks of life: a shepherd and a rabbi; a soldier and a general; a peasant girl and a lawyer. Some of the stories are factually true; others may have the whiff of legend. Some prayers, such as the prayer for Bastogne, may have had an immediate impact on history; others, such as the prayer of St. Francis, were more subtle and took decades to make their influence felt. What they do have in common is that they all changed the world in a significant way, purely on the strength of a spiritual experience.

WHAT DO YOU THINK OF WHEN you hear the word *history*? You think of textbooks in school or articles in a scholarly journal. But that's not how history was passed on in centuries past. For thousands of years, it was relayed in the form of *stories*—stories told around a campfire by the elders of the tribe while the young watched and listened, committing the stories to memory—ready for the day when they too would pass it on to their children and grandchildren. Modern neuroscience has revealed why they did that; why the collective wisdom of a clan, a tribe, or a nation was handed down in the form of epics, of heroic stories. The reason is that unlike a textbook, a story appeals to two parts of our brain: our cognitive faculties and our emotional intelligence.

In other words, when we listen to a story, we become emotionally invested. We begin to identify with the characters. We root for them as they embark on their journey, stay with them through their trials, and rejoice with them when they triumph in the end. That is why the elders of Mesopotamia and Egypt, of Greece and Rome, of medieval France and the pre-Columbian societies of the Americas couched the wisdom of their native cultures in narrative form: so that their children would remember and pass them on.

It therefore seems entirely appropriate that in writing this book, I should respect that tradition. That is why the ten stories that follow are anchored in one special moment from the character's life. Although I have dramatized the stories to some extent, as any storyteller would, the action and dialogue are inspired by historical sources, which I detail at the back of this book. At the end of each story, I switch hats and examine the story from the critical perspective of a historian and see what verifiable impact the story had on the course of history.

So let us gather around the campfire and listen to the stories of these remarkable women and men. Perhaps it will help us to better understand why they set out to make their mark, inspired by the whispers of a divine mind, and shaped the course of history in ways that resonate with us today.

JEAN-PIERRE ISBOUTS

Caravaggio painted this portrait of Abraham as he is about to sacrifice his son Isaac.

CHAPTER 1

ABRAHAM'S PLEA

Do not lay your hand
on the boy or do anything to him;
for now I know that you fear God,
since you have not withheld your son,
your only son, from me.

HIGHLANDS OF RUSHALIMUM,
Canaan
CA 1950 B.C.E.

At first he isn't quite sure. But then, by the first light of dawn, he recognizes the looming shape and knows it's the place that they've been seeking. It isn't a particularly tall mountain as hills go in this part of the country. That's probably why he didn't see it until they had traveled for three days, and he was beginning to think he was lost. But, no, there it is, this hill that the locals call Mount Moriah, washed by the soft orange light of the rising sun. He rubs his eyes and sits up. Around him, the ground is still covered by a cocoon of mist, while the air carries the scent of pine resin and dew.

It looks familiar, this mound. Perhaps he's passed it before, during his first journey across this mountain ridge, now so many decades ago. He was much younger then, as was his wife; and the train of servants and flock had been a fraction of the wealth he has accumulated since. Today he is the owner of herds too numerous to count, the lord of a sprawling camp as large as a city, the leader of a major tribe. He is a wealthy man, it is true—a man of condition, of consequence. And yet he would gladly give it up, all of it, if only he does not have to climb the hill in the distance.

He sighs and picks up the bundle of wood, swinging it on his back with more force than necessary. The sharp points of the branches cut into his flesh, but he accepts the pain without demur.

He turns to look for his son but the boy is already up, his eyes full of excitement over this unexpected adventure.

He nods and begins the ascent as his son runs ahead of him. There is a path that, with luck, should take them close to the summit before midday. But it is hard going; his breath is labored, and he must will his old legs to continue as the dust fills his nostrils and the sweat runs full on his brow. He briefly thinks of the donkey and the comfort of the saddle that he's left behind with his servants down in the valley, but he forces it from his mind. What he is about to do will bear no witness, will not suffer the sight of human eyes, for it is too terrible to contemplate.

"Father?" says the boy walking slightly ahead of him.

"I am here, my son."

The boy stops and turns. "The fire and the wood are here," he says, "but where is the lamb for a burnt offering?" And then he tilts his head and smiles, as if amused by his old father's dimwittedness.

"God himself will provide the lamb for a burnt offering, my son," he replies, and looks at the boy more closely. *How beautiful he is,* he thinks. *How young and handsome.*

HE NEVER WANTED ANY OF THIS. He never dreamed of being a great tribal lord. His father, Terah, was a merchant. What could he possibly expect from life? He was not like the young men he'd known back in Ur, boys who belonged to noble families, the old aristocracy that traced its lineage back to the kings before the Sumerian Flood. He never had the benefit of tutors, sages, and astrologers who drilled the young lords about Ur's great history, how it had risen as the first great civilization on Earth, fed by the miracle of irrigation when much of Mesopotamia was still desert and shrub. Or how the men from Sumer were the first to develop a written script. The first to invent the wheel to propel a wagon. The first to create brick to build a towering ziggurat and draft laws to rule justly over the people.

What he did know is what his father had taught him: that for centuries, traders had come from lands far beyond the Euphrates to trade their obsidian, copper, and carnelian for the harvest bounty of Sumer's fields. How this wealth had made the city strong and rich and how it had spawned a class of men that the world had never seen before: scientists, engineers, astronomers, artists, builders.

And then, inevitably, his father would turn to tales of Sumer's gods. He still remembered the story of Tiamat, the ocean goddess whose evil schemes had forced the other gods to rally around a young deity named Marduk. They begged Marduk to get rid of her, and Marduk complied. Sometimes, in his dreams, Abram still recited the lilting verses of the great creation epic, the story of Marduk creating the Earth and the heavens:

> *He constructed stations for the great gods,*
> *Fixing their astral likeness as constellations.*
> *The Moon he caused to shine, the night (to him) entrusting.*
> *He appointed him a creature of the night to signify the days:*
> *Thou shalt have luminous horns to signify six days.*

And then, on the seventh day, Marduk created something new: a savage, a beast walking on two legs. How should he call this creature? *"Man* shall be his name," the epic said, "and he shall be charged with the service of the gods."

To service the gods: That's what his father drilled into him and his brothers, Nahor and Haran. Whatever happened to humanity, Terah said, was the will of the gods. That's why the people should serve them and obey them in all that they did.

And then, one day, his brother Haran died. The family was devastated. They grieved not only for Haran but also for his young family, including his newborn son, Lot. Terah, too, wept over his son's grave, but he never questioned the reason for his passing. It was the will of the gods, and nothing more needed to be said.

But worse was to come. They lived in dangerous and unsettled times. The territory of Ur was slowly being torn asunder by the pressure of invaders, particularly the powerful forces of Amorite tribes. Some of the traders who had visited Amorite territory told bloodcurdling tales of violence and chaos, of untended fields and streets running with blood. It was whispered that the Amorites never buried their dead, leaving them to serve as carrion. But Terah was phlegmatic. It was all the will of the gods, he said, even if the caravan trade that had sustained Ur's *tamkaru,* its merchant class, for so long was now draining away.

In the end, they faced the inevitable. With fewer caravans making the long trek along the Euphrates, Ur's great prosperity was no more. Many people in the city had already left. Some had moved to the city of Larsa, Ur's principal rival. Others had settled in a new and rapidly growing city farther north, known as Babylon.

Terah tried to hold out as long as possible. He had large landholdings around the city, the yields of which he used to barter with traders from regions as far as Sippar, Ashur, and Mari. But when the news arrived that Amorite forces were less than a hundred leagues from the city itself, he knew the time had come. By the time the Amorite army broke through the last Sumerian defensive line, Terah and his family were already far to the north. They had fled with the few possessions that their donkeys and their servants could carry, heading northeast toward Harran.

He was called Abram then, the oldest of Terah's sons, and married to a lovely young woman named Sarai. They were very much in love, Sarai and he, even though he already knew that she was probably barren and could not give him a son and heir. To compensate for that fact, Terah had given him custody over Lot, the young son of his deceased brother, Haran. Together with Nahor and his wife, Milcah, accompanied by their servants and retainers, the family had slogged north along the Euphrates River, pausing only to rest and offer sacrifice to Terah's ancestral gods.

The choice for Harran made sense. A bustling trade center in the region of Aram, Harran was one of the last great outposts of the Sumerian commonwealth, and Terah knew he could count on the hospitality of merchants whom he had known and traded with for most of his life. But when they finally arrived in the city, Terah was utterly exhausted. The loss of his property, his lands, and his trading network had left him a mere shadow of his former self. Though Abram and Nahor were able to secure good land on which to pitch their tents and graze their donkeys, Terah slowly withdrew into himself. Most of the time he sat at the opening of his tent, staring hollow-eyed toward the horizon, ignoring the plates of food that Sarai put in front of him. One night he went into his tent, lay down on his roll, and never rose again—a broken man, left with nothing but the memory of his estates in Ur.

That's when he, Abram, realized that Terah's gods didn't particularly care for humans. For these gods, people were mere playthings, pawns to be moved and toppled on a chessboard, simply as a source of amusement.

In the meantime, he had other things to worry about. With the death of his father, the mantle of leadership had passed to him. What should they do? Stay in Harran? Trade was out of the question. They no longer had the capital to take equity in the trade caravans that came and went, even if they knew anything about the markets of Aram, which they did not. Agriculture was not an option either. Terah had always relied on his tenants to seed the barley and wheat on his irrigated fields. Besides, whatever agricultural experience they might have had was of no use on Harran's dry and sandy topsoil, good only for dry farming.

What remained was animal husbandry. There was, he knew, always a need for milk, meat, wool, and the hides of goats and sheep, no matter where one went. Sarai's handmaidens had never milked a goat before, but they could learn.

And so the family of Terah became pastoralists. As the months passed and the herd grew, they began to look for new grazing fields beyond Harran, moving along the River Balikh to the fields of Hanhum, or westward toward Urshum, Emar, and Carchemish.

In time, they settled into their new life and were content. Though Sarai was still unable to bear children, Nahor's wife was blessed with many sons, beginning with Uz. He was followed by Buz, Kemuel, Chesed, Hazo, Pildash, and, finally, the twins, Jidlaph and Bethuel. The camp was now filled with the cries and laughter of small children darting between the taut ropes of the tents or hiding among the soft wool of the sheep. Sarai was happy for her sister-in-law, but sometimes, by the fading light of the sun, Abram could see the pain in her eyes, the deep yearning for her body to bring forth life as well.

THE ENCOUNTER WITH GOD took place shortly after dawn. Abram was standing on high ground, watching his flocks drink from a stream in the valley below, when he heard the voice and felt the presence. From one moment to the next, the birdsong stopped and the wind in the trees died away. He felt the hairs stand up on the back of his neck. It was as if he had entered a space without air or sound, sucked dry by a power far beyond his comprehension.

And then God spoke. He called Abram and said, "Go now from your country and your kindred and your father's house to the land that I will show you."

He still remembers his first reaction, the sense of shock and dismay, the *panic* at the thought of being uprooted again, he and Sarai and the rest of the family, just when they had made a new home for themselves.

But God sensed his fear. "I will make of you a great nation," he explained, "and I will bless you, and make your name great, so that you will be a blessing."

Even now, looking back, Abram remembers that moment as he stood, mute and dumb, on the top of the hill while a hundred questions ran through his mind. *Why? Why me? What is it that this God expects of me, a lowly shepherd with a barren wife? How could I possibly become the head of a great nation? I don't even have a son.*

But that's not how Terah had raised him. One never questioned the will of the Divine, his father had taught. And so Abram didn't.

By the time he made his way back to the mud-brick homes they'd built to weather the winter season, he'd made up his mind and told his beloved, his Sarai. And Sarai, bless her, didn't argue. She merely asked the most basic, most logical question, as women invariably can: *But who is this God you intend to follow?*

They spent the rest of the evening and most of the night debating the matter. Was it Marduk? Or Anu, the god of creation? Or Enlil, who ruled over all that moved across the Earth? Or was it Enlil's son Nanna, the moon god, for whom the priests of Ur had once built a huge ziggurat in the center of the city?

No, it was none of these gods; he was sure of that.

Why not?

Because in Abram's mind, ancestral gods would never talk to humans like that. They would never bother with giving them any promises, for they didn't care what humans did. Who'd ever heard of a Sumerian or Akkadian god telling a man he would become a great leader? It was too absurd for words. The gods they had been taught to worship were concerned only with themselves, with their pleasures and intrigues.

No, this God was different; he had known that from the start. He had not seen God, but he had *sensed* him, had felt his presence so acutely as if God had been standing right in front of him, though he only heard his voice. This was a true God, a God wholly beholden to his Creation, and the well-being of the men and women who dwelt in it.

Sarai was satisfied. She'd always trusted her husband, and as she listened to his words, she could almost feel the power of the Divine that had spoken to him. When they shared the news with young Lot, their adopted son, he was excited beyond words, perhaps at the opportunity to get away from the boredom of tending sheep in Harran.

But Nahor felt differently, as Abram had feared all along. Nahor and Milcah had built a new life for themselves. They had young children to take care of and plenty of livestock that filled the pens around their home.

Life was good in Harran. Why should they abandon all that for an uncertain future, in a land unknown? After all, Nahor said, it was *you*, Abram, whom this mysterious God had talked to, not to him.

Abram accepted his decision, though there were tears in his eyes when he embraced his brother. He was the only blood relation he had left. It pained him to depart from him.

Soon after, they split up the herd, packed their donkeys, and embarked on their journey to a land that God would show him.

How MANY YEARS HAVE PASSED since then? He tries to remember, but his memory fails him. He does recall that for weeks they traveled south, along the great caravan route that led to Pelusium and the borders of Egypt, until they entered a country of stark hills and dry brush known as Canaan. At Shechem, in a holy place marked by an oak tree, this new God appeared to him once again. To this day he could recite, word for word, what God told him that day: "To your offspring I will give this land."

The words stirred his heart. They gave him that sense of purpose that he had yearned for since they had left Ur. *To your offspring I will give this land.* Here, in the land called Canaan, the great nation that God had spoken about would be built. Here, they would live and prosper and become a beacon to the world.

But things did not turn out the way he had hoped. First, his flocks struggled to find any edible shrub in these highlands, lashed by sun during the day and cold by night. Not that there wasn't any good land in Canaan. There was plenty of it down in the valleys, vast pastures rich with grass and stalks of grain. Sometimes he and his herd came so close he could almost touch them.

But those were Canaanite lands. Those fields and wells were defended by Canaanite militia, armed to the teeth and deeply hostile to nomads and their thirsty flocks. Abram and his retinue, they didn't have any arms to defend themselves other than the odd knife or spear. The idea of having to fight for land had never occurred to him, which meant that against these natives, he was essentially powerless.

To make matters worse, a famine spread across the land. Crops withered, wells ran dry, and dust covered the fields. Abram and Sarai had no choice but to follow the other nomads on the long coastal road to Egypt where, it was said, there was water aplenty. It broke his heart to leave Canaan, the Promised Land, before they even had a chance to possess it. Was this all part of God's plan? To what purpose?

It confused and troubled him, this sudden turn of events. He was supposed to be the leader of his clan, the man to whom everyone looked for guidance, but he felt himself rudderless, lost, swept up in the flotsam of refugees streaming toward Egypt's borders. And then his confusion turned to *fear*—not fear for his people, but for himself. As soon as they crossed the frontier, he noticed how the local officials made eyes at Sarai, with her flawless vanilla skin, her bright emerald eyes, and her long brown hair flecked with gold. Who is this beautiful woman, they asked him. Where did she come from? Pharaoh, their king, was known to favor beautiful women. Perhaps she should be taken to Pharaoh's court. Did he, Abram, have any objection? They certainly hoped that he did not.

Abram had always feared that something like this could happen. So as they were about to enter Egypt he told Sarai, "Say you are my sister, so that it may go well with me because of you, and that my life may be spared on your account." Technically it was not a lie; Sarai was his half sister as well as his spouse, not uncommon in Mesopotamia. But she was also married to him; *that* bit of information he withheld from the Egyptians. And so, within days, Sarai found herself in the harem at Ankh-Tawy, the king's capital near Saqqara, sharing the luxury of his palace with other exotic beauties.

Why would he, Abram, do such a thing? Why had he allowed his own wife to become a concubine? The answer was simple: He was a coward. He wanted to save his own skin. The thought plunged him into despair. He felt ashamed—not just because his wife now shared Pharaoh's bed, but because he had consented to the arrangement, even encouraged it.

Was this the behavior of a man destined to become "a great nation"? Was this the sort of thing a man would do to become a blessing of humanity? He had searched his soul for answers, wracked his mind for the reason that he had done something so shameful, but all he found was silence. Silence, too, from the God that had brought him to Canaan. Had he forfeited God's trust?

It got worse when Pharaoh began to deliver all sorts of "gifts" as a token of his boundless gratitude. Clearly Sarai must have pleased him greatly. Every slave, oxen, donkey, or sheep brought to his tent merely served to deepen his self-loathing. Though he was now a rich man and getting richer by the minute, there was nothing he wanted more than to hold his beloved wife in his arms and to return to their adopted home, to Canaan.

AND THEN ABRAM DID SOMETHING that he had never done before in his life: He prayed to God. He didn't know the proper form, how one prayed to an unseen power, unlike the deities in Mesopotamia whose idols were shaped just like human beings. But at times he thought he felt God's presence, and when that happened, he poured his heart out. He prayed to God for forgiveness. He prayed to God for guidance. And he prayed that God save his wife, his beloved Sarai.

And God heard him.

Great plagues began to affect Pharaoh and his house, including his wives, his children, and his retinue of counselors, servants, and slaves. The king promptly ordered an investigation, and so it was discovered that Sarai was a married woman, after all. Pharaoh rose in anger. He ordered his soldiers to summon Abram forthwith.

"What is this you have done to me?" he roared as Abram was ushered into the throne room. "Why did you not tell me that she was your wife?"

Abram was silent, his eyes downcast. Now that his deceit was exposed, he only wished for the king to be merciful toward Sarai. As for him, well, Pharaoh could do as he pleased. He said so to the king.

But Pharaoh's anger was spent. He was fond of Sarai, it was true, but there were other lovely young women in his harem. What was one more, or less? Should he punish this man, this goat herder from Canaan, for all the pleasure that his wife had given him? No, the king decided; being cuckolded was punishment enough. He raised his hand and ordered Sarai to be brought to the audience chamber. As soon as she entered, Abram gasped. He barely recognized her. Her eyes were lined with dark kohl, her lips were painted red, and her hair, tied with ribbons of gold, cascaded riotously over her shoulders. She looked like an Egyptian princess.

"Now then," Pharaoh said, "here is your wife. Take her, and be gone."

The counselors were shocked. Was the king really going to let this insubordinate shepherd get away with deceiving the majesty of Egypt? It would set a dangerous precedent, especially now, with so many foreign tribes on Egyptian soil. But Pharaoh held up his hand and stifled their protest.

But what about the royal gifts? the counselors retorted. What about the slaves, the oxen, the donkeys, and the sheep? Surely, all of this should be returned to the Crown?

But Pharaoh sternly ordered his men to set Abram on his way, "with his wife and all that he had," ending the discussion.

IN HINDSIGHT, THAT WAS the turning point. Abram recognizes that now. When they returned to Canaan with their vast train of booty, he was no longer a furtive nomad, moving in the shadow of the hills, in fear of Canaanite ire. He had become a rich and powerful chieftain. The

Canaanites looked on him with new respect. And when he offered to purchase some of their land, they eagerly took his gold.

But soon his herds grew so vast there weren't enough pastures to sustain them. The situation became so bad that some of his retainers began to quarrel with Lot's men over access to the few wells in the vicinity. The time had come to part ways with Lot.

"Let there be no strife between you and me," he told Lot. "If you take the left hand, then I will go to the right."

With the careless selfishness that comes naturally to the young, Lot picked the best part of the land: the well-watered plain of Jordan to the east. Abram had no choice but to move south, to the hill country of the Judean Mountains, and pitch his tents by the oaks of Mamre, near the Canaanite city of Hebron. And here God reaffirmed his covenant to Abram. "Raise your eyes now," God said, "for all the land that you see I will give to you and to your offspring forever." Abram was grateful. It seemed that God's promise would finally come to pass.

Yet, there was still a problem. How was he going to have descendants when Sarai was childless?

Fortunately, she was a resourceful woman. A true daughter of Mesopotamia, Sarai knew that by law she had to procure a surrogate for her husband if she could not bear a child herself. For years she had hoped that she might still conceive, that her womb would be opened by the sheer power of her desire, but it was not to be. Though it pained her, she chose a girl from among the Egyptian slaves whom Pharaoh had given her.

Her name was Hagar. She was a dark and comely girl, young, mature beyond her years. There was also a streak of rebelliousness in her. She always threw a certain look when she was told to fetch water from the well or wash their linen, but Sarai dismissed it as youthful impudence, not uncommon in young girls.

One night, Sarai brought the girl to Abram's tent and told him that she would serve as his *'ishshâ*, his concubine. Abram was taken by surprise, but after a moment, he nodded and beckoned the girl to his bedroll. As Hagar went in and closed the tent, Sarai walked away under the star-strewn sky, to be alone with her tears and her sorrow.

The girl conceived. But as her belly swelled with child, she began to take on airs. She walked about the camp as if she owned it, knowing full well that this was not far from the truth. She was carrying the future of the tribe. And then it went from bad to worse. She snubbed Sarai, taunting her that she could not give her husband what he wanted. She refused to carry water from the well. In fact, she refused to do most chores, always claiming that the effort was too much for her, that it might endanger the child.

At last, Sarai rounded on her husband. "I gave my slave girl to your embrace, and when she saw that she had conceived, she looked on me with contempt!" she railed.

Abram tried to equivocate, as men sometimes do when caught between two strong-willed women. "Your slave-girl is in your power," he mumbled defensively; "do to her as you please."

But Sarai knew there were limits. The same laws that required her to procure a surrogate also restrained her from dealing harshly with that surrogate. "If a female slave has claimed equality with her mistress because she bore children," the Mesopotamian code noted, "her mistress may not sell her." What Sarai could do, however, is give the girl a good tongue-lashing, and that she did. She was the wife of a chieftain, the former lover of the king of Egypt, and she was not going to let this slave girl run all over her.

Hagar fled. Shocked by the fury of her mistress, she ran into the wilderness—which was tantamount to suicide. A young girl had no chance of surviving in the desert, certainly not if she was with child. Fortunately, God chose to intervene—the first of two such intercessions to save the life of Hagar and her son. An angel was sent to locate her, and found the stricken girl near a spring of water.

"Where have you come from?" the angel asked.

"I am running away from my mistress Sarai," Hagar said.

Inwardly, the angel smiled. "Return to your mistress, and submit to her," he counseled.

Hagar, a stubborn girl, shook her head. She refused. She was not going back to Mamre to be humiliated by her mistress. She knew all too well that as soon as she gave birth, she would be discarded—or worse.

And then something extraordinary happened. The angel bent down to the girl's ear and said, "I will so greatly multiply your offspring that they cannot be counted for multitude."

An astonishing pledge. The girl's eyes opened wide. She sat up. Was God giving her the same promise that he had given to Abram?

"Now you have conceived and shall bear a son," the angel continued, seeing the surprise on the girl's face. "You shall call him Ishmael, for the Lord has given heed to your affliction."

The girl ran back to Mamre and told Abram what had happened and why they had to call their child "Ishmael." She didn't know what it meant, but Abram did. He smiled. *Ishma'el* was a composite of two words: *El,* the word for "God," and *shama',* a verb that meant "hearing." Ishmael, in short, meant "God hears (me)."

And God did hear. Once more, he appeared to Abram to confirm his covenant. "You shall be the ancestor of a multitude of nations," he said. "I will make you exceedingly fruitful; and I will make nations of you, and kings shall come from you."

And to seal his covenant, God did two things. First, he gave Abram and Sarai new names. Abram was henceforth to be known as Abraham, from *abh* (father) and *raham* (nations), or "father of a multitude of nations." Sarai would be called Sarah, rooted in the Akkadian word *sharratu,* which means "princess."

And second, as a token of their covenantal relationship with God, every male descendant should from now on be circumcised, beginning with Abraham and Ishmael. "So shall my covenant be in your flesh," God explained.

Abraham. He liked the name. It rolled nicely off the tongue and gave him a sense of gravitas, as befitted the head of a large clan. But God wasn't done yet.

"As for Sarah your wife," he said, "I will bless her."

This pleased Abraham. Sarah was 90 years old and often infirm. He worried about her, particularly here, in the harsh climate of the Judean Hills. "And moreover," God continued, "I will give you a son by her."

Abraham's jaw dropped. Did he hear that right? At 90 years of age, long after her menses had stopped, Sarah was going to bear a child? Was God joking? And before he could help himself, Abraham fell on his face and laughed so hard that tears rolled down his cheeks.

But the Lord was serious, and suddenly Abraham understood the beauty and simplicity of God's plan. The whole purpose of his journey from Harran had been to show that he was deserving of God's trust. All the trials they had faced—it had all been part of God's plan to test his faith, to prove that he was worthy of the covenant, and worthy of the son who would be heir to that covenant. His steadfast loyalty would be rewarded. God would grant what he and Sarah had so fervently desired: a son of their own. And when, in due course, that child was born, they called him Yishaq, or Isaac, which means "[he] laughs"—as a playful reminder of their incredulity at God's bounty.

THAT WAS THE ZENITH, the high point of his life; he sees that now. How happy they were, he and Sarah and their newborn son. It felt as if everything had come full circle, that all wrongs were made right. He could see himself in the years to come, sitting contentedly at the opening to his tent, watching his little boy grow into a man.

And then it all came to naught. The wonderful life he had built, the servants and luxury and wealth, it crumbled around him. And looking back, he knows he has no one to blame but himself. That is the hardest part. He has brought it on himself. He has eroded God's trust and now must face the consequences.

It began with rumors that something was amiss in the tribal communities on the plain of Jordan, south of the Dead Sea. This was a rich land, well watered by streams from the mountains of Moab, lush enough to sustain large herds. And yet vile things were happening there, particularly in the cities of Sodom and Gomorrah, where men were doing unspeakable things, acts of cruelty beyond words.

"How great is the outcry against Sodom and Gomorrah," God said to Abraham. "How very grave their sin!" Therefore, the cities would be destroyed. God would send three of his angels down to the plain to verify the wickedness of the people and punish them.

The news struck Abraham like a bolt of lightning. Lot, his nephew— the boy he had raised as their own—was also living in Sodom, together with his wife and children. Whatever these evil people had done, he knew that Lot could not be one of them. His first impulse was to stop it, to try to resist whatever the angels were planning to do. And so he did something foolish.

He started to argue.

"Would you indeed sweep away the righteous with the wicked?" he said, using a tone of voice he'd never used with God before.

God was silent.

"Suppose there are fifty righteous men in the city," Abraham went on, improvising now, not knowing whether there actually *were* righteous people in Sodom other than Lot and his family. "Will you then sweep away the place and not forgive it for the fifty righteous who are in it?"

God was quiet, taken aback, perhaps, by Abraham's insolence.

Regardless, Abraham plunged on; better to push on and, he hoped, change God's mind. "Far be it from you to do such a thing," he said before he could stop himself. "Shall not the Judge of all the Earth do what is just?"

For a moment, it seemed as if all of Creation held its breath. No one, neither angel nor mortal, had *ever* spoken to God like that. Abraham waited, his heart beating in his chest, wondering, *knowing,* that he had gone too far.

At last, the Lord spoke, in measured, deliberate words, drained of their habitual warmth. "If I find at Sodom fifty righteous in the city," God said, "I will forgive the whole place for their sake."

A wiser man would have stopped right there. But Abraham couldn't help himself; the thought of his nephew and his family being destroyed by God's vengeance was too much to bear. Besides, there was no guarantee that the angels would indeed find as many as 50 honorable people in the place.

And so he started to negotiate, as if God were a carpet seller or a peddler of sheep, and he, Abraham, could get him down to the lowest price. Now, thinking back to that horrible episode, he wonders what had gotten into him, how he could do such an outrageous thing. But he hadn't been himself. Other than Sarah, Lot was his only kin from his family back in Ur.

Even when the haggling reduced the number to 20 righteous people, when every fiber in his body screamed at him to shut up and not test God any further, Abraham kept on going. He couldn't help it.

"Oh, do not let the Lord be angry if I speak just once more," he pleaded, knowing full well that the Lord was already furious and getting angrier by the minute. "Suppose that only ten are found there?"

A stony silence. At last, God said, "For the sake of ten I will not destroy it." And then he disappeared without another word, leaving Abraham to ponder what he had done.

And the worst thing was, the whole exercise turned out to be pointless anyway. Because not even ten righteous people could be found.

Fortunately, God was merciful with Lot, as he'd always planned to be, long before Abraham decided to challenge him, for he knew the great love that Abraham bore toward his nephew. And so the Lord made sure that the angels rescued Lot and his family from the city. Only then did he rain sulfur and fire from heaven and destroy everyone and everything on the plain.

Such was the wrath of God.

As the sun rose on the next day, Abraham climbed a hill and looked down on the settlements in the valley. All of the cities of the plain had been burned to the ground, down to the last cinder. And then he saw the waters of the Dead Sea rise and cover the ruins, wiping out all traces of this abomination.

And Abraham knew he had gone too far.

A BETTER MAN WOULD HAVE tried to make amends. A better man would have offered contrition, would have pleaded with God for forgiveness. But he, Abraham, was too wrapped up in his own affairs to dwell on such thoughts. In fact, just when it seemed that it couldn't get any worse, he did the vilest thing of all. He committed a crime so great that all others paled by comparison: He sent Hagar and his son Ishmael off into the desert, there to die a certain death.

That it was Sarah who suggested it in the first place did not diminish his guilt in the least.

"Cast out this slave woman with her son," Sarah told him in no uncertain terms, "for the son of this slave woman shall not inherit along with my son Isaac."

He'd worried about that himself. Now that he had two sons, Ishmael and Isaac, who would become his heir? Who would lead the tribe after his death? More to the point, who would inherit the covenant? There was, he admitted, some logic in what Sarah said; many tribes had been destroyed because two sons had contested the mantle of leadership.

But why did he have to send them *into the desert*? With little more than a piece of bread and a skin of water, which he knew wouldn't last for more than a day? Why had he forced them into the wilderness of Beersheba when he could have sent them to a distant land with servants, sheep, and cattle, as he had done with Lot?

Is THAT WHY GOD HAS DECIDED to punish him and given him this horrific task? Why he has sent him to Mount Moriah to sacrifice what he loves above all else?

He is tired and needs to rest. He sees a pile of rocks along the path and sits down, takes a deep breath. Only then does he remember the branches on his back; the pain has become so dull he's forgotten about it. He pulls the bundle from his shoulders and flings it into the dirt.

Up ahead, Isaac is watching him carefully, uncertain now, the first glimpse of dread in his eyes. Abraham sees it and decides it must be done, *right* now, right here. There is no point in making the boy suffer. Up ahead is a cluster of boulders; it will do as a makeshift altar.

For a brief moment he is reminded of the altars he built when he first arrived in this land, in places like Shechem and Bethel. They were sacred places; he could tell the stone altars had been used, probably by Canaanites sacrificing to their gods.

Had they ever killed a human being, even a child? He knows that some of the local deities, like the cult of Baal, demand it. He is no stranger to it; there was human sacrifice in Ur too. Not to expiate the gods; the Mesopotamian deities were far too haughty to bother with that. No, such immolation was usually performed for the king. When a royal died, all those who had served him followed him in death: his wives, his servants, his slaves, his animals, even his favorite horse. And for what? To serve the king in the afterlife? What utter nonsense.

Abraham sighs, gets up, and pulls the henna rope from his belt. The boy knows. He sees the shadow of fear on his son's youthful face, the confusion, the bewilderment. But Isaac won't run away. He knows his son. Isaac will not fail him, not now.

He is right.

The boy stands frozen in place, trembling slightly, as he begins to tie the heavy rope around his lithe arms and shoulders. How impossibly young he is, he thinks; just a child, skin over bones, not yet fully formed, with eyes that can still look at him with devotion.

When it is done, he must turn the knife on himself. That he's known from the start. No one will leave this place alive. If God wants his son to die in order to absolve the sins of his father, then the father shall follow in death. Without Isaac, there is no point in living. Besides, Sarah will never forgive him, just as he will never forgive himself.

As soon as the boy is bound, he places him on top of the branches, gently, as if he is putting him to sleep, making sure that none of the sticks can cut in his flesh.

Isaac opens his mouth but Abraham shakes his head, weeping freely now, overcome with grief, and puts his finger on the boy's mouth. No more words. He unsheathes his knife, holds it high, but his tears obscure his eyesight; he can't see. He grips the dagger with both hands, his feet wide apart, and takes a deep breath, the sharp blade poised over the naked belly. Summoning the strength to do it.

But he can't.

Filled with anguish, he lifts his head and cries with all his strength, "Here I am, my Lord, here I am!"

I am here, my Lord. I beg of you, do not force me to strike the knife. Do not let me kill what I love and cherish above all. Know that I fear you. Know that I am sorry for all that I've done. Know that I cannot refuse you, not even the sacrifice of my son, if you will it. But I beg you, take me instead. Let me die in my son's stead, so that all my guilt will be washed away. Hear my plea, I beg of you.

Thus, Abraham prays, with all his heart, all his soul, all his strength and all his mind, while Isaac lies trembling on the kindling and the sun slowly tracks across the killing ground. And then, at long last, comes the familiar sensation: the feeling as if everything around him stops and holds still, as if the space empties itself to make way for the presence.

"Do not lay your hand on the boy," a voice whispers in his ear, "for now I know that you fear God."

A cry escapes from Abraham's lips as he crumples to the ground, overcome by the power of God's grace and mercy.

✡

NEARLY FOUR MILLENNIA AFTER these events reportedly took place, the story of Abraham's "Sacrifice of Isaac" continues to fascinate scholars across the religious spectrum.

Who was Abraham? A tribal chieftain? A Mesopotamian lord? A Canaanite herdsman? Did he even exist? And if so, when did this great epic take place? Who was the pharaoh who took such a keen interest in Sarah, his wife? Is there any evidence for the hail of sulfur that destroyed the cities of Sodom and Gomorrah? Is there *anything* that can corroborate these amazing stories?

We can't help it. We are children of the modern media age. For us, nothing is real unless we read about it in the newspapers or watch the live footage on CNN. For us, truth must be based on facts, tangible facts that can be parsed, broken down, analyzed, and spun. Only then do we accord it credibility; only then does it become meaningful for us.

But we tend to forget that matters were very different between the Late Stone Age and the Early Bronze Age—the period around the year 2000 B.C.E., the time in which I think the story is set. The people who came after Abraham did not have the benefit of the Internet, or television, or newspapers. They didn't have the ability to verify whether a story was factually true, and as a result they didn't particularly care.

For these people, huddled around their campfires at night, it was the *stories* that mattered. Stories that had been transmitted from one generation to the next, accumulating wisdom, experience, and values. These sagas were no mere "folktales" as we sometimes think of them today, like myths or fables; these stories carried real meaning that lent a tribe its history, its identity, its raison d'être. Yes, there was truth in these stories, but it was a moral truth. Long before there were laws, these stories sustained the social fabric of the Habiru, the "sand dwellers" as the Egyptians called them (which may, perhaps, be the root of the word *Hebrews*), and served the tribe as its foundational text.

Therefore, the question of whether Abraham was a historical figure is actually beside the point, because it brings a 21st-century mind to a Bronze Age question. The elders who told these stories, and the youngsters who listened and memorized them, didn't care if Abraham was an actual person or a composite of several characters, or simply a projection of the hopes and dreams of a community as it tried to define a way of life under El, their God. For them, the story of Abraham was a living reality because it validated their faith in a single divine power, as compared to the mixed bag of greater and lesser deities that ruled nations far more powerful then they.

It took guts to do that, and the stories of Abraham, Isaac, and Jacob gave them that courage. It gave them the strength to remain true to their faith even as they were swept into Egypt, the most developed polytheistic civilization of their time, there to succumb to suppression and slavery. And these stories would sustain them again when they returned to Canaan, there to build the kingdom that the God of Abraham had told them about so many centuries ago.

But that is not the only reason I think that Abraham's story is perhaps the first spiritual event to change history in ways that reverberate to our modern day: Judaism is not the only community that traces its foundation to Abraham; two other mainstream traditions do so as well.

The first, of course, is Christianity.

Christians, too, consider Abraham the archetype of a believer who follows God's instructions, even though they don't make much sense at first. As the angel tells Abraham, "Do not lay your hand on the boy or do anything to him; *for now I know that you fear God.*" This message of absolute trust and faith is particularly relevant for Christians, for they see it as a foreshadowing of the sacrifice of Jesus on the cross. Paul wrote that the most important attribute of Abraham was his faith in God's grace, and that is why God bestowed his covenant upon him. That is also the essential difference between the Jewish and Christian perspective: Whereas Jews see themselves as Abraham's children through birth and circumcision, Christians consider themselves descendants by virtue of faith.

The third major tradition that traces its origins to Abraham is Islam. This will surprise some readers, who may think that Muhammad is the key figure. That is certainly true, but for Muslims, Muhammad is only the seal on a long line of prophets that began with Adam and culminated in Abraham, or Ibrahim as he is called in the Quran.

In fact, Islam's Scripture, the Quran, includes many stories that also appear in the Hebrew Bible and the New Testament. For example, there are *suras,* or chapters, about Isaac, who is called Ishaq in the Arabic, just like the Hebrew name. Moses is Musa, David is Dawud, and Solomon is named Suleiman. The Quran even features many stories about Jesus (Isa) and Mary (Maryam), including the story of the Virgin birth.

But for Muslims, Abraham is a special case. He appears in 35 chapters, more than any other biblical figure with the exception of Moses. Islam looks at the stories of Abraham through a different lens as well because in the Muslim tradition, the covenant is passed not through Isaac but through Ishmael.

That means that Hagar also plays a far more important role. Hagar is never mentioned by name in the Quran, but there are many stories about her in the various Hadith, an oral tradition of great spiritual and legal authority known as "sayings of the Prophet." According to one such saying, Abraham decides to go with Hagar and Ishmael when they are cast out into the desert. Together, they travel south and eventually reach Paran (Faran in Arabic). But unlike the location of Paran in Genesis, this oasis is not located in Sinai but in Arabia proper, close to the future city of Mecca.

Here, God decides to test Abraham. He orders him to abandon Hagar and Ishmael. Abraham reluctantly does so, and before long, the scene from Genesis is repeated, albeit in an Arabic setting: Ishmael (Ishmail in Arabic) lies dying, while Hagar frantically searches for water. As it happens, Paran is located in a valley surrounded by hills. Desperate to save Ishmael, Hagar runs back and forth between two mountains, al-Safa and al-Marwa, in the hope of finding a well. When she climbs the mountain a seventh time, the angel Gabriel finally intervenes. He strikes the earth with his staff, water pours forth, and Hagar and her boy are saved. This sacred well, located in today's Mecca, is called Zamzam, and the rite of walking between the two mountains seven times, known as the *sa'y*, is reenacted every year as part of the hajj, the pilgrimage to Mecca.

Soon after this episode, God puts Abraham to the same test that we find in Genesis: He is ordered to sacrifice his own son. This story is known as the "Binding of Isaac," the *Akedah* in Judaism and *Dhabih* in Arabic. But just before Abraham gets ready to plunge the knife in his son's body, God intervenes. "You have indeed shown the truth of the vision," God says, "and so we will reward the doers of good. This was indeed an important test" (Q 27:104-6). So important is this story in the Islamic tradition that it is celebrated every year as part of the Eid ul-Adha festival. During this feast, Muslims roast the meat of a sheep, cow, or camel and share it with their family, as well as the poor and needy.

Meanwhile, the story of Ishmael continues. Together with Abraham, he builds the Kaaba, the square monument in the heart of Mecca, which includes a sacred Black Stone known as the Hajar al-Aswad. Ishmael then becomes the ancestor of many great Arab nations, all the way down to the Adnanite tribe of Muhammad himself.

Surprising, you might say? Not really. Amazing though it may be, the root of this prophecy actually appears in Genesis. Here is what happens after Abraham casts Hagar and Ishmael out into the desert: God intervenes for the second time to save her and makes good on his promise to make Ishmael "fruitful and exceedingly numerous." Ishmael, Genesis tells us, "shall be the father of twelve princes, and I will make him a great nation" (Genesis 17:20-21).

Later, Genesis specifies the Arab tribes that descend from Ishmael, including the Nebajoth, the Kedar, and the Tema (Genesis 25:13-15). The Nebajoth would reappear as the Nabaiati in Assyrian war records and become known as the Nabataeans in Roman times. The Kedar, also mentioned in the Psalms, have been associated with the eighth-century tribal group of the Qedarites (Qaydhar in Arabic), located in northwestern Arabia. Tema has been linked to the oasis northeast of Dedan, which straddles the caravan route between southern Arabia and Mesopotamia.

What this means is that roughly around the first millennium B.C.E., when the earliest stories of Genesis began to emerge in the Kingdom of Israel, Ishmael's descendants were already associated with Arab nations living throughout northern Arabia and as far south as the caravan routes on the fringes of the Hijaz.

Indeed, it is a caravan of Arab "Ishmaelites" that in a later Genesis story will carry off Isaac's grandson Joseph to the slave markets of Egypt. In sum, the roots of Islam can actually be found in the story of Abraham in the Judeo-Christian Bible.

And so the figure of Abraham would shape a world that continues to this day. Though it is sometimes difficult to believe in an age tormented by al Qaeda, the Islamic State, and other forms of fundamentalist terrorism, Jews, Christians, and Muslims are children of the same father.

They are cousins, united in their faith in one God.

Rembrandt van Rijn's portrait captures Jesus' deep human compassion.

CHAPTER 2

JESUS' PRAYER TO ABBA

✝

Father,

hallowed be your name.

Your Kingdom come.

Our daily bread give us today.

And forgive us our debts,

for we forgive our debtors.

And do not lead us to the test.

CAPERNAUM ON THE SEA OF GINOSAR
Lower Galilee
29 C.E.

Jesus rises well before dawn, careful not to wake the others, and leaves the house wearing little more than his tunic and a blanket. The Sea of Ginosar is just a few steps away, but there's a better spot, just up the coastal road toward Bethsaida. There he sits, on a rock jutting into the surf, alone with the stars and the soft murmur of waves lapping onto the pebble-strewn beach.

A magical time, this hour—not yet dawn but no longer night either, a precious twilight of reflection, a haven of perfect solitude. He always looks forward to this moment, this brief spell in the morning, to ponder the things that have happened and to look ahead to what might still come.

Was it only three months ago that he and his four companions from John the Baptist's camp stumbled onto the beach of Bethsaida, hungry and haggard, with little more than the clothes on their backs? Those were tense days, with the Herodian militia running amok in Perea, along the eastern bank of the Jordan, chasing down anyone suspected of being part of the Baptist's "mob," as Herod Antipas called it.

He sighs and shakes his head. How often had he not warned the Baptist? And every time, his entreaties were dismissed out of hand. John was not a Galilean; he didn't know what it was like to grow up under the rule of a Herodian. But he, a man from Nazareth, he knew what Antipas was capable of, with this obsession to match the glory of his father, King Herod the Great. For years he, Jesus, son of Joseph (or Yeshua bar Josef in Aramaic), had labored in the work pits of Sepphoris alongside his father, forced to build Antipas's new capital city in Galilee. Herod Antipas may be a mere tetrarch, a ruler of just a quarter of what was once his father's kingdom, but he is a dangerous tetrarch, a pseudo-king who suspects treason in every corner, under every bed, just as his father did.

The Baptist did not listen, firm in the belief that Herod Antipas could not touch him. Instead he would turn to the crowds, the hundreds of men and women who'd come to hear him, many from Jerusalem but many more from villages and townships throughout Judea. Look, the Baptist would say, pointing at the Pharisees, the high-ranking officers, and the Levites who came to be lashed by his words. With such a powerful following, what was an upstart Galilean tetrarch going to do? Scare him?

Well, yes. Perhaps the Baptist wasn't afraid, but Antipas most surely was. He knew all about the multitudes who flocked to the Baptist's camp in Bethany, on the eastern bank of the Jordan, just a day's walk from Jerusalem. The problem was that Bethany-in-Jordan happened to be in Perea, not Judea—a territory that by a quirk of fate had been appended to the lands under *his* rule. That made the Baptist *his* problem. And Antipas knew all too well how Rome dealt with governors who couldn't keep their territories under control.

Take his older brother Archelaus, for example. Augustus had kicked him off his throne and sent him into exile in Vienne, a city on the Rhône in Gaul, precisely because he had failed to maintain law and order in Judea. Antipas was determined not to let that happen to him, especially when there were people like the Baptist running around, railing about the coming of the Messiah who would "clear his threshing floor" with his winnowing fork, and "burn the chaff with unquenchable fire."

Antipas had a good idea what sort of "chaff" the Baptist had in mind. That would be him, the tetrarch, at the top of the list, together with all other elites who collaborated with the Romans to keep the restive Jewish nation in check.

And so, inevitably, a company of the tetrarch's mounted militia rode into the camp one morning. They summoned the Baptist, charged him with sedition, and put him in chains—his work of a lifetime cut short in the span of minutes. And as soon as the soldiers disappeared over the hills, his followers scattered in all directions—men, woman, and children, too terrified to gather up what few belongings they had brought to the camp.

He, Jesus, left as well, together with three other disciples, all Galileans—Simon, Andrew, and Philip—as well as a Judean named Nathanael. They debated their options and in the end agreed with Simon: It was best to go back to Galilee. There was a house in Capernaum, Simon said, on the northern bank of the Sea of Ginosar. Technically it was the house of his mother-in-law, but she was old and ill, so his wife now owned it in all but name.

Jesus agreed. He knew the time had come to return to Galilee, but he had underestimated how much time it would take. They didn't know if Antipas's patrols were still looking for them, so they traveled only by night, holing up in stables or caves during the day. It took them almost a fortnight to reach the southern shore of the sea, not far from Hammat Gader, but there their luck held. They found a fisherman from Bethsaida who was willing to take them across, provided each of them agreed to take the oars, for the wind was still.

That's when Philip had another idea. He suggested they stay in Bethsaida rather than move on to Capernaum. He had family in Bethsaida; he was sure they would offer them hospitality.

Nathanael frowned. He was a Judean; for him, everything north of the plain was *galil ha-goyim,* the countryside, the sticks. What difference did it make where they settled?

A big difference, as it turned out. Capernaum was in Galilee, the territory ruled by Herod Antipas. But Bethsaida lay just on the other side of the Jordan, in the Gaulanitis. That was the area ruled by Herod Philip. And Philip did not want anything to do with Antipas. They would be safe there, for the time being.

Ah, Nathanael nodded, and then they all turned toward him, waiting for his decision. With the Baptist gone, he was now their leader, their Teacher. It was to him that they looked for guidance. The thought filled him with pride—the idea that he, the Nazarene, was forming his own movement. But it also filled him with dread, knowing the grave responsibility that now rested on his shoulders.

One night as they sat around a campfire, he overheard Andrew whispering in Simon's ear, "We have found the Messiah."

The next months would determine if Simon was right.

THEY STAYED IN BETHSAIDA FOR 40 DAYS. In hindsight, that respite was a blessing. While Simon and Andrew put their ear to the ground, trying to find out what was happening in Galilee, Jesus went in search of solitude, walking deep into the wilderness. It was a wild country, this side of the Jordan, more harsh and rugged than the soft, rolling hills of Galilee. Instead of lush fields perfumed with the scent of jasmine and coriander, the lower Gaulanitis was cleft by sharp and jagged ridges, carved from the charcoal-colored basalt that the locals quarried to build their homes.

Here, he prayed to Abba, the Father. Day after day he prayed, nights even, not bothering with food or drink, waiting for guidance. If God had called them to serve his people, then what was it that he should teach them? Was it true, as Andrew said, that he was the Messiah, the "anointed one" who would redeem Israel? If so, how exactly was he going to do that? He did not have an army; he was a poor *chasid*, a rural preacher. What good news could he possibly bring to this region, these Galileans who had been plundered by Herod and his henchmen for more than half a century?

The evidence was plain to see, no matter where you looked. The poor, the dispossessed, the sick, the hungry were everywhere. Like miserable clusters of humanity, they sat along the road or outside their village compounds, families with three or four malnourished children, staring with their hollow, uncomprehending eyes.

That was the price that Galilee had paid for the vainglorious ambition of King Herod the Great. Ever since he had doubled the tax burden on Galilee—not only to pay the Romans but also to fund his massive construction projects in Judea—scores of farmers had seen their lands forfeited by the tax collectors, the *telones*. Most of these plots had then been sold for a song to the landed gentry in Jerusalem, the *kurioi*, and consolidated into large estates run by professional "stewards."

And now, hundreds, even thousands, of these landless peasants roamed the hills. While their women and children tried to subsist on husks of barley, the men stood around in village squares, often for weeks on end, hoping for a day's work at rates far below the norm. Some of them—the lucky ones—were hired to work as tenant farmers on the land that had once been theirs, in exchange for a pitiful share of the harvest.

What could Jesus bring to this ravaged land? What could he tell these people? That the end of their suffering was at hand? That he, the Messiah, would come with a winnowing fork in his hand to sweep the Romans and their collaborators into the fire and restore this land to God and his people?

That's what the Baptist had believed. A great cataclysm would cleanse the land, John had said; a great and terrifying judgment would destroy the Gentiles and punish everyone who had failed to repent. It's what prompted Herod Antipas to have him beheaded. But some of the prophets in Scripture had foretold the same thing: Isaiah and Ezekiel, Jeremiah and Daniel.

Was that all Jesus could promise the people of Galilee? To wait for a great cataclysm? To hope for the ouster of the Gentiles?

And so he prayed, day after day. And there, in the wilderness, Abba answered him, and gave him his mission.

A fortnight later, during the Sabbath, he stood up in the synagogue of Capernaum. He asked for a scroll from one of the elders, as visitors were often invited to do. It was, he saw, not one of the Torah scrolls but a text from the Nevi'im, the Prophets, with the words of Isaiah. He quickly located the passage he wanted, cleared his throat, and read in a clear voice, "The Spirit of the Lord is upon me, for he has anointed me."

A murmur swept through the synagogue. Who was this young rabbi? Where did he come from? From Nazareth, you say? What good can come from Nazareth? Listen to the lad; he almost sounds as if the passage refers to *him;* as if *he* is the anointed one.

Undeterred, Jesus, continued in the same firm voice, saying, "He has sent me to bring good news to the oppressed, and heal the brokenhearted."

He closed the scroll and returned it, well aware that the eyes of everyone in the synagogue were upon him. He took a deep breath, turned to the congregation, and said, "Today, this scripture has been fulfilled in your hearing." And with that he sat down.

The people gasped. Everyone turned to their neighbors and began to talk, shocked by the sheer gall of this young rabbi. Others stood up and shook their fists. "What have you to do with us, Jesus of Nazareth?" one man cried. "Have you come to destroy us?"

That caught everyone's attention. The man who'd spoken was well known in Capernaum. He was a tormented figure, mentally unstable, undoubtedly possessed by demons. That's when Jesus performed his first miracle. In front of everybody he took the man and rebuked him harshly, until the demon was gone out of him. He knew that was what they all needed to see: a sign. That's what people always wanted to see: a *semeion,* an omen, some tangible proof that he was what he claimed to be. A prophet. A man blessed by God.

No sooner did the congregation file out of the synagogue than the news began to ripple across town. Within hours, a long line began to form outside the house of Simon Peter's wife—all of the sick, the infirm, the disabled, the demoniacs, the epileptics, and the paralytics who lived in Capernaum and the surrounding countryside, all hoping to be cured. And since it was after sunset, marking the end of the Sabbath, Jesus welcomed them and healed them to the best of his ability.

In the days that followed, word of his deeds spread from Capernaum like wildfire, touching all of the villages and townships in the Valley of Ginosar. And the line in front of Peter's house became a stream of hundreds, and then thousands, flocking to the healer's words, following him wherever he went, hoping for a miracle.

That's when he told them about the Kingdom of God.

HE PICKED A MOUND JUST OUTSIDE CAPERNAUM, not far from the spot where he is sitting now. The hill gently sloped down to the water, so that everyone could feel the cooling breeze as it swept in from the north, carrying his words with it. There were so many people that his followers finally gave up trying to count them.

What a pitiable, heartbreaking crowd it was. Most of the people were mere skin and bones, their hair long and dirty, their clothes reduced to rags. And yet they looked up at him with bright eyes, full of hope, holding pitiful bundles close to their chest, rocking them while they listened.

"Blessed are you," he roared from that mountaintop, "Blessed are you who are poor, for yours is the Kingdom of God."

His listeners frowned, momentarily confused. Blessed? No one had ever called them blessed. They were outcasts, landless and penniless, doomed to a life of poverty and hunger. Who in his right mind would ever call them blessed?

"Blessed are you who are hungry now," he said, as if he read their minds, and was rewarded with numerous heads nodding in response. Yes, they were hungry indeed.

"Blessed are you," he said, "for you will be filled."

He now had their attention. Some of the men and women moved closer so as not to miss a word he said. Some reached out to him as if to touch him and feel the power of his presence.

"Blessed are you who weep now," he continued, his voice choking with emotion at the sight of the wretched little ones, clinging to their mothers, "for soon you will laugh." And then he smiled, and the children smiled back at him. It was getting hot; he could see the reflection of the sun glistening on the waves of the sea, but no one seemed to notice.

"Blessed are you when people hate you," he said, stretching out his hands, "when they exclude you, revile you, and defame you."

More nods now. These paupers, they knew what it meant to be marginalized. Most of them had been evicted from their villages because of their illness or their unpaid taxes, condemned to a life of beggary.

"But woe to you who are rich," he continued, his voice rising, "for you have received your consolation!"

A few muted cheers rose from the crowd.

"Woe to you who are full now, for you will be hungry!"

More cheering now, punctuated by cries of *Yes!* and *That's right!*

"Woe to you who are laughing now," he cried, "for you will mourn and weep!"

And at that the crowd rose to its feet, clapping and cheering. Some of the women began to dance, singing psalms. *Truly God is good to the upright,* they chanted; *to those who are pure in heart.*

His followers did not understand a word of it.

Later that night, after they had labored to feed the crowd with barley bread and sardines caught in the sea, they gathered around him as he sat at a fire, reflecting on the events of the day. There were more of them now, his *shaliach,* his disciples. Most of them were fishermen. Not the type of people you would expect to see in a Jerusalem *yeshiva,* he thought, or in the *beit midrash* of Sepphoris, where so many years ago, kind men had taught him to read the scrolls. But what these fishermen lacked in intellect or education, they made up in common sense, in a fierce belief in what was right and wrong.

They had finished their supper, but no one wanted to be the first to speak. In the end, it fell on Simon to express their concerns. What was this Kingdom of God that he was talking about this afternoon? What on earth was he promising these people? After all, they were just fishermen, with wives and children. They weren't soldiers. They didn't have horses, or weapons. So how were they going to establish this kingdom that he was talking about? By staging a rebellion? Kick that tyrant Antipas from his throne?

Did he need to remind the rabbi of what happened to the Baptist? Aye, the other Apostles said, nodding in agreement. Perhaps the rabbi was not aware of the fact that there was a cohort of soldiers, right here in Capernaum. Did he have any idea of what these soldiers would do if they chose to make trouble?

No one needed to be reminded. In the last 30 years, there had been not one, but two peasant uprisings, both in Galilee. The first one, led by Judas bar Hezekiah after the death of King Herod, had left Sepphoris and all the surrounding villages, including Nazareth, a smoking ruin. And the second one, led by Judas the Galilean during the Roman census of Quirinius, had led to brutal reprisals by Roman forces. All that these revolts had accomplished was more death, more misery, and more fields and homes destroyed. Is that what he was asking them to do?

Jesus smiled at them and shook his head. "What is the Kingdom of God like?" he said. "And to what should I compare it?"

They waited patiently. They knew what would come next: one of the rabbi's beautiful parables. Beautiful, yes, but also a bit difficult to follow sometimes.

"It is the smallest of all the seeds," Jesus continued, "but when it has grown it is the greatest of shrubs and becomes a tree, so that the birds of the air come and make nests in its branches."

Ah, they said, nodding, though no one had the faintest idea of what he was talking about. What did that mean, a mustard seed? So it grows and becomes a great shrub. A nuisance really, mustard plants, when you come to think of it. There were too many of them in Galilee. What did that have to do with establishing a Kingdom of God?

He tried again.

"The Kingdom of God," he said, "is as if someone scattered seed on the ground and went on to sleep and rise, day and night. And the seed would sprout and grow, even though he doesn't know it."

Mmm, the followers said.

"You see," he said, "the earth produces of itself, first the stalk, then the head, then the full grain in the head. But when the grain is ripe, at once he goes in with his sickle, because the harvest has come."

The disciples looked at each other, thinking, *Do you understand a word of what he's saying?*

He sighed. He knew it was difficult, this idea of the kingdom as a spontaneous movement, as a groundswell of people power. So he told them another story.

"A sower went out to sow," he said. "And when he sowed, some seeds fell on the path, some fell on rocky ground, and others fell among the thorns. Other seeds fell into good soil and brought forth grain, and then it yielded thirty, sixty, even a hundredfold."

By now the disciples were getting restless. What was the point of these stories about sowers and seeds? What did that have to do with building a kingdom right here in Galilee? They all knew their Scripture, at least some of it. They knew that whenever Israel suffered under a foreign boot, whenever it was ruled by Gentiles who defiled the land, there were always prophets who gave the people hope. As long as the people had faith, these prophets said, the nation would be restored, just as the king of Persia had released them from bondage and allowed them to rebuild the Temple. Just as the Maccabees had thrown off the yoke of the Syrian tyrant and established a Jewish kingdom, after a long and bloody struggle.

These were stories they could understand. Kingdoms were the business of powerful people, rulers with armies, and treasure to back up their claims. What did that have to do with them—a ragged band of followers?

"Do you not understand this parable?" Jesus said. "Then how will you understand all the parables?"

SOON THEREAFTER THEY WERE JOINED by some of the Pharisees who had listened to his sermon on the mount. Rabbi, they said, "when is this Kingdom of God coming?"

All eyes swiveled back to Jesus. This was a question his followers could understand, and they were eager to hear his answer. They loved the rabbi dearly, but sometimes he spoke in such impenetrable terms that it was hard for them to follow him. They had also discovered that some of the Pharisees were quite intrigued by the things Jesus was saying. Like John the Baptist and his followers, the Pharisees were somewhat of a dissident movement in a land that was now split between several Jewish sects, several different factions. There were those who believed that the sacrificial rites in the Temple were the only path to redemption and those who didn't. There were those who accepted the high priest as the highest religious authority, and those who rejected him as a corrupt collaborationist, a henchman of the Herodians.

The Pharisees were a bit in between. They loathed the Sadducees, the wealthy priesthood that controlled the Temple, but when the festivals came, they went down to the Temple nonetheless. They observed the Torah, but they also tried to reinterpret its meaning for everyday life. That's why some Pharisees were beginning to listen to the rabbi's teachings, because in a way, the Master was doing the same thing.

"The Kingdom of God is not coming with things that can be observed," Jesus replied, "nor will they say, 'Look, here it is!' or 'There it is!'"

Ah, the Pharisees said. Why not?

"Because, in fact, the Kingdom of God is among you."

That struck everyone dumb. Among *us*? Us, fishermen and tradesmen from Galilee?

One of the scribes who had listened to their discussion spoke up. In this Kingdom of God, he asked, what is the greatest commandment? Which *mitzvah* is the first of all?

Jesus answered, "The first is, 'Hear, O Israel: the Lord our God, the Lord is one; you shall love the Lord your God with all your heart, and with all your soul, and with all your mind, and with all your strength.'"

Midway through the verse all the followers fell in, reciting the words from memory, words they had mumbled since they were toddlers. For this was the Jewish profession of faith, the *V'ahavta*.

"But," Jesus continued, "the second is this, 'You shall love your neighbor as yourself,'" now quoting from Leviticus. "There is no other commandment greater than these."

He sat down among them, sensing their rapt attention, and explained that these were the pillars on which the new society, the Kingdom of God, would be built.

It would not be an earthly kingdom, a polity that would challenge the rule of the Romans or that of Herod Antipas, but a nation of faith, based on social justice and compassion, as a reflection of heaven. "So therefore render to Caesar the things that are Caesar's, and to God the things that are God's," he added.

They were quiet after that, each man trying to absorb the rabbi's words and wrap his mind around their meaning. It was slowly beginning to dawn upon them what the rabbi had meant with his sermons and parables. For a long time, there was no sound but the crackling and popping of the dry olive wood over the fire.

They were reaching a turning point, Jesus realized. Looking back, he recalls that this was the moment they were beginning to grasp the enormity of the task that lay ahead of them. Would they be up to it? Would they still agree to follow him?

Most of these men had families and mouths to feed. Others cared for their parents and siblings, or struggled to keep up payments on the large boat that they had leased together. But he needed them. Without shaliach, without delegates like these salt-of-the-earth men and women from Galilee, he could never build the kingdom that Abba had charged him with.

And yet, it was a lot to take in. They were fishermen, not educated men. Most of them couldn't read, let alone write. Finally, one of the Apostles cleared his throat.

"Lord," he said, "teach us to pray, as John taught his disciples."

Everyone nodded at that. Yes, a prayer. That would help them to remember, to remind themselves what it was God wanted them to do.

"Well then," Jesus said, and spread his hands. "Repeat after me. 'Abba.'"

And all the followers did as he told them. They closed their eyes and raised their hands, while a chorus of "Abba" rose to the heavens.

Father,
hallowed be your name.
Your Kingdom come.
Our daily bread give us today.
And forgive us our debts,
for we forgive our debtors.
And do not lead us to the test.

THE SUN IS SLOWLY CREEPING OVER the rim of the mountains of Jordan, turning the deep mauve of the night into a peerless blue. How long has he been sitting here? Half the night? By now the women will be up, mixing yeast with three measures of flour, rolling the dough into flat cakes. In his mind he sees the small oven in the courtyard of Simon Peter's house, and he can almost smell the delicious scent of freshly baking bread. *Give us today our daily bread.*

Suddenly a voice rings out.

He turns and sees Simon Peter walking briskly toward him, a worried expression on his face.

The rabbi smiles. If someone else had interrupted him in his meditation he might have been cross, but Simon, his *kêfa,* his "Rocky," can do no wrong.

"Master," he says, breathless from his run, "Everyone is looking for you. We didn't know where you were." And then he points to the hill, where a number of people have already gathered, hoping for another sermon, or perhaps another miracle.

But Rabbi Jesus shakes his head. He takes the blanket from his shoulders and turns to the Sea of Ginosar. In his mind he sees the scattered towns and villages that lie just beyond the horizon.

"Let us go on to the neighboring towns," he says, placing his hand on Simon's shoulder. "I want to proclaim the message there also."

He pauses and adds, "For that is what I came out to do."

✝

Of course, my depiction of these events, of the days following Jesus' great sermon, is a composite of several different episodes in the Gospels. But there is no question that the Kingdom of God concept was the primary focus of Jesus' ministry. That's also what makes the Our Father so exceptional—not only that it was composed by Jesus himself, but also that in just five brief sentences, it effectively summarized the full scope of Jesus' teachings.

Though deceptively simple, each of these five verses carries a special meaning, starting with the opening: *Abba, hallowed be your name.* In Judaism, the name of God played a unique role. Unlike the cults and religions that surrounded ancient Israel, Judaism refused to allow anyone to depict God in a painting or sculpture. That was rather unprecedented. In Canaan, El was worshipped in the shape of a bull. In Egypt, gods were depicted in a variety of forms, human or animal. And the Greeks and Romans believed that the gods looked just like human beings, but with a physical beauty and perfection beyond the grasp of mere mortals. When early Christianity moved out of Palestine and into the Roman Empire, it inherited these expectations, because people in Asia Minor, Greece, and Rome were used to seeing the god they were praying to. Thus, the earliest depictions of Jesus appear not in Israel but in the catacombs of Rome or on Christian sarcophagi uncovered in Turkey. Depictions of God, as well as of the Apostles and the saints, soon followed.

The ancient Jewish world did not tolerate such a tradition. One could argue, perhaps, that the Asian mind—and Israel is part of Asia, after all—is more comfortable with contemplating God in transcendent terms than the European mind, which, conditioned by centuries of Greek and Roman iconography, requires a devotional image.

That may also be the reason that in Jewish worship, the name by which people prayed to God has a very special meaning, for it was only through this form of address that believers could turn their mind to the Divine.

In the Torah, the first part of Hebrew Scripture, God is referred to by two names: the four-letter construct known as YHWH (Yahweh) or the title *El* and its plural, *Elohim.* Some two centuries before Jesus, the term *Adonai* became the accepted form, which in English is usually translated as "the Lord," a custom that would be continued in the Gospels. Finally, in the first century, another form of address emerged: Ha-Shem, literally "the Name"—a term as mysterious as God itself.

When you see it in this context, Jesus' idea of referring to God as "Papa" was actually a daring and radical innovation. By doing so, Jesus tried to eliminate the great distance that existed between God and human beings. The use of "Father" as an epithet of God also appears in the Hebrew Bible, but there it is used in a metaphorical sense: God as the father of the 12 tribes of Israel. Jesus did the exact opposite. He deliberately used the term Abba, or Papa, to forge a deep intimacy between God and the individual, which would have been anathema for many Jews of the time.

Your Kingdom come. For Jesus, the "Kingdom of God" concept was the central focus of his activity as a preacher and rabbi. Today, that's not always understood. Our idea of who Jesus is and what his ministry was about is to a very great extent determined by the writings of Paul, which are known as epistles, or letters. Paul was an Apostle who never knew Jesus in the flesh but developed a unique interpretation of what Jesus was about in the years following his conversion, roughly in the latter part of the 30s.

Paul explained that Jesus was sent from heaven to be crucified as atonement for the sins of humanity, to be resurrected on the third day. Paul argued that all who believed in Jesus as the source of salvation would share in this redemption and be granted eternal life with Christ after death. As Paul emphasized in one of his letters, "If Christ has not been raised, then our preaching is in vain and your faith is in vain."

This idea is somewhat different from what the Apostles were saying at the time, and indeed, what the synoptic Gospels (those of Mark, Matthew, and Luke) are telling us about Jesus. For them, the paramount message is that Jesus was—and is—the Messiah. In Jewish writings, the Messiah (*Mashiach* in Hebrew, meaning "Anointed One") is a figure who, by military or supernatural means, will restore the sovereignty of Israel as a nation under God's law. The evangelists therefore draw an explicit inference between the Jewish concept of Messiah, as a king and commander from the line of David, and the idea of the Kingdom of God that obviously permeated the oral traditions about Jesus' teachings.

The inherent problem with this equation, and possibly the reason that most Jews in first-century Palestine rejected Jesus as the Messiah, is that the prophesy of the Anointed One promised a liberation from foreign occupation in both a political and a religious sense. The Kingdom of God concept that Jesus espoused was more of a social and spiritual construct, not strictly limited to Jewish aspirations.

Therefore, the words *your Kingdom come* are not an appeal for liberation or redemption in a political sense, but rather a petition, as well as an article of faith. To be a disciple of Jesus, the prayer says, you must believe in the possibility of the Kingdom of God as a society based on faith, love, and social justice. Only then can this kingdom become a tangible reality.

Our daily bread give us today. For us, this is perhaps the most obvious verse in the prayer. Naturally a human being cannot live without nutrition. And clearly bread was a major staple in Jesus' time, as it is today.

The difference is that the ministry of Jesus took place in the midst of a socioeconomic crisis that mainstream biblical scholars have yet to fully acknowledge. There is no other way to explain the frequent references to hunger and poverty in the Gospels and the fact that the Beatitudes—the Sermon on the Mount—are specifically addressed to people who are poor, disenfranchised, hungry, and miserable.

We might say that's not all that surprising. There was obviously a vast gulf between the elite of wealthy priests, noblemen, and officials and the vast majority of peasants and laborers. Life in antiquity was not a walk in the park.

That's true. But we should also remember that Galilee was a special case. Since the days of the Patriarchs, this region had been renowned for its exceptional fertility. The first-century Jewish historian Josephus wrote that virtually everyone in Galilee was engaged in agriculture. But that changed in 37 B.C.E., when King Herod rose to the throne. Herod was eager to demonstrate his bona fides to the Roman emperor and wanted to turn the Jewish kingdom, a rather insignificant corner of the Roman Empire, into a splendid nation filled with the blessings of Greco-Roman culture. He began to build new cities and monuments at a feverish rate. To fund all this, he turned to the one capital asset that the region possessed: Galilean agriculture.

Taxes on farmers were doubled, not only to finance the tribute to Rome but also to fund Herod's ambitious projects in Judea. As the biblical historian Richard Horsley has shown, farmers who succumbed to this tax burden inevitably lost their indebted land to forfeiture.

The upshot of this development is that by the time Jesus launched his ministry, large numbers of homeless and dispossessed families roamed the land, unable to properly feed their families. This is vividly illustrated by the story of the miraculous multiplication of loaves and fishes. Then and now, most bread consumed in the Middle East is leavened flatbread, or pita bread. Bread made from wheat was the principal staple of people's diet in Jesus' time, and we know that such bread is an important source of calories and vitamins. But the story of the miraculous multiplication specifically refers to loaves made from barley. In the first century, barley was grown not for human consumption but as feed for farm animals.

In other words, the miraculous multiplication story tells us that the crisis in Galilee had reduced people to eating animal fodder. The verse *Give us today our daily bread* is therefore not only an urgent petition to God to feed ourselves, but also an invocation to feed those in need. In fact, the Gospels are full of stories of Jesus breaking bread with others. In Jesus' view, such is not only an act of kindness; it is an essential affirmation of our human dignity.

And forgive us our debts, / for we forgive our debtors. This verse differs in Matthew and in Luke, and this has given rise to a lot of different interpretations. Matthew refers to *debts*, but Luke refers to *sins*, perhaps prompted by the fact that the Aramaic word *ḥôbâ* can mean both "debt" and "sin."

The case for "debt" is supported by numerous references in the Gospels to debt in a monetary sense. The parables of the Talents and Pounds (Matthew 25:14-30), the Creditor (Luke 7:41-43), the Rich Fool (Luke 12:16-21), and the Pharisee and the Tax Collector (Luke 18:9-14) all illustrate the erosive impact of debt on Galilean society. The heavy tax burden Herod and his successors placed on farmers in Galilee forced these people to borrow heavily, so as to satisfy the tax collector. Debt, in other words, was a daily source of concern for most Galileans, if not an existential threat. What Matthew's version seems to say is that we should share this burden equally, and that in the Kingdom of God, we should be willing to forgive our debtors as readily as we would expect debt relief from others.

Luke's version takes the verse into the moral domain, into *sin*. It acknowledges that as human beings, we are bound to be fallible, therefore prone to mistakes, or *trespasses,* to use the word used in Catholic, Anglican, and Methodist liturgy. We are sinners, all of us, and only God is able to forgive the sins we have committed. But Luke's version suggests that in the Kingdom of God, this requires reciprocity. In other words, if we expect God to be merciful toward us, then we have the moral duty to extend that same mercy and forgiveness to those who may have done us wrong.

And do not lead us to the test. This last verse in the original Aramaic version of the Our Father has also prompted an intense scholarly debate. One view interprets the word *test* as an apocalyptic clash, a colossal battle between good and evil that, as many believed in Jesus' time, would herald the Kingdom of God at the End Times, the day of Last Judgment. The Gospels tell us that John the Baptist was one of those who believed in such a final test and urged his followers to repent and prepare. The same view is expressed in the Dead Sea Scrolls. Some scholars see something similar in the Book of Revelation, which uses the same Greek word for *test, peirasmos,* as "trial": "Because you have kept my word about patient endurance, I will keep you from the hour of *trial* that is coming on the whole world" (Revelation 3:10). In this view, *And do not lead us to the test* is a petition to God to save the faithful from the horrors of the Last Judgment and allow the righteous to enter the Kingdom on the strength of their faith.

The problem is that this appears to be in conflict with what Jesus himself said on the subject. For Jesus, the Kingdom was a matter of the heart: a perfect state of faith and goodwill toward one another, as a reflection of the Kingdom of Heaven to come. For Jesus, such a Kingdom did not need a massive apocalypse to bring it about.

That is why many historians believe that the word *peirasmos,* a Greek translation of the Aramaic *lenisyôn,* should not be translated as "test" but as "temptation." Not surprisingly, this version has found broad acceptance in Christian liturgy. Who is the source of this temptation? Satan, of course. As it happens, Satan and his acolytes, the demons, appear frequently in the Gospel stories because they represent the exact opposite of what the Kingdom is about: a world ruled by selfishness, lust, and base desires.

In this interpretation, the verse *do not lead us to the test* asks God for strength in resisting any form of temptation of a material or physical nature. "Each person is tempted when he is lured and enticed by his own desire," says the Letter of James, and that is as valid today as it was in Jesus' time.

However we interpret the Our Father, there is no question that the prayer shaped the growth of early Christianity. Many communities throughout the Mediterranean world continued to recite it, and that's how it found its way into the Gospels. The story doesn't end there. As the early Church began to expand across the Roman Empire and into foreign lands never touched by Roman culture, the prayer often served as a vanguard. Especially in places where no one spoke Greek or Latin, the Our Father was usually the first Christian text to be translated, long before the Gospels became available in the local tongue. For example, the first English version of the prayer was composed as early as 650 C.E.

The power of the Our Father to inspire the faithful continues to this day. Although Christianity is the largest religion in the world, with more than 2.4 billion followers, it is splintered over countless traditions and factions with sharply different views on doctrine and liturgical practice. But one thing that is shared across all confessions is the Our Father.

To this day, it is the one prayer all those who call themselves followers of Christ recite.

This heroic head of Emperor Constantine was once part of a colossal statue in Rome.

CHAPTER 3

THE DREAM OF CONSTANTINE

Supreme God:
We beseech you.
We commend all justice to you,
we commend our safety to you,
we commend our empire to you.
Through you we live,
through you we emerge
victorious and fortunate.
Supreme, holy God, hear our prayers,
we stretch our arms to you;
listen, holy, Supreme God.

Via Flaminia, near Rome
October 313 c.e.

I t is late, and the wind from the north carries the bitter taste of rain, but the emperor refuses to step from the opening to his tent. It soothes him, this hour, just to listen to the familiar sounds of an army settling in for the night: the digging of trenches and latrines; the clatter of pots and plates; the idle banter of battle-hardened men, relieved that they have made it through another day. High above, the stars are obscured by thick columns of smoke wafting up from a hundred campfires, carrying the scent of rabbits, chickens, and heaven knows what else being roasted on spits.

A slave brings him a cup of wine, but he waves it away; he wants to be left alone. In the distance, a cohort begins to sing one of their bawdy marching songs, full of expletives and exaggerated accounts of their conquests. He smiles; it is a good sign. Despite their battle scars and obvious fatigue, the men are in good spirits. Morale, he knows, is not a mystery. It all depends on good generalship. *His* generalship. Unlike other Roman commanders, he always insists on taking his forces into battle himself, usually by leading his *cataphractii,* his armored cavalry, into a devastating head-on attack. He'd learned such tactics while serving as a young officer in Diocletian's army. Diocletian was no friend of his family, but even the wizened old emperor was impressed with the way young Constantine led his men into the field, sending entire barbarian armies to whatever afterlife they believed in.

But the morale among his general officers, well, that's another story. In a few moments, they will gather in his tent for the nightly war council, and no doubt he will get another earful of their gripes: the staggering casualties, the loss of trained cavalry horses, the endless problems with supply. How many troops does he still have? He started out with well over 50,000, but after five months of hard campaigning, he'll be lucky if he still has 30,000 battle-worthy men left.

No one could have foreseen that it would last so long. Back in 305, no one expected Rome to be plunged into another civil war. The house that Augustus had built, the imperial system of worldwide governance, had stood for nearly three centuries. Emperors came and went—some because they were toppled, others because they were killed, some because they died of old age—yet through it all, the Roman Empire kept humming as if nothing was amiss. Even through the worst of civil war and foreign invasion, tributes were collected, favors dispensed, and salaries paid by countless unseen bureaucrats, far removed from either politics or battle.

That changed when the barbarian invasions, always a nuisance, started to become an existential threat. That's when Emperor Diocletian decided that a major management reorganization was in order. Instead of *one,* the realm needed *four* rulers, to ensure that every border was protected: two emperors and two vice-emperors, or *Caesars,* each placed in a strategic corner of the empire. Thus was born the Tetrarchy, the "Rule of Four."

But then Diocletian suddenly announced that he wanted to retire. It was true, he was in poor health and looked forward to spending his final years in a sumptuous palace he had built in the city of Spoleto on the Adriatic Sea. The problem was that this forced his co-emperor, Maximian, to retire as well, so as to allow both their Caesars to advance to the highest office. That's when things got out of hand, for everyone with a half-decent claim on the throne decided to join the fray. For example, when Constantius, the emperor in the West, suddenly died, his army elevated his son Constantine to the throne. But that prompted the Praetorian Guard in Rome to declare for *their* candidate, whose name was Maxentius, the son of Maximian. There followed many years of turmoil and battle, but in 313 came a turning point: Constantine was able to push Maxentius, his last rival in the West, from the north of Italy.

And now it is October 27, and Constantine finds himself standing on the threshold of Rome. Encamped along the Via Flaminia, they're at a stone's throw from the Tiber River, the historical boundary that marks the city precinct. A single span crosses the river at this point. The locals referred to it as the Milvian Bridge.

He himself cares little for the place—he has hardly spent any time in the city and considers it a relic of the past— but he is well aware of its psychological significance for Rome's enemies and friends throughout the world. Whoever controls the city of Rome controls the realm, even though the Tetrarchy has long since moved its main command centers to more strategic locations. That is why he *has* to defeat Maxentius on the morrow and crush the old aristocracy with which the pretender surrounds himself. That is why he has to win the coming battle—decisively, irrevocably.

He knows his army still has one good fight in it, that morale is high, and yet, and yet—he is troubled. Earlier in the day, he saw . . . well, *something,* though he is not sure what it was: a natural phenomenon perhaps. Or some bizarre anomaly, not unusual in these parts. Or a vision, a sign from above. Who would know? Who can explain it to him? No one else seems to have seen it, or they would have reported it, wouldn't they? Should he share it with his generals? Or will they think he's gone soft in the head?

He sighs and decides he needs a drink after all. Walking back into the imperial tent, the same slave is still waiting with his cup. He takes it wordlessly, gulps the wine—and promptly makes a face. This Italian stuff is not at all like the sweet variety he's developed a taste for at his imperial residence in Trier, on the Moselle River.

His tent is large, much bigger than the small *contubernia* that his soldiers are forced to squeeze into, eight men to a tent. The imperial tent, by contrast, boasts a suite of rooms, each separated by stiff walls made from calfskin. As usual, the entrance is decorated with rows of battle *vexelli,* tattered emblems of the units he's commanded since his earliest days as a general officer. Below them hangs a row of flags and trophies, including the sword that was taken from the body of Ruricius Pompeianus, Maxentius's ablest general, killed in the Battle of Verona just last year.

There are also a few private items, but these he keeps out of sight of his officers. On the small table next to his bed, for example, is the portrait of his son Crispus by his first wife, Minervina. A much smaller portrait of his current wife, Fausta, stands beside it. Unfortunately, his second marriage is under a cloud. It's been five years since they were wed, and she has still not borne him a child. His friends have written him that back in Trier, it is widely rumored that she is barren.

And then, at the third hour of the night, his senior commanders troop in for the evening conference. Everyone is keen to hear the scout reports, for no one has actually seen, let alone made contact with, the enemy. That the morning will bring battle, of that there is no doubt. The River Tiber is the last defensive line before Rome, save for the city walls proper. One way or another, Maxentius will have to make a stand. That worries them. They know that without the benefit of surprise, the advantage is always with the defender, given his shorter lines of supply and the ability to entrench his forces at leisure. What's more, the generals know that Maxentius has far more men, including the fanatical Praetorian Guard, sworn to protect the life of the emperor.

Though every officer tries to ignore it, the tension in the air is almost palpable. No one doubts that the battle on the morrow will be the biggest and most difficult fight of their campaign. It is going to be a closely run matter, and the commanders know it.

One by one, the officers array themselves around the map table, chatting with one another or motioning a slave for a cup of wine. Most have fought together for years, some going back to the war of 306 in northern Britain. But as soon as one of the slaves brings in a map of the area and spreads it on the table, the conversation stops. The map is old and wrinkled, obviously pulled with haste from the cartographic library of the senior legate, but there is no indication, no clue whatsoever of the enemy's positions. Clearly the scouting vanguard has not yet returned. The officers are still in the dark.

Moments later, Constantine enters the room. Never one to stand on protocol, he absentmindedly acknowledges the stiff salutes and motions to the table. A desultory conversation follows, the emperor inquiring into this and that while everyone waits for the reconnaissance reports. Time and again, the commander of the *exploratores,* the mounted reconnaissance unit, steps outside to inquire about his scouts. *Where the hell are they? The emperor is waiting.* But to no avail. The reconnaissance detail is nowhere to be seen.

Inside the tent, the emperor becomes taciturn and withdrawn, immersed in his thoughts. The generals pretend not to notice and keep their conversation going as best they can. They all know about the true condition of the army. All one has to do is step outside and take a look. The battles of the Po Valley have turned the campaign into a hard slog, the type of attritional warfare that consumes men regardless of whether you are winning or losing. Horses are in short supply. Yes, special details are out corralling whatever they can get their hands on, but clearly these new horses will be untrained, hardly fit for battle. Food supply is not much better, since Maxentius has purged the countryside of anything that can be used to feed an army. Scorched-earth tactic—they are all familiar with it, having done it themselves when the need called for it. And yet morale is surprising high, considering the state that the legions are in; of course, that can change in a heartbeat.

WHEN AT MIDNIGHT THE SCOUTS have still not returned, the generals start to debate how *they* would organize the defense if they were in Maxentius's shoes. Everyone agrees that the most sensible thing is to entrench right behind the Tiber. It is textbook, this type of defense, and Maxentius is no fool. For this reason, they should plan accordingly.

That means that Constantine's favorite opening gambit, the flying cavalry attack, will not work. Instead, they will have to scour the area for boats at first light—not a welcome prospect, since Maxentius has probably thought of that too. And even if they do find a way to get the infantry across in one piece, it will be the devil of a task to get them in battle order and attack in echelon—all under withering fire from Maxentius's archers, no doubt. The longer the generals talk about it, the more serious they become. Not pessimistic, never that—simply *aware* of the tremendous odds they will face.

Constantine suddenly wakes from his reverie and startles them all with a question: Have they seen it?

The generals look at each other. Seen what, exactly?

The . . . *thing,* Constantine says, his eyes unfocused, as if he is reliving the vision afresh. Whatever it was. From one moment to the next, it looked as if the sun had split into three parts like a giant orb or perhaps like a cross, formed by light.

The generals clear their throats, scratch their beards. Like most military men, they are superstitious and firmly believe in the importance of omens.

Was it a sign? A heavenly sign? Perhaps. But if so, from whom?

They know that Constantine is a monotheist, a man devoted to one god. This is Sol Invictus, the "Unconquered Sun God," a great Apollo-like deity whose birth date is celebrated on the winter solstice, December 25. Constantine's panegyrists have made much hay of that, the idea that Sol is Constantine's patron god, since it ties his imperial claim to the imperial House of the Flavians. In Gaul, Constantine even had some coins struck showing him side by side with the victorious sun god.

But there are other rumors as well, both at court and in the barracks. These rumors claim that this is all outward show. That in his heart, Constantine is leaning more and more toward the Christian cult like his mother, Dowager Empress Helena.

Is that the reason the auguries were so poor on their departure from Trier? *Do not attempt the invasion of Italy*, the priests told

Constantine—not now, not when the omens were so unfavorable. News of the disastrous augury rapidly spread among the troops, and many were apprehensive.

But Constantine dismissed the auguries out of hand. He was in touch with "the divine mind" himself, he proclaimed to his soldiers; meaning, *That is why I know our cause is just, and that victory will be ours.* The speech worked. But that's because everybody assumed that the emperor was talking about the sun god. What if he was talking about the Christian God? Would Constantine risk such an outrageous thing?

Constantius, Constantine's father, may have stopped the persecutions begun by Diocletian, but most people still treat Christians with suspicion. Prejudice against them is rife both in government circles and among the officer ranks of the legions. And outside of Constantine's territory—particularly in Italy, North Africa, and Asia—Christians continue to be oppressed as a dangerous, subversive sect. The very idea that the emperor could be sympathetic toward these people, these *Chrestians,* is simply preposterous, unthinkable.

Rome will stand or fall by the grace of its ancient gods; everyone knows that. To lose faith in their power is to lose faith in the idea of Rome itself. To even suggest such, on the eve of battle, when the fate of the realm hangs in the balance, is tantamount to treason.

Was there anything special about this vision, a general asks. Anything that could help us decipher its meaning? Is it not true, as he's been told, that Apollo himself once appeared to the emperor? Accompanied by the goddess of victory, carrying a laurel wreath with the Roman numeral XXX?

A silent, noncommittal nod from the emperor. Now is not the time to reveal that he'd made that story up out of whole cloth, as any imperial claimant is expected to do. In the battle for the Roman Empire, propaganda is as important as the power of the sword. But this vision—this is different. It did not look like a freak accident of nature. It didn't look like something that can be explained away as some optical effect, a reflection of some sort, a cloud formation lit from behind by the sun. To Constantine, it looked like the real thing. "A most marvelous sign," he calls it.

Plus, the fact that some text appeared right below it.

A piece of text? In writing? In *Greek*?

Yes, the emperor says. *En toutoi nika,* it read. "Conquer by this."

A pause, then everyone begins to talk at once. Of course, the generals are relieved beyond measure. They know that an omen, *any* omen, can spell doom or victory, but if the god has written these words across the sky, that can only signal divine sanction of their cause. Smiles begin to appear, the generals clasping each other's arms. Sol Invictus smiles on our venture, our victory! Cups of wine are raised; toasts are drunk.

Except for Constantine. He does not share their confidence, and for this reason: The message in the sky makes no sense. What does it mean, "Conquer by this?" By the sun? The sun god himself? By Jove, he and almost every other general officer already carry the symbol of the victorious sun god on every surface they can think of: their breastplates, their shields, their battle standards. And not only because Sol Invictus is Constantine's patron god; the radiant sun is also a motif as old as Alexander the Great, to try to blind the enemy with its reflected light. So what is the vision telling him? What does this god want him to do that he hasn't done already?

A few commanders see the emperor's frown and quietly nod toward the exit of the tent. The emperor is tired; they should retire, wait for news from the scouts in the morning. All salute briskly and leave. Constantine waves them off, then stretches on a nearby couch. His fingers probe the numbing fatigue behind his eyes. Yes, he is tired, but the riddle of the sign nags him, won't leave him alone. A slave offers him another cup of wine, but he shakes his head. What he needs now is sleep: the sweet oblivion of a long, undisturbed rest. Perhaps tonight, it will finally be granted to him.

But even as he stretches on his bed and surrenders himself to the slaves, untying his sandals and the clasps of his tunic, he knows the respite will be brief, that he will be up long before sunrise.

THE DREAM IS VERY SHORT, or perhaps that's how it seems in retrospect. Time, like logic, doesn't seem to matter in dreams; things happen from one moment to the next without any apparent connection. He dreams that he stands in an open field and watches the sun rise, then split into an orb, exactly what he saw the day before. And then, suddenly, the three lights carve a sign in the sky as clearly as if someone is drawing it with a pen on a scroll. It looks like the letter *X*, but one perpendicular line rises up and curves outward, forming the letter *P*, pronounced "rho" in Greek. He recognizes the sign. It is the *chi rho* emblem, the first two letters of the Greek word *Christos*. The symbol of Christianity.

A voice rises from heaven. "Go and order your soldiers to paint the heavenly sign on their shields," it says, "and so to proceed to battle." And then, in an instant, the dream vanishes, taking the luminous apparition with it. He wakes up, rubs his eyes, and sees the familiar calfskin of his tent. He runs his hand over his face. Is this a dream, a vision, or both?

A slave, half asleep on a stool in the corner, awakes and offers him a cup of water. He pushes him away, and wearing nothing but a silk robe over his loincloth, runs through the tent and into the cold of the early dawn, calling for his legate.

They need paint; lots of it.

Later that morning, after each of his soldiers has hastily painted the Christogram on his shield with lime plaster from a nearby quarry, Constantine force-marches his army down the Via Flaminia, covering the last few miles to the Milvian Bridge that spans the River Tiber, the last obstacle before Rome. It is October 28; the sun is shrouded in fog, and the air is damp from the nearby marshes. He can see the breath of his men. Fall has come early this day.

As usual, Constantine rides at the head of his main cavalry unit, but his mind is in turmoil. The dream has unsettled him. He knows all about the Christian God, of course. His mother is a pious woman, a devoted Christian, and she would have baptized him too if his father, Constantius, had not put a stop to it. Christianity is still a *religio illicita,* a banned faith, and proclaiming oneself as a Christian is tantamount to committing professional suicide.

He knows the reason: Most Christians shun military service. What's more, they refuse to sacrifice to statues of the emperor. That's why people think of them as an alien cult, unpatriotic, hostile to Roman interests. But deep in his heart, Constantine knows that Christian communities pose no threat to anyone. On the contrary, many cities rely on their charitable works, such as feeding the poor and burying the dead.

And now, the Christ of his mother's faith has spoken to him in a dream. It rattles him, the idea that a divinity would truly want to communicate with him. The question is, Why? Why *now*?

A shout shakes him from his reverie. The exploratores, the unit that everyone has been waiting for, have finally reappeared and are racing toward the head of the army. Their horses are flecked with foam; they must have been riding all night. A tribune on Constantine's staff meets them and escorts them to the emperor.

The report is brief, a mere sentence or two, but it strikes like a thunderbolt from the sky. At first, Constantine refuses to believe it, but the decurion insists. He has seen the enemy's order of battle with his own eyes. There is no doubt whatsoever. Maxentius has destroyed the Milvian Bridge and placed his forces in a long line *in front of the river.*

Constantine shakes his head in disbelief. If the report is true and not a ruse, then Maxentius has committed a major blunder. Rather than defending the city from behind its ancient walls, as his forces in Turin and

Verona did, he has moved out to meet him in the open. And rather than placing his forces behind the Tiber River, he has moved them in front of it. That not only robs him of the room to maneuver but also denies him the use of the river as a defensive line.

Why would Maxentius, an experienced general, do such a thing? Is he worried about defections? Is that why he has destroyed the Milvian Bridge, to deny his soldiers a means to escape? If so, then morale in his ranks must be a lot worse than anyone surmised.

And suddenly Constantine's spirits begin to rise. Perhaps it is true, he thinks; perhaps the God of Christ is truly protecting him, confusing his enemy, showing him the path to victory. And if that is the case, then he, Constantine, will remember this day for the rest of his life.

He looks around, pleased to see the grins on the faces of his officers. The news has given them the shot in the arm that they need.

He signals the commander of the imperial cavalry.

"Sir!"

"You may commence the attack," Constantine says calmly.

"At your command, *imperator*," the officer replies, salutes, and spurs his horse. Moments later, the trumpets sound, the men form up, and the tight mass of the heavy cavalry rides out. A splendid sight, the way these cataphractii begin their assault: first moving at a steady trot, in perfect formation, colors and pennants flying; then gradually picking up speed, the hooves drumming on the hard-packed earth, the noise overwhelming, giving the enemy a good look of the juggernaut that is heading straight toward them.

The move takes Maxentius by surprise. He knows that the frontal cavalry attack is Constantine's favorite opening. That's why he has spaced his forces out along the Tiber in an effort to thwart it. This way, a narrow frontal assault would merely push through a thin screen of soldiers before plunging headlong into the river. But then he sees Constantine's cavalry split and fan out, and he realizes his mistake. He opens his mouth, turns to his tribune to unleash his own cavalry, but it is too late; at that moment the first units of the enemy crash into his center like an avalanche.

A furious battle ensues. Without waiting for the outcome of the cavalry attack, Constantine sends his infantry into the fray. Though outnumbered by far, they march briskly, ready and eager for the fight, brandishing the chi rho symbol on their shields as battle ensigns, as emblems of divine justice. Watching his soldiers, Constantine is reminded of something Diocletian once told him. The greatest weapon a soldier can ever yield, Diocletian said, is his *mind:* his will to win, his absolute and unshakable faith in victory. And that, Constantine knows, is what the Christian God has given them.

He realizes that he owes this God a debt. As soon as he is inside Rome's walls, he vows, he will acknowledge it. And once he's finished, the Roman Empire will never be the same.

As the sun rises high and the battle becomes a furious melee of Roman soldiers fighting each other to the death, it looks as if Maxentius's soldiers will rally. They have superior numbers and may still carry the day. They certainly fight bravely, Constantine has to give them that. But they are not veterans, not like the fine soldiers they fought at Segusium and Verona: experienced men, the cream of Maxentius's forces. And so, almost imperceptibly, the ranks at the river begin to give way, like stalks of corn under the scythe.

The first soldiers to break are those closest to a rickety pontoon bridge that Maxentius has ordered built to bring up supplies. With the escape route so near, so tantalizingly close, the temptation becomes irresistible. They break, turn, and run, dropping their shields and weapons before pounding on the improvised bridge, ignoring the shouts of the engineers who were still busy anchoring the boats.

Within minutes, Maxentius's battle line begins to collapse. Instead of fighting the enemy, the soldiers turn on each other, pushing and shoving their comrades out of the way in a dash for the pontoon bridge and the safety of the opposite river bank. The retreat becomes a rout.

As more and more men fight their way onto the delicate footbridge, the planks give way, the boats take on water, and the bridge starts to collapse. Constantine holds his breath as hundreds of men plunge into the swirling waters of the Tiber before his very eyes, their heavy armor dragging them down into the murky water.

Later that evening, as the burial details begin their grim job, Maxentius's body is located as well. In the end, he too dropped his sword and joined his men in a desperate rush for the rear. His body is found not far from the spot where his horse has cast him into the water, surrounded by the corpses of men who swore to defend him.

Rome now belongs to Constantine.

Five months later, Constantine is in Milan, getting ready for the wedding of his half sister Constantia to Licinius, his co-emperor in the East. Ever since the Battle of the Milvian Bridge, Constantine has been mulling over the best way to repay his debt to the Christian God. The obvious solution, he believes, is to legitimize Christianity once and for all as a recognized faith of the Roman Empire. The planned visit of Licinius to Milan is the perfect opportunity to do so, for there are also many Christian communities in the East, including Asia Minor. In this way, the new decree can be promulgated by both emperors, for both East and West, ensuring that all Christians will henceforth be freed from discrimination and oppression.

The text for the new decree is carefully drafted and reviewed by his counselors. But for Constantine, the legalese does not quite capture the great significance of the moment or the sense of deep debt he owes this Christian God. He feels it needs to be accompanied by a *votum,* a national vow or prayer, traditionally drafted by either the emperor or Senate to invoke the blessing of a god. But this votum will be dedicated to one God only, the Supreme God, in the hope that he will continue to favor Constantine's reign.

"Supreme God," the prayer begins,

> *We beseech you. We commend all justice to you, we commend our*
> *safety to you, we commend our empire to you. Through you we*
> *live, through you we emerge victorious and fortunate.*
> *Supreme, holy God, hear our prayers, we stretch our arms to you;*
> *listen, holy, Supreme God.*

And so it comes to pass. In February 313, Constantine welcomes Licinius to Milan. They agree on the final text of the declaration, and at the end of the wedding celebrations, both co-emperors jointly announce the Edict of Milan, granting full religious freedom to all citizens under their imperial sway.

☧

WHAT REALLY HAPPENED ON THE VIA FLAMINIA on the eve of the great Battle of the Milvian Bridge? Two different accounts have come down to us, and my reconstruction of the story is essentially a composite of both. Lactantius, a scholar who converted to Christianity as early as 303 C.E. and served as tutor to Constantine's son Crispus, gives us one version. He wrote that in the night before the battle, Constantine was commanded in a dream to "delineate the heavenly sign on the shields of his soldiers" prior to battle, though the shape of that sign was not specified in any detail.

Bishop Eusebius of Caesarea, one of Constantine's biographers, offers another version. He wrote that on the day before the battle, Constantine had a vision of a luminescent cross in the sky, just above the sun, blazing with the Greek words *en toutoi nika* ("by this [sign] conquer"). The exact nature of this phenomenon continues to be debated. Some recent authors

have suggested that Constantine may have witnessed a celestial phenomenon known as a parhelion, whereby sunlight is refracted through ice
crystals to create a luminous ring, anchored on bright spots on either side
of the sun.

These accounts are not necessarily in conflict. The dream Lactantius
described could have served to explain the vision that Constantine reportedly saw earlier that day. What matters, though, is that Constantine
himself firmly believed he had experienced a spiritual encounter with the
Christian God and that this encounter helped him to defeat his rival in
the West.

The day after the battle was October 29, 312. According to Roman
custom, Constantine marched his forces into Rome in a triumphal procession known as an *adventus*. Ancient tradition required that such victory
parades end at the temple of Jupiter Optimus Maximus on Capitoline
Hill. Here, at Rome's most important religious shrine, the victorious
general was expected to offer a sacrifice to Jupiter in thanksgiving. But
according to the panegyrist describing the parade, Constantine declined
to do so. He scrupulously avoided the temple, refusing to credit a pagan
god with his victory.

More signs of Constantine's new spiritual allegiance began to emerge
in the weeks and months to come. He disbanded the Praetorian Guard,
one of the oldest military units in the history of the empire, since they
were the ones who had proclaimed Maxentius as emperor to begin with.
Constantine also abolished the Imperial Horse Guard, which remained
loyal to Maxentius until the very end, and he ordered their large fort on
Caelian Hill, the Castra Nova, torn down. In its place he built a large civic
hall known as a basilica, similar to the one he had built in Trier, in the
Rhineland of today's Germany. Shortly after, he presented the building to
the bishop of Rome. It became known as the church of St. John Lateran.
It still stands on the Piazza di San Giovanni in Laterano, the oldest of five
papal basilicas still in existence.

The graveyard that the Horse Guard used was also destined for demolition. In its place rose a church dedicated to St. Marcellinus and St. Peter, just as the graveyard of the Praetorian Guard was used for the construction of a church dedicated to St. Agnes and St. Constantius. As Paul Stephenson has suggested, it would seem that in his vengeance against his former rival, Constantine specifically earmarked the property of imperial guards for the construction of Christian churches.

Other monuments built by Maxentius were repurposed for Constantine's use. The massive Basilica of Maxentius on the Roman Forum, begun in 308, was completed by Constantine and given his name instead. The building's northern aisle still stands on the Forum today, the greatest monument of Roman secular architecture in late antiquity.

In February 313, Constantine did meet his co-emperor in the East, Licinius, in Milan. Diocletian's original system of dividing the empire into an eastern and a western half, each to be ruled by an emperor and a deputy known as a Caesar, was still in force. Constantine did not expect any objection from Licinius to his proposed edict of religious freedom, and in this he was not disappointed. As it happened, Licinius also faced a challenge to his rule, in the form of his Caesar, Maximinus Daia. Soon after his elevation in 308, Maximinus began to challenge his superior for the supreme post of emperor. A temporary truce was agreed on in 311 by carving up the Eastern Empire between themselves. But unlike Licinius, who took a tolerant attitude toward Christians, Maximinus was a committed pagan who continued to persecute Christians with a vengeance. Licinius knew that it was only a matter of time before he came to blows with his rival. A declaration of tolerance, as Constantine suggested, would therefore become a valuable piece of propaganda—particularly because there were many Christian communities in the territory ruled by Maximinus.

Thus, the two emperors in Milan, now joined as brothers through marriage, issued the famous Edict of Milan—prompted, as they said, by "reverence for the divinity."

"We thought," Constantine wrote, "that we might grant to the Christians and others full authority to observe that religion which one prefers." The edict therefore granted "both to Christians and to all others the freedom to follow whichever religion they might wish; whereby whatsoever divinity dwells in heaven may be appeased." Constantine was well aware that the people now under his sway followed many different religions, not in the least those who continued to venerate Rome's ancient gods. But that the emperor favored monotheism, of that there was no doubt. "We thought to arrange that no one whatsoever should be denied the opportunity to give his heart to the observance of the Christian religion," he added, "so that the Supreme Deity, to whose worship we freely yield our hearts, may show his favor in all things."

The edict has rightfully been acknowledged as a watershed in the history of the Roman Empire. But the fact that it was accompanied by a public prayer to the "Supreme God" is not generally known. Why was it excised from later records, including Eusebius's *Ecclesiastical History*? Shortly after the Milan wedding, Licinius was forced to rush back to the borders of his eastern realm. His rival, Maximinus, had exploited the emperor's absence to invade his territory. By the time Licinius was able to scrape together 30,000 men near the city of Adrianople (modern Edirne on the Greek-Bulgarian border), he found himself facing a force more than double in size, some 70,000 men, commanded by Maximinus himself.

Facing such odds, the historian Lactantius later wrote, Licinius ordered Constantine's prayer to be "distributed to all the officers and tribunes, so that they could all teach them to their own troops. Confidence then grew among them all with the belief that victory had been announced to them from heaven." Apparently this is exactly what happened: The troops fell to their knees and said the prayer three times. They then turned on

Maximinus's forces and dealt them a decisive defeat. Two months later, on April 30, Licinius formally abrogated the persecution of Christians in all the lands formerly ruled by his foe.

An amazing turn of events. Why, then, is this prayer not better known? Why don't we remember it as a pivotal moment in the history of Christianity?

The answer is that soon after, tensions rose between Constantine and Licinius, notwithstanding their familial relations through marriage. The reasons don't concern us here, other than that Constantine's control over Rome was a major point of contention, as was his choice of Caesars to be groomed as his eventual successors. In truth, the two men were both fed up with the cumbersome Tetrarchy, the Rule of Four, and wanted to rule in his own right. By 316, three years after the Edict of Milan, the two emperors were openly at war.

Despite a temporary truce, hostilities flared up again, and in 324, Constantine defeated his rival in Adrianople, not far from the field where Licinius had triumphed over Maximinus. Acceding to the desperate pleas of his sister Constantia, Licinius's wife, Constantine allowed Licinius to retire to Thessalonica. But when he discovered that Licinius was plotting against him once more, this time by rallying barbarian troops, Constantine had him hanged. Licinius's role in history was excised, and so was the prayer that had become so closely associated with his victory over Maximinus—even though most likely, it had been composed by Constantine after the Battle of the Milvian Bridge.

Constantine was true to his word. Now in sole command of the empire, both East and West, he moved to rehabilitate all Christians and to nurture the growth of a Christian Church within his realm. All Christian property that had been confiscated in the preceding decades was returned to their owners. Officials and clerks who had been dismissed from their positions in the imperial government were invited back. Churches were restored, and others were built from scratch.

In this, Constantine encouraged his architects to use the basilica form, traditionally used as a civic center, rather than the typical Roman design for a temple, since temples were invariably associated with pagan gods. What's more, pagan worship was usually done in private, by individuals, whereas Christian liturgy was performed in the presence of a large community. The paradigm of a Roman temple was simply not large enough to contain the rapidly growing Christian community of Rome. Thus, the basilica, a building that in Roman history had always served as a city hall, became the favored design for a Christian church.

As the years progressed, Constantine became more active in guiding the early Church, creating a precedent that would be followed by Byzantine emperors in the decades and centuries to come. He established a new seven-day calendar, starting with Sunday as the *Dies Domini,* or Day of the Lord, which is reflected in the French word *dimanche* and the Italian *domenica.* He also decreed the development of a liturgical calendar, regulating the various Christian festivals and feast days that culminated in Holy Week and Easter. Up to this point, church services had been rather informal, since they were often celebrated in secret, in home chapels. Now, Christian worship was formalized into a liturgy filled with litanies, hymns, and prayers; many of these rites still survive in the Eastern Orthodox Church today.

Constantine's greatest monument to Christianity, however, was the basilica he ordered built on a hill known as the Ager Vaticanus, Vatican Hill, previously used as a large necropolis that reportedly held the remains of the Apostle Peter. The construction of St. Peter's Basilica took 25 years, but the building would stand for more than a millennium—powerful testimony to the supremacy of Roman engineering in late antiquity. It was in this church that Charlemagne was crowned emperor of the Holy Roman Empire in 800. And the church still stood at the dawn of the high Renaissance, when Pope Julius II ordered Donato Bramante to design a new basilica from scratch.

Constantine the Great had changed the Roman Empire beyond recognition. Though he himself would not be baptized until he lay on his deathbed, he had prepared the empire for the moment, some 50 years later, when Christianity became the sole religion of the realm, and by extension, the basis for Western civilization.

John Everett Millais's portrait shows Joan of Arc as a humble young woman, called to arms.

CHAPTER 4

THE VOICES OF JOAN OF ARC

✝

And suddenly I heard a voice, on my right.
It was accompanied by a light,
coming from the same side as the voice.
It spoke French in soft and gentle tones,
and there was no doubt in my mind
that it came from God.
It said that I must come to France
and raise the siege laid
to the city of Orléans.

DOMRÉMY, THE DUCHY OF BAR
France
1425

At first glance, there's nothing unusual or remarkable about Joan. Like most other young women from the village of Domrémy, she is a farmer's daughter who faithfully does her chores, such as feeding the animals, cleaning the stable, or herding the livestock to better pastures. Her parents aren't rich, but neither are they poor. Her father, Jacques, it is rumored, owns as many as 50 acres, and even so he complements his income with minor administrative duties in the surrounding villages. What sets Joan—little Jehanette—apart is an unusual, all-consuming piety.

When questioned, the curé, Father Guillaume Fronté, agrees. "When she was 12, Jehanette was a good and sincere girl," he says, "pious, of good morals, fearing God, so good that there had never been the like in the village." But he admits that it is rather unsettling, the way she insists on attending every Mass that he celebrates in the small village church, even if she is in meadows yonder, tending the cattle. "When she heard the bell toll while in the fields," another villager remembers, "she came running to the church to hear the Mass, as I have seen her do."

It gets even stranger when Jehanette starts to show up for confession on a daily basis, even though confession is usually heard a few times a year, before the great religious feasts. Even stranger, she exhibits no interest in playing, dancing, or any of the other things that young girls are supposed to do.

"She would go off on her own sometimes," Jean Waterin, a local boy, would later say, "and speak to God." And when she did, he added shame-faced, "We all made fun of her." "True" said another boy, the son of Jean Colin. "She was always praying to God and the Virgin. And of course we would tease her about it."

THEN CAME THE SUMMER OF 1425: the 88th year of the war between England and France, between the Plantagenets and the House of Valois, for control of the French kingdom. In centuries to come, historians would refer to the conflict as the Hundred Years' War. The population of France saw it somewhat differently. For them, it was an unending scourge of pillage, destruction, and death, made even more horrific by the plague of 1348, which lasted two years and carried off almost a third of the country's population.

As if this wasn't enough, the Church was once again going through a crisis as well. Back in 1305, the newly elected pope, Clement V, stunned Christendom by refusing to settle in Rome. Instead, he moved to the admittedly more pleasant surroundings of Avignon in Provence, in southern France. It was not until 1377 that Pope Gregory XI agreed to return to Rome, and then only in response to the urgent pleas of the mystic Catherine of Siena. Alas, when he died barely a year later, rival factions decided to elect *two* popes: the Italian Urban VI who resided in Rome and the French Clement VII who went back to Avignon. By the time a special council was called to Pisa in 1409 to resolve the matter, there were actually *three* popes, each claiming to be the legitimate heir of St. Peter.

And then the Hundred Years' War took an ominous turn. Cunningly, the English king, Henry V, found a way to gather a fleet of 1,500 ships, the largest naval force ever assembled, which crossed the Channel and poured into the French countryside. In the months that followed, the English king—with his ally, the Duke of Burgundy—was able to seize large swaths of northern France, stretching from Rouen to Paris. The French were virtually powerless, since their king, Charles VI, was too wracked by mental illness to organize a concerted defense. That left the kingdom in the hands of Queen Isabeau, a well-intentioned but weak-willed woman, with dire consequences for the nation.

As it happened, the English king was not satisfied with occupying the north. He wanted *all* of France. To that end, he forced poor Isabeau to disinherit her own son, Crown Prince Charles, and accept him, Henry V, as the heir, the dauphin, instead. To make things nice and legal, he agreed to marry Isabeau's daughter, Princess Marie. This deft maneuver would go down in history as the Treaty of Troyes of 1420.

But fate had something entirely different in mind. Two years later, Europe was stunned by the news that both the English king and the French king (now thoroughly mad) died within two months of each other. Their untimely passing left two claimants to the French throne: Henry's infant son by his French wife, Marie, and the original dauphin, Charles VII. The latter, needless to say, had refused to submit to the Treaty of Troyes and still claimed to be the legitimate prince of France, even though his French forces had suffered one humiliating defeat after another.

Small wonder, perhaps, that these perilous times saw the rise of a number of mystics, seers, and soothsayers. One seer, Bridget of Sweden, warned the people of France that they themselves bore the blame for their political troubles. "Only when the French acquire true humility, shall the kingdom devolve to the true heir and experience a good peace," she said.

But the prophecy that would soon be on everyone's lips was uttered by another mystic, Marie of Avignon. She declared that "France, ruined by a woman, would be restored by a virgin from the marches of Lorraine." No one needed to be told what she meant by the "woman": Obviously, that was Queen Isabeau, who had sold out the nation to the English king. But who was this mysterious "virgin from Lorraine"?

THE WORLD WOULD SOON FIND OUT, BECAUSE IN 1425 the Hundred Years' War finally comes to the village of Domrémy. As it happens, Jehanette's family lives on one of the fault lines of the war. This is the Meuse River, which divides those who have pledged their fealty to Burgundy (in alliance with the English invaders) and the so-called Armagnacs, people who remain loyal to the French dauphin. One day, a group of Anglo-Burgundian militants crashes into the village and brutally kills or burns everything they can lay their hands on. Fortunately, Jehanette and the rest of her family are able to gather their livestock in the nick of time and flee to Neufchâteau, where they stay for a fortnight, until it is safe to return.

The voices begin soon after.

"It happened toward noon," she would remember later. "It was summer, and I was in my father's garden. I remember it well, because I had not fasted during the previous day. And suddenly I heard a voice, on my right, in the direction of the church. It was accompanied by a light, coming from the same side as the voice."

What sort of voice was this?

"It was . . . it was a *worthy* voice," she would recall. "It spoke French in soft and gentle tones, and there was no doubt in my mind that it came from God. When I heard it a second, and then a third time, I knew that it was the voice of an angel."

But what did the voice say?

"That I should be good," Jehanette said, at the time just 13 years old. "That I should be obedient and go to church often. And that the day would come when I would have to come to France." By "France" she means the heartland of the kingdom, the royal region of the Loire.

She tells her parents about the voice, but does not get the reaction she hopes for. Her father, Jacques, has observed with growing concern the obsessive devotion of his daughter. He also notes that Jeanne has begun to take an unusual interest in the soldiers who pass through the region. This sudden concern for arms, combined with a voice that insists she "come to France," fills him with alarm. He shares his misgivings with his wife, Isabelle, who promptly relates them to Jehanette, now known as "Jeanne."

"Your father has had a dream again," she whispers to her daughter one morning.

"Oh? What kind of dream?"

"The one in which you decide to leave us, so that you can join some men-at-arms. It worries him to no end."

Jeanne shakes her head. "He shouldn't. There is no need."

"Well," Isabelle says, "I certainly hope so. For he told your brothers that if you ever got it in your head to do so, he'd wish they would drown you."

Jeanne is shocked. "They wouldn't!"

"No, I think he knows that. Because he also said that if your brothers didn't do it, he would drown you himself."

THAT SAME SUMMER, some important changes are taking place in the crown council of the French dauphin, which thus far has been unable to resist the English occupation of northern France. The principal agent of this management shakeup is a woman. Known as Yolande, Queen of Aragon, she has raised Charles from an early age after his own mother, Queen Isabeau of France, lost interest in a boy who was then only the fifth in line to the French throne. Yolande lavished much love on the young prince and was rewarded for her care when Charles started to take a keen interest in her own daughter, Marie. Much to her delight, Charles and Marie were wed in 1422. But soon after, a series of defeats against English and Burgundian forces, including the disastrous Battle of Verneuil, once again placed the fate of the dauphin in serious peril.

So just as Jeanne starts hearing her voices, Yolande decides to move to Charles's court in Bourges in order to clean house. She ruthlessly evicts all councillors whom she deems inept and deploys her considerable tact and charm to woo important French noblemen to the dauphin's cause, including the Duke of Brittany, Arthur de Richemont. Unfortunately, one of these new appointees is a far less fortunate choice. This is Georges de la Trémoïlle, a highly corrupt and manipulative man who instantly recognizes the dauphin's vacillating nature and wastes no time to exploit it to his own advantage.

In 1427, it is Trémoïlle's turn to stage a palace coup. He ousts both the Duke of Brittany and Yolande. He then moves the court to the Castle of

Chinon, on the River Vienne, where he and his councillors engage in daily squabbles while the world around them continues to crumble.

Through their network of informants, the English are very much aware of these developments. They judge, correctly, that the growing isolation of the dauphin offers a splendid opportunity. One big push, or so the English Duke of Bedford believes, and his forces will be able to push into the south, capture the dauphin, and secure their mastery of all of France for centuries to come.

One of his commanders, the Earl of Salisbury, comes up with a bold plan. He will stage an attack on one of the last remaining redoubts protecting the territory of the dauphin. This is the fortress city of Orléans, the gateway to the south of France.

REMARKABLY, IT'S AROUND THIS TIME THAT the voices visiting Jeanne gain a new urgency.

"You can no longer stay where you are," she is told. "It is time to come to France."

But where in France?

"You have to go to Orléans," the voice says. "Go to Orléans to raise the siege that the English have laid around the city."

"But," Jeanne stammers, "I am a poor girl. I know not how to ride, nor lead in war."

"You should make your way to Robert de Baudricourt, in the fortress of Vaucouleurs," the voice replies. "He will show you and give you people to take you to the dauphin."

Jeanne is familiar with the name. Baudricourt is the captain of a small garrison at Vaucouleurs that has remained loyal to the dauphin. That is why her father recently went to Vaucouleurs to ask for protection for his village, since he fears the English will launch another raid soon.

Jeanne duly obeys the voice. In May 1428, she asks her parents if she can visit her dear uncle Durand. No one suspects that, serendipitously, Uncle

Durand's house happens to be halfway between Domrémy and Vaucouleurs. Soon after she arrives at her uncle's house, she is back on the road to Vaucouleurs. On May 14, she presents herself to Captain Baudricourt.

"Who are you?" he asks.

"I am Jeanne, Jeanne d'Arc from Domrémy. I believe you met my father last year."

The captain grunts. "And what is it you want?"

Jeanne takes a deep breath. "I have come to you because I have been sent by my Lord. I want to bring word to the dauphin."

"And what might that be?"

"The Lord wants the dauphin to be made king. To make that happen, he must place his kingdom at my command."

Baudricourt nearly falls off his chair. "He wants . . . *you* to be put in charge of the kingdom?"

"Yes. In spite of all the enemies he might face, the dauphin should be made king. And I will lead him to his coronation."

According to one eyewitness, that's as far as the interview gets. Within minutes, Jeanne is back on the street, and the captain sends word to her uncle that "he should cuff her soundly, and then send her back to her father's house."

But soon after, Baudricourt finds he has other things to worry about. In July, Burgundian forces launch a surprise attack on the region of Bar and Lorraine, with the goal of capturing the fortress of Vaucouleurs. Jeanne and her family are once again forced to seek sanctuary in Neufchâteau, while Baudricourt and his small garrison fight a heroic battle to stave off the enemy. They succeed and send the Burgundians back to their home base in the Champagne, although the retreating troops leave a trail of burned and ravished villages in their wake.

There is, however, a silver lining to this episode. Alarmed by the boldness of the Burgundian attack, Charles insists that his mother-in-law, Queen Yolande, be returned to the crown council. As soon as she is back in power, she persuades three French noblemen, all "princes of the blood," to come to the dauphin's aid and raise a new army. Yolande herself sets an example by selling much of her plate of gold and silver.

Back in Vaucouleurs, meanwhile, Jeanne tries for a second time to persuade Captain Baudricourt of the righteousness of her cause. This attempt is also unsuccessful, but she is undeterred. In the intervening months, she has quietly begun to gather a group of supporters who are impressed with her intelligence and her grasp of the political situation, so unusual for a 15-year-old girl. Many believe that her story is credible, that she is truly communicating with God in her prayers, and that God speaks to her in turn. Among those who come to listen to her are two of Baudricourt's officers, Jean de Metz and Bertrand de Poulengy.

"I *must* be at the king's side before Lent," she tells them, "even if I have to lose my legs to do so. Believe me, no one else, neither kings nor dukes, can recover the realm of France. His only hope comes through me. Although I'd rather have stayed at my mother's side, spinning wool, this is not my destiny. I must go and do this thing, for my Lord wills that I do so."

"Who is this lord that you speak of?" Poulengy asks.

"The King of Heaven," Jeanne replies.

Metz and Poulengy, two officers who will later ride into battle with her, are impressed. They persuade a reluctant Baudricourt to meet with Jeanne for a third time. When she appears, Baudricourt expects to hear more of the same, of how "she is guided by divine voices" and more of such nonsense, but Jeanne surprises him. She asks him, "Do you know what day it is?"

"Yes," he says, "February 12. What of it?"

"Don't you know that on this very day, the siege of Orléans has taken a turn for the worse?"

Baudricourt is taken aback. "How would you know that?" he stammers, knowing full well that Orléans is more than 200 miles away. "I've heard no such thing."

Jeanne merely smiles. "I have. The voice has told me."

And she's right. Earlier that morning, a poorly planned ambush of an English supply train at Rouvray resulted into a stunning defeat for the French.

When news soon arrives by messenger that French forces have indeed suffered a major check, the captain is stunned. Incredible though it may be, this young girl in her peasant's smock does appear to be guided by the voice of God. Now convinced, Baudricourt pledges his full support in getting her to Chinon to see the dauphin.

As Jeanne prepares to take her leave from Vaucouleurs, the captain gives her a sword. It's the first weapon she has ever had.

"Go, go," he says, "and let what is to be come to pass."

CHINON ON THE VIENNE, FEBRUARY 23, 1429. Another day, another crown council. The dauphin comes in and sits at the head of the table, frowning, sulking. Around him, the usual battle lines are drawn: Georges de la Trémoïlle and his retainers on one side; Yolande of Aragon, the Count of Vendôme, and Arthur de Richemont on the other. Depressingly, the topic is the same as before: the steadily deteriorating situation in Orléans.

A senior officer reports on the readiness of the troops. After the setback at Rouvray, the dauphin now has slightly fewer than 3,000 men, including knights, bowmen, and men-at-arms, not counting the militia from the villages. On a good day, this may add another 500 men or so—not an altogether impressive force, but a force nevertheless. More to the point, it is a force that is ready be put into the field once more, to relieve the pressure on Orléans. *Today.*

But the dauphin dithers and stalls, as is his wont. The debacle of Rouvray has affected him deeply, making him even less inclined to risk whatever remains of his arms. Seeing the prince flail about, la Trémoïlle comes to his aid. A new offensive is a weighty matter that should not be decided hastily, he argues. And clearly the English and their allies still command far superior forces.

But the group around Richemont has new information. The defeat at Rouvray, as it turns out, has had a silver lining. The failed ambush has prompted the Earl of Suffolk, the new English commander at Orléans, to parcel his troops out over the surrounding countryside to defend the roads against future raids. By Richemont's best estimates, there are now fewer than 3,000 men defending the English outworks, including the various *bastides,* or strongholds, that Suffolk has built around the city.

In other words, if it comes to a clash, the French and English forces will be evenly matched.

Emboldened, the noblemen pounce on the table. The attack should be ordered forthwith *now,* before this opportunity slips away.

But Charles refuses to be pressured. He has lost the will to fight because deep down inside, he has lost faith in his own cause. *Perhaps,* he thinks, *I was never meant to rule. Perhaps I should submit to the overwhelming forces that are arrayed against me.* Though few people know it, he has already put out feelers to leave France and seek sanctuary in Scotland.

No, he says, the moment has not yet come. I will only send forth the army when I know the time is right.

And when will that be? the noblemen want to know.

When I receive a sign, the Dauphin replies. When God gives me a sign.

THEY HAVE TRAVELED FOR 11 DAYS straight, pushing the horses to their limit while avoiding the roads that are patrolled by English pikemen. What's more, Poulengy insists that they travel only by night. He knows that the Burgundians pose as much a danger as their allies, the English, and unlike the English, the Burgundians know the lay of the land.

And so they ride through occupied territory for hours on end, with nothing but the moon and the stars to guide them, hoping and praying that they will not be detected. For this reason also, Jean de Metz has dressed Jeanne in men's clothes—a simple surcoat and hose, tied together with string—because the sight of a woman traveling by horse at night is sure to raise the alarm. This simple subterfuge would later, at her trial in Rouen, become a major issue and form the backbone of the prosecutor's case, since cross-dressing is prohibited by the Bible as the work of Satan.

The man's attire serves another purpose. It discourages any soldier in her escort to take a pass at her, to try to lie with her carnally. The taut string that keeps her tunic and hose firmly wired up is an effective deterrent. But after the first few nights, that danger slowly evaporates. Every man who rides with her soon recognizes her virtue, her unfathomable faith.

"She never swore, and I myself was much stimulated by her voices," Poulengy would later testify, "for it seemed to be that she was sent by God, and I never saw in her any evil. She was so virtuous a girl that she seemed a saint."

At long last, just after noon on February 23, they spot the Château de Chinon, its crenellated towers sharply etched against the metal-gray sky. But they are in no condition to present themselves to the dauphin. Poulengy directs the party to a local inn where they can rest, bathe, and prepare themselves to meet the crown prince.

Poulengy is concerned. He knows that Queen Yolande and her party are well aware of the maid's journey and will readily grant her access to the dauphin. But he also surmises, correctly, that other members at court are not so inclined, and will do their utmost to prevent her from meeting the prince—for no reason other than that it might give the Yolande faction an advantage.

In the end, it is decided that Jeanne should write a letter, formally asking the dauphin for an audience. "I sent letters to my king," she would later testify, telling him, "I had made my way 150 leagues to come to him and bring him succour, and that I knew many good things touching him."

As soon as it is written, the letter is dispatched to the château with haste.

It creates quite a stir. Within the hour, the news runs riot from one chamber to the next, until all the court is abuzz. Rumors of the Maid from

Lorraine have been circulating for weeks. And now the virgin is here, in Chinon! For the courtiers, long accustomed to an endless litany of bad tidings, the news produces a frisson of excitement, especially because it provokes another delightful spectacle: the two factions at court, embroiled in heated dispute.

Georges de la Trémoïlle is adamantly opposed to giving Jeanne access to the dauphin. He hints that the maid is a plant, a Burgundian spy who is trying to infiltrate the court. But inwardly he is convinced that the whole story is a trick, a ploy by Aragon and her henchmen to bring Charles under their control once more.

During the long debate that follows, a compromise is reached: They will send a delegation to the inn where Jeanne is staying and ask about her purpose. Satisfied, the noblemen sit back and wait for their report, which is not long in coming.

"She claims," the emissaries say, "that her intentions are twofold, for which she has the mandate from the King of Heaven. One is to raise the siege of Orléans, and the other to lead the king to Reims for his coronation."

A fierce argument ensues once more. On no account should the dauphin have faith in her, says the la Trémoïlle party. Nonsense, says the Richemont faction. If she was sent by God and she has something to say, the dauphin should at least listen to her. The debate continues all afternoon, while Charles himself hedges and stalls, unable to make up his mind.

And then, according to one eyewitness, the clerk Simon Charles, there arrives another letter. This one comes from the pen of Robert de Baudricourt, the very man who launched Jeanne on her mission to Chinon to begin with.

"I am sending you a woman," he writes, "and have given her an escort to try to conduct her safely through enemy territory. She claims she has two orders from God: to lift the siege of Orléans and to take the dauphin to Reims for his coronation. And if, by some miracle, she is able to cross the many rivers and fords on her way and arrive unarmed, that in itself should be a sign of divine protection."

A sign. This is the word the dauphin has been waiting for. He desperately craves a sign, any omen that suggests divine approbation. With surprising firmness of voice, he orders that Jeanne be brought into his presence this very night.

La Trémoïlle protests, and as a result, a compromise is reached: No one is to tell her who the dauphin is. He will be hiding among the noblemen and courtiers in the audience hall. If she is indeed guided by the hand of God, then God himself should lead her to him. If she cannot recognize him, then everyone will know that she is not who she claims to be.

This stratagem, at once so simple and so cunning, delights everyone on the council. The court loves a game, a mystery—particularly when it pits an illiterate peasant girl against the sophisticated snobs of the royal court.

SOON AFTER, THE DOOR TO THE audience chamber opens and Jeanne walks in, guided by the Count de Vendôme. She stops, momentarily overwhelmed by the splendor of the court of Valois. She has never seen a crowd larger than the congregation of her small parish church. Now she is in the presence of more than 300 men and women, all wearing silk, satin, and damask, eyeing her as if she were some exotic animal caught in the nearby hunting forest. Vendôme bends over to whisper something in her ear, then steps back.

She turns to him questioningly. But Vendôme merely extends his hand, inviting her to find the dauphin.

She hesitates, then slowly steps forward, passing through the large hall. The throne itself is empty. That means that the dauphin, the man she has struggled so long to meet, must be somewhere in the crowd.

The hall is silent as the councillors, advisors, and clergy size up the elfin figure in front of them. They are not impressed. Shockingly, the girl is dressed like a boy, wearing a tunic and hose, even though the swell of her full breasts, unusual for a girl so young, leaves no doubt about the nature of her sex. She has piercing dark eyes that bespeak of a certain intelligence, and her dark hair is cut in the shape of a bowl, which makes her look like a page. On her head she wears a wool cap that has seen better days. And yet there is something unsettling about her. Perhaps it's the delicate features of her face, which exudes a strange aura of grace.

As Jeanne slowly walks past the assembled courtiers, moving her penetrating gaze from one man to the next, there is a tangible tension in the air. Women fidget and finger their jewelry; men clear their throats, stroke their beards, and exchange knowing glances. As she approaches the dauphin, leaning against a large pillar out of the light of the chandeliers, the whole court holds its breath. Her gaze passes over him, moves on to the next man, then swivels back. Alarmed, the dauphin turns his face, which gives him away. Jeanne stops. She knows, beyond any doubt, that she has found the prince.

She pushes herself forward and falls to her knees, at his feet. The court gasps as if they have just witnessed a miracle.

"Very noble lord Dauphin," she says in a clear voice, "I have come, and I have been sent by God, to bring aid to you and to the kingdom."

The dauphin is shaken. He hesitates, then asks her in a quivering voice, "And who are you, *ma fille?*"

"Gentle Dauphin, I am Jeanne the Maid," she continues, her confident voice echoing in the packed chamber, "and the King of Heaven commands that through me, you be anointed and crowned in the city of Reims as a lieutenant of the King of Heaven, who is king of France."

The dauphin is lost for words. Uncertain of what to do, he looks at la Trémoïlle, who is shaking his head, then at the other noblemen, some of whom are crossing themselves, entranced by the unfolding drama.

Reluctantly, he turns back to the girl. He finds it difficult to meet her strong gaze. "Why should I believe you?" he asks.

She rises, steps forward, and whispers in his ear. No one can hear what she says, but everyone can see the expression on the dauphin's face. He blanches visibly. When she steps back, he remains standing, motionless. The hall is quiet.

The dauphin clears his throat.

"Jeanne has told me certain secrets," he declares. "Secrets that no one knows, or could know except for God." He pauses. "Therefore, I have great confidence in her."

A stunned silence follows. Then some of the noblemen begin to applaud. Everyone starts to talk at once.

And for the first time in many months, Jeanne d'Arc smiles.

THUS, THE MAID FROM LORRAINE PERSUADES the dauphin of her divine mission and secures the command to orchestrate the liberation of Orléans. Much more lies ahead, including an in-depth examination by scholars in Poitiers and two months of grueling training in the arts of war.

On April 29, 1429, Jeanne d'Arc, or "Joan of Arc" in English, arrives in Orléans at the head of a convoy that brings desperately needed supplies to the besieged city. Cheering wildly, the population receives her as a savior. There follow nine days of intense fighting between the French and English forces—nine bloody days in which the specter of victory moves back and forth between the two opponents, the ebb and flow of war. But whenever it seems that the English are gaining the upper hand, Joan rallies her soldiers with her battle cry, *"Ou Nom Dei*—In the name of God." At long last, on May 8, the Earl of Suffolk realizes that this has become a battle of attrition that he is bound to lose. He orders the withdrawal of the remaining English troops to Beaugency and Jargeau. The siege of Orléans is lifted.

Emboldened by Joan's victory and convinced that God is now on their side, the French army embarks on a series of stunning victories. They steadily push the English from Lorraine territory, culminating in a major triumph at the Battle of Patay.

Eager to exploit her momentum, Joan immediately launches a march on Reims, traditionally the place where all French kings must be crowned. Although this is Burgundian territory, fiercely defended by local troops, Joan makes rapid progress. Troyes, the place forever associated with the treaty that robbed the dauphin of his legitimacy, falls on July 11. Châlons-sur-Marne follows a mere four days later. On July 16, the dauphin triumphantly enters the holy city of Reims, with Joan of Arc at his side. The next day he is crowned King Charles VII of France.

†

AN AMAZING STORY. And yet why would God charge a young, uneducated peasant girl with the liberation of France? And even more astonishing, what led the Crown Prince of France, Charles VII, to believe her? Much has been written about this mystery, including two recent books by Nancy Goldstone and Larissa Taylor. And countless more theories and hypotheses have been floated to explain it.

The first thing we should remember is that these events took place in the Middle Ages, when even the most devout Christians firmly believed in supernatural phenomena such as spirits, gnomes, elves, and fairies. It is difficult for us, in our modern times, to imagine this aspect of the medieval age. We are surrounded by all sorts of media and technologies that keep us up-to-date about events taking place around the globe. Medieval men and women, particularly in rural areas like the Lorraine, had no such connection to the outside world. Their only frame of reference was nature, and as a result, natural phenomena gained a special meaning as a conduit of signs from above. Similarly, they readily accepted dreams and visions as the medium for saints and demons to speak to ordinary people. Even Martin Luther was convinced of the existence of demons. "Prussia is full of them," he wrote, "just as Lapland is the abode of witches."

The idea that some people, particularly women, had a gift for visions that were inspired by God or the saints was therefore eminently plausible. In the late 13th century, for example, a German seer named Mechthild of Magdeburg had become a European sensation when she published her visions in a book, *The Flowing Light of the Divine*.

Almost everyone who met Joan of Arc—even highly educated people— became convinced that she was a legitimate medium for divine whispers. As related in our story, she first associated these voices with God or with an angel of God. But eventually she believed that the voice belonged to the archangel St. Michael. "The first time I had great doubt if it was St. Michael who spoke to me, and I was very much afraid," she testified at her trial, "and I saw him afterward several times."

"How did you know it was him?" her judges asked.

"St. Michael taught me and showed me and proved to me that I must believe firmly that it was him," she replied.

The idea that it was the archangel Michael who, on God's orders, spoke to Joan of Arc would later become the bedrock of her legend, and with good reason. In medieval France, St. Michael was revered as the principal angel, as God's general who led the heavenly host in its battles with Satan. The French propaganda machine, which went into high gear after Charles VII was crowned, strongly abetted this notion, since it affirmed the dauphin's legitimacy while casting his opponents, the English and the Burgundians, as demons led by the devil.

Predictably, modern historians have cast doubt on the suggestion that God—or saints—spoke to Joan directly. Some scholars have tried to interpret the voices as symptoms of a mental or physical illness, such as schizophrenia, epilepsy, or even tuberculosis, with little success. Joan's contemporaries had no such doubts. Once they recognized Joan's sincerity, they had no trouble accepting the idea that God would choose a humble young woman and instruct her directly. Moreover, the suggestion that Joan suffered from some sort of mental illness is refuted by eyewitness accounts. Nearly everyone who met her praised her composure, her intelligence, and her highly articulate defense in front of her judges.

One thing we do know is that the story of Joan of Arc is one of the best documented annals in medieval history due to the fact that she was tried in the court of law—not once, but twice.

The first trial took place after she rushed to Compiègne in 1430 to relieve an English siege, only to be captured by Burgundian troops. She tried several times to escape, but to no avail. The Burgundians then committed the inexcusable treachery of handing her over to the English in exchange for a sum of 10,000 livres. The English naturally relished the idea of taking their revenge on the young woman who was the primary cause of their defeats the previous year. Rather than killing her outright, it was decided to stage a "trial" in Rouen, so as to give the affair a sheen of legitimacy. A collaborationist bishop named Pierre Cauchon agreed to preside over the trial.

These proceedings were stacked against Joan from the beginning. The tribunal consisted exclusively of Burgundian and English sympathizers. The principal charge was heresy, but there was no evidence to support it. What's more, Bishop Cauchon did not exercise any authority in this jurisdiction. Even so, the tribunal struggled mightily to find any legal grounds to condemn Joan, particularly when most witnesses on the stand refused to incriminate her. In the end, it was decided to convict her of cross-dressing, of wearing male attire and cutting her hair, even though she argued that it was done to protect her from her jailers, who repeatedly tried to rape her. Cauchon condemned her to a heretic's death by being burned at the stake.

The Armagnacs, the party of the dauphin, did not sit still. They launched several attacks against Rouen in desperate attempts to rescue Joan. The last offensive took place just days before her execution, but each attack was beaten back.

The sentence was carried out on May 30, 1431, on the Place du Vieux-Marché, the Old Market Square in the heart of Rouen. Just before the flames leaped up, Joan asked two priests to hold a crucifix before her eyes, to sustain her in her suffering. Many of the people who stood around the pyre later remembered her dignity and courage as she slowly succumbed to the fire. She was just 19 years old.

To add insult to injury, the English twice burned her remains to ensure that nothing was left, then tossed the ashes into the Seine. Even a proper burial was denied to her.

Twenty-one years later, at the end of the war, Pope Callixtus III formally ordered an investigation into the charges against Joan of Arc. This led to her full rehabilitation—albeit posthumously. This retrial, also known as the "nullification trial," reportedly put 115 people on the stand. All of their testimony was scrupulously documented. Remarkably, these records have survived to this day, which allows us to reconstruct these events in great detail.

Nevertheless, many mysteries about the story of Joan of Arc remain unanswered. One question that historians continue to debate is what she told the dauphin during their first meeting. What "secrets" did she impart to him? Why would the prince claim that Joan knew things that no one could know, except for God?

The most obvious answer, it seems to me, is that Joan knew about the dauphin's deep insecurity, born from doubts about his legitimacy, and that she firmly put those qualms to rest. A highly impressionable man, Charles was much affected by English propaganda that suggested that he was a bastard, the result of his mother's presumed affair with the Duke of Anjou, rather than the legitimate issue of her marriage to King Charles VI. In his tormented mind, that notion was proved by his mother's willingness to sign the Treaty of Troyes, disqualifying him for the crown of France. Similarly, he believed that the string of military defeats his troops suffered was a sign of God's displeasure. According to a groom of his chamber, Charles would often pray to God that "if he were truly the heir of the royal house of France, that God should reveal such, and help him defend his cause. But if he wasn't, then God should grant him grace and allow him to escape to Spain or Scotland."

Joan must have known this, either because her voices had told her or because it was divulged to her by people in a position to know—such as Yolande of Aragon and her entourage. By revealing her knowledge of his doubts and by strongly affirming his legitimacy, Joan essentially gave Charles the sign from God that he had craved for so long. This would have sealed his belief in her as a divine emissary and her ability to lead his troops to victory.

The mystery of how she was able to identify the dauphin from more than 300 sumptuously dressed people has also been the topic of much speculation, both then and now. This too was seen by her contemporaries as evidence of her divine guidance. My suggestion is perhaps more mundane. As the Count de Vendôme led her into the audience hall, as we know he did, he may have whispered in her ear, "Look for a crooked nose. He's got the biggest crooked nose in the hall." This physical attribute, so typical of members of the House of Valois, is vividly attested in portraits of the king. But of course we will never know for sure.

After the great triumphs of 1429 and Joan's tragic end on the scaffold of Rouen, the Hundred Years' War would continue for another 24 years, ending with the Treaty of Picquigny. But France would never again face the mortal danger that it did in those dark winter months, thanks to the voices of Joan of Arc. Eventually England lost all of its major holdings on the Continent and once again became an island nation, while France would emerge as the dominant monarchy in northern Europe.

From that point on, the balance of power between England and France would determine much of European history. As France became the undisputed center of European art and culture, Britain gained mastery of the seas and much of its international commerce. They would remain sworn rivals, all through the Napoleonic era and the battles at Trafalgar and Waterloo, until at the dawn of the 20th century, England rushed to France's aid in the opening days of World War I. Britain would do so again during World War II, forever ending the 600-year enmity between the two nations.

Lucas Cranach the Elder painted this highly realistic portrait of his close friend Martin Luther.

CHAPTER 5

MARTIN LUTHER'S HYMN

A mighty fortress is our God,
a sword and shield victorious.
He breaks the cruel oppressor's rod
and wins salvation glorious.
The old satanic foe
has sworn to work us woe.
With craft and dreadful might
he arms himself to fight.
On Earth he has no equal.

WORMS, RHINELAND-PALATINATE
February 1521

A trumpet blares, the people rise, and the Holy Roman Emperor walks in, trailed by his entourage of German worthies and heralds in Habsburg livery. A hush falls over the hall. All eyes turn to the figure who is, at that moment, the most powerful man in the world, the successor of dynasties that have ruled Europe for centuries: the Habsburgs, the dukes of Burgundy, the House of Valois, the kings of Castille and Aragon. His dominions stretch from the shores of the Atlantic to the alpine peaks of Austria, from the hills of Naples to the Hanse ports on the Baltic. He is also master over vast territories in Asia and the Americas, with colonies that pour forth an endless stream of gold and spices, much to the envy of other European royals who have to make do with taxes levied on their subjects.

It is said that the sun never sets on the empire of Charles V and that some part of the world is always laboring to magnify the glory of his house. He is an absolute king over millions of people, the architect of Europe's first modern standing army, soon to become the savior who stops the Islamic conqueror Suleiman the Magnificent at the gates of Vienna.

That is why so many people in the hall have trouble believing that this legendary monarch, this heir to the glory of the Roman Caesars, is none other than the ungainly young man now shuffling to the platform that holds his throne, with his bent nose, gaping mouth, and ridiculously long chin. It is well known that Charles does not have a very pleasant countenance, but few people had realized until now how truly ugly the poor man is.

Of course, none of these facial flaws are his fault. The Habsburg family is cursed with what many centuries later, modern science would diagnose as hereditary mandibular prognathism, a condition whereby the lower jaw is grossly extended. Charles is severely affected by this condition, to the point that he often leaves his mouth wide open, which gives him a rather dull and dimwitted look. This has sometimes caused his opponents to underestimate him, which they soon learn to regret, for behind this grotesque face with its malformed nose and thick lower lip is a brilliant and calculating mind that nurtures one ambition: to merge all of Europe, indeed all of the world, under the benign rule of the House of Habsburg, unified by the Catholic faith.

In fact, this is the reason that he has come to Worms, though only with the greatest reluctance, for it has come to his attention that a lowly monk from Wittenberg, an Augustinian friar named Martin Luther, has seen fit to attack the holy edifice of the Church that has kept Europe together for more than a thousand years. At first, Charles believed the matter should be left to lower courts, if not the Church itself. But then he remembered the case of Jan Hus, a heretic who had dared to argue that salvation could be had outside the Church. In 1415, Hus was invited to the Council of Constance, under solemn promise of safe conduct. Upon his arrival, he was promptly tried and condemned to the stake by the presiding judge—none other than one of Charles's predecessors, the Holy Roman Emperor Sigismund. As Thomas More used to say, a promise to a heretic is not a promise at all. But Hus's execution led to widespread turmoil in Bohemia.

The precedent convinced Charles that he should intervene himself, that the suppression of heresy is too important a matter to be left to the clutch of dukes and princes that rule northern Europe. Indeed, he has been reliably informed that several of these local *Kurfürsten,* or princeelectors, including Frederick III of Saxony, are not unsympathetic to the monk's ideas. They too believe that the excesses of the papacy, particularly under Italian popes like Julius II and Leo X, have reached truly appalling proportions.

Secretly, Charles agrees with them. Ever since the 13th century, church and state, pope and emperor, have engaged in a proxy war for the hearts and minds of Europe, since no one quite knew where the domain of temporal powers ended and the realm of the spiritual began. And in the case of Leo X, it has been difficult to determine any concern for spiritual matters at all.

For much of his reign, this Medici pope has devoted himself to sensuous pursuits, such as the hosting of lavish banquets and masks, the creation of magnificent works of art, or the raising of troops to conquer territory for the Papal States. That is what galvanized this monk, Martin Luther, into rebellion: the sale of indulgences to finance one of Leo X's most ambitious projects, the completion of the new St. Peter's Basilica in Rome.

Of course, indulgences are nothing new. They offer the bearer, or whomever one designates as the beneficiary, a respite from the time spent in purgatory. What is this place? The simple answer is that unless you are utterly free of sin, which very few people are, you're not allowed into heaven on your death unless you first do penance in this realm. Purgatory is therefore sort of a halfway house, a probationary state between death and heaven, with facilities that are believed to be not very comfortable.

The idea to grant such indulgences began during the Crusades. To every knight and footman who set out to liberate the Holy Land from Muslim rule, Pope Urban II offered "plenary indulgence." This meant that these warriors had the license to pillage, plunder, and kill to their heart's content, without fear of retribution in the form of a long sentence to hell.

In time, these certificates became available to the average Christian as well, provided one had the means to acquire them. But no one knew how long, exactly, souls were expected to suffer while being "purified" in this netherworld. One reason: The idea of purgatory itself was a fairly novel invention, developed at the Council of Lyon in 1245. Clearly, the length of time was related to the severity of the sins that the sufferer had committed in life. Some clerics believed that it could take many thousands of years before one was admitted to the heavenly bliss of paradise, a daunting prospect that called for some form of mitigation. That is why many years ago, the Church issued a rate card that matched the amount invested in indulgences to the number of years that would be reduced from one's stay in purgatory. As the sale of these indulgences grew, many institutions, temporal and sacred, rushed to get involved. By the time the Borgia pope Alexander VI ascended the throne of St. Peter near the end of the 15th century, the sale of indulgences had become the primary source of income for clergy throughout Europe.

As it happened, one of these clerics was Bishop Albert of Mainz, a man who was deep in debt. When he had asked Pope Leo X to buy his bishopric, the pope demanded the staggering price of 10,000 ducats (roughly two million dollars in today's currency). Albert therefore turned to his sales agents, notably the Dominican friar Johann Tetzel, to boost the sale of indulgences in his territory in the hope that his share of the proceeds would help him pay off his debt.

Tetzel was very good at selling indulgences. In fact, it was his energetic marketing pitch that provoked Luther's ire.

AT THE TIME, MARTIN LUTHER WAS SERVING as a member of the faculty of the University of Wittenberg. This was not at all what his father, Hans Luther, had in mind for him. From an early age, Martin had been groomed for a career as a lawyer. But soon after enrolling in law at the University of Erfurt, Martin found himself drawn to theology and philosophy.

Then, on July 12, 1505, he experienced something that would change his life—and, indeed, the course of Christianity. He had just visited his parents and was on his way back to university when the skies grew dark and a lightning bolt struck very close to the path he was walking on. The sheer power of the blast lifted him off his feet. "St. Anne, help me!" he cried. "I will become a monk!"

Martin made good on his vow, for less than a week later, he entered the Augustinian monastery in Erfurt. His father would never forgive him.

"Have you not read in the Bible that you should honor your father and your mother?" he flung at his son. "And here you have left me and your dear mother to look after ourselves in our old age!"

"But father," Martin protested, "I could do you more good by prayers than if I had stayed in the world."

Luther Senior would remain firmly opposed to his son's career choice. And for Martin, the entry into the monastic life did not turn out so well either, a source of much distress for the young man. "I was indeed a good monk," he later recalled, "and kept the rules of my order so strictly that I can say: If ever a monk got to heaven through monasticism, I should have been that man." But even after he was ordained a priest in 1507, the strict rites and rituals of the Augustinian Order failed to temper the storms in his heart, his desperate search for Christ, no matter how hard he prayed.

"If I had remained a monk much longer," he ruefully wrote, "I would have become a martyr through fasting, prayer, reading, and other good works." The experience would later color Luther's depreciative attitude toward the Catholic emphasis on such "good works."

But then an opportunity presented itself. Three years earlier, Frederick III had decided to establish a university in Wittenberg, one of the first in the region, and was looking for faculty to teach the medieval curriculum, which included theology. A post as instructor was offered to Martin, who accepted gladly. The position allowed him to continue his own academic studies—in theology, that is, rather than law. In 1512, he received his doctorate, which gave him the right to be recognized as a "Doctor in Bible."

Just four years later, Johann Tetzel launched his campaign for the sales of indulgences among the German faithful.

When he heard of this activity, Martin was shocked to the core. He strongly believed that no man, neither priest nor pope, could promise relief from purgatory. The reason was that no human being had the power to forgive sins. Only God could do that.

This was not the only matter that upset Martin. He also denounced the veneration of relics, the presumed mortal remains of saints, since it prompted vast numbers of pilgrims to spend their meager savings on pilgrimages to places like Saxony itself, which was reputed to hold more than 19,000 relics. Martin did not denounce the veneration as such, but rather the fact that the vast majority of these relics were fake, a cruel hoax perpetrated on gullible pilgrims, including such items as a "vial of mother's milk" from the Virgin Mary or straw from the Bethlehem manger.

What's more, the pilgrimage to relics in Saxony was closely intertwined with the practice of indulgences, though in this case, the proceeds flowed to Frederick III, the prince-elector of Saxony himself, rather than to St. Peter's in Rome. Frederick had declared that whoever visited the relics on All Saints Day (and paid the stipulated fee, of course) would receive a reduction of 1.9 million years in purgatory, for themselves or their loved ones as they so chose. How the *Kurfürst,* the prince-elector, had arrived at this staggering number was not explained. But such was the fear of the flames of purgatory, actively fanned by skilled orators such as Johann Tetzel, that people literally stood in line to purchase them.

"Listen to the voices of your dear dead relatives and friends, beseeching you," Tetzel railed from the pulpit; "they're saying, 'Pity us, pity us. We are in dire torment from which you can redeem us for a pittance.'"

Well, a pittance it wasn't. A certificate of indulgence, issued by Bishop Albert, typically cost a minimum of three gold ducats (about $600 in today's currency) and as much as twenty ducats for the well-to-do, including noblemen and prelates.

ANY SANE INDIVIDUAL WOULD HAVE concluded that there was something rotten in the state of Rome and that the Church had strayed very far from the noble poverty and social compassion embraced by Jesus. Martin Luther was that individual. But he did more than denounce the sale of indulgences, or the veneration of questionable relics for financial gain.

For Martin, the practice exemplified the baseness and venality of the papacy in the hands of Italians like the Medici and the Rovere. What was needed, he believed, was a total reform of the Mother Church to cleanse it of these odious practices and return it to the spiritual message of the Gospels. This was the thrust of a document that he nailed to the door of the castle church at Wittenberg in 1517, known as the Ninety-Five Theses.

In principle, there was nothing particularly new or heretical about the call to reform the Church. Other prominent Catholic intellectuals had also pleaded for change, including the English scholar John Colet and the Dutch humanist Erasmus. But when Luther's Theses spread through Europe like wildfire, magnified by the invention of the printing press, it kindled a long-suppressed resentment against the financial abuses of the Church among both the commons and the local aristocracy.

"Look at the ghastly shedding of blood by [Pope] Julius II," Martin wrote to a Roman prelate who challenged his ideas. "Look at the outrageous tyranny of Boniface VIII, who, as the proverb declares, 'came in as a wolf, reigned as a lion, and died as a dog.' And you call me a leper?"

In 1518, Martin was summoned to Rome to explain himself. He refused, safe in the knowledge that he still enjoyed the protection of Frederick III of Saxony. This gave Pope Leo X pause; he did not want a conflict with the German states. But when Martin continued to publish books espousing his views, the pope responded. He issued a papal bull—a decree issued by the pope—entitled *Exsurge Domine* ("Arise, O Lord"), which found that Martin's Theses were "riddled with errors." As a result, Luther was warned he would be excommunicated within 60 days unless he recanted. Which, of course, he didn't.

If anything, the papal bull encouraged him to widen his protest. Inspired by a close reading of Paul's Letter to the Romans, Martin argued that the saving grace of God's love could be received through faith and faith alone, rather than through good works, as the Catholic Church preached. That also meant that only the three sacraments ordained by God in the Bible—baptism, confession, and the Eucharist—should be considered holy sacraments.

Many of these ideas appealed to the sober-minded German princes, who were repelled by the sensuousness of the Renaissance papacy. But what they really liked about Martin was his suggestion that German rulers should stop paying ecclesiastic tribute to Rome and rethink the way the Church should operate in their domains—under their personal supervision, of course. This was no longer a call to reform; this was an open invitation to create a new movement, a *Lutheran* church in German lands, no longer governed by the vicar of Rome. And that was something that the Holy Roman Emperor, Charles V, would never accept.

On November 28, 1520, the emperor sent a letter to his "beloved Uncle Frederick," ruler of Saxony, to prevail on Luther to appear before a tribunal during the Imperial Diet, or assembly, in the city of Worms, which was scheduled to begin in February 1521.

"We are desirous that you should bring the abovementioned Luther to the diet," Charles V wrote, "that there he may be thoroughly investigated by competent persons, that no injustice be done nor anything contrary to the law."

Next, the emperor surprised his councillors by writing a letter to Martin himself. Perhaps he felt he needed to assure the friar that no harm would come to him. "Honorable, beloved, and devoted [Luther]," his message began, using the unctuous style of the Habsburg court, "Since we and the estates of the Holy Empire . . . have proposed and decided to obtain information about you and your doctrines and books, we give you safe conduct . . . with the desire that you should set out, and that under our protection you will appear here among us and not stay away."

In many ways, the emperor's personal intervention was nothing short of extraordinary. In fact, Pope Leo X had already ruled on the case in

Exsurge Domine and had excommunicated the friar. By convening another inquiry, Charles essentially signaled that his authority superseded that of the pope, and that his verdict would be the last word on the subject.

But the emperor also recognized his rather uncomfortable predicament. Less than two years earlier, the coveted title of Holy Roman Emperor had been bestowed on him by many of the same German princes, like Frederick III, who would now serve on his tribunal. They were called prince-electors precisely because of their right to bestow the title on whomever they chose—and they had chosen Charles rather than the French king, François I, despite fierce lobbying on his behalf. Charles also knew that many of these German noblemen were rather sympathetic to Luther's ideas. If he decided to condemn Luther as a heretic, he ran the real risk of alienating the very princes on whose authority rested his legitimacy as Holy Roman Emperor.

Martin was torn as well. While flattered by the idea of defending his ideas in front of the emperor, he knew that he could be snatched and burned like poor Jan Hus despite the promise of safe conduct. What's more, he questioned the emperor's motives. Was Charles genuinely interested in hearing his ideas about theology and the Church, or did he merely expect him to recant?

"I will reply to the emperor that if I am being invited simply to recant, I will not come," he wrote to an imperial intermediary, George Spalatin. "But if he is inviting me to my death, then I will come. The Lord's will be done."

In the end, Martin recognized that this was a historic opportunity to make his case in full view of the leading princes of the land. "I will go, even if I am too sick to stand on my feet," he wrote to Frederick III. "This is no time to think of safety."

And so he finds himself in Worms.

The formal inquiry opens on April 17, 1521. It is an unusually cold day, with rain lashing the lead-lined panes of the windows. Just the day before,

Martin arrived at the city gate of Worms with an escort of eight horse-men—on the off chance that he might change his mind at the last moment.

"When he stepped out of his coach," one eyewitness reported to the papal legate, Jerome Aleander, "a priest embraced him and touched his habit three times, and shouted with joy, as if he had had a relic of the greatest saint in his hands." For Martin's prosecutors, it was not a very auspicious beginning.

"Indeed," the eyewitness went on to say, "as soon as he entered the inn, he was visited by many men, ten or twelve or so, with whom he ate; and after the meal, all the world ran there to see him."

But looks can be deceiving. In fact, Martin is under intense pressure. For the first time, he will face the full force of imperial authority, backed by the finest legal minds of Europe. There is no way to predict the outcome.

And so, when he first appears in front of the emperor and the German princes, his nerves fail him. He stands silently in front of the tribunal, fidgeting, while he listens to the charges. The lords wonder, Is this the man who threatens to destroy the Church? This stocky figure in his brown habit, with his mop of dark hair and deep-set eyes, hooded by such bushy eyebrows? They are not impressed.

"The fool entered with a smile on his face and kept moving his head back and forth, up and down, in the presence of the emperor," Aleander would later note derisively. Alas, soon he had reason to eat his words.

Johann von Eck, an official from the bishopric of Trier, is in charge of the proceedings, while the emperor quietly sits on his throne in the back of the room. With the panache of a modern prosecutor, von Eck has set up an impressive display: the people's exhibit number one, a table covered with books, all by Luther's hand.

"Are you the author of these books?" von Eck demands sternly.

"The books are all mine," Martin whispers, in a voice so low that many have to lean forward to hear. "And I have written more," he adds unnecessarily.

"Do you defend them all, or do you care to reject a part?" von Eck asks—a calculated question, because by recanting any part of his writings, no matter how small, the defendant would effectively allow the first breach in his defense, by accepting that his ideas could be in error.

But Martin recognizes the legal trap for what it is. He pauses, then says, "I beg you, give me time to think it over."

The tribunal debates the request. Von Eck is against it. He wants to push for a debate right now. After all, he argues, the monk has had enough time to prepare for his defense. But Charles V, eager to avoid any precipitous action that might offend the princes, overrules him. Luther is given leave until tomorrow to develop his case.

And so the actual debate does not begin until April 18. Martin has stayed up most of the night, surrendering himself to prayer. No doubt he has asked God for succor and spiritual guidance. If so, his wish must have been granted, for the figure who presents himself before the tribunal at 4 p.m. is a changed man: clear of mind, standing tall, with a light in his eyes.

"Yes, the books are all mine," he declares in a strong voice, "but they are not all of one sort."

And with that, Martin launches into his defense. Some of his books, he says, deal "with faith and life so simply and evangelically that my very enemies are compelled to regard them as worthy." Those in a second category, he argues, attack the abuses of the papacy and inveigh "against the desolation of the Christian world." He also wrote a third class of books: works that inveigh against the actions of certain individuals. "I confess I have been more caustic than what befits my profession," he says, "but I am being judged not on my life, but for the teaching of Christ, and I cannot renounce these works either without increasing tyranny and impiety." Doing otherwise, he argues, is tantamount to allowing these abuses to continue.

In summation he says, "I am bound by the Scriptures I have quoted, and my conscience is captive to the Word of God. I cannot and will not recant anything, since it is neither safe nor right to go against conscience. May God help me."

Many in the audience are impressed. It has been a passionate and most articulate defense. But von Eck is unruffled and immediately goes on the attack. "You have not sufficiently characterized your works, Martin," he retorts. "The earlier books were bad, but the later ones are much worse." And then he cuts to the heart of the matter. "Your plea to be heard from Scripture is the one always made by heretics," he says dismissively. "You do nothing but renew the errors of Wycliffe and Hus."

There it is: the dreaded reference to Jan Hus, the man who was invited by an emperor under false promises and wound up being burned as a heretic. Von Eck's tirade goes on for a good deal longer, but Martin knows his cause is lost. He has failed to move the hearts of his judges. He realizes that their minds were made up long before he set foot in this hall.

When von Eck ends his summation by asking him, one last time, "Do you, or do you not repudiate your books and the errors which they contain?" Martin takes a deep breath. He turns to the emperor and says, "Since Your Majesty and your lordships desire a simple reply, I will answer without horns and without teeth. My conscience is captive to the Word of God. I cannot and I will not recant anything."

According to legend, Martin then says, "Here I stand. I cannot do otherwise." It does not appear in the transcripts or in any of the eyewitness accounts, but the sentiment accurately captures Martin's state of mind. He knows the die has been cast.

And it has.

The next day, rumors leak from the closed chamber that all six prince-electors are ready to denounce Martin as a heretic. Though he is much troubled, Frederick III feels he has no choice but to go along with his princely brethren. And so does Charles V.

"I am descended from a long line of Christian emperors of this noble German nation," he declares ponderously from his throne, with a brief nod to the German nobility arrayed before him, "and they were all faithful to the Church of Rome. I have resolved to follow in their steps. A single friar who goes counter to all Christianity for a thousand years must be wrong."

The princes take a deep breath. Though no one is truly in doubt about the outcome, some wonder—hope, perhaps—whether Martin's fiery rhetoric would make an impression on the young lord.

"Having heard Luther's obstinate defense yesterday," the emperor continues, "I regret that I have so long delayed in proceeding against him. I will have no more to do with him."

Charles V then takes a breath and issues his verdict. "He may return under his safe conduct," he says, glancing toward Frederick III, who bows in gratitude, "but without preaching or making any tumult, I will proceed against him as a notorious heretic."

The German lords exchange a quick glance. They know that with these words, Martin Luther is a marked man.

The session continues for weeks, while the electors, lawyers, and councillors debate the exact wording of the edict to condemn Martin for all time. But one after the other, the princes steal away and repair to their provinces. And suddenly a mysterious poster has appeared on doors all over Worms, bearing the image of a wooden clog, a *Bundshuh,* symbol of the peasantry. In effect, the placard is an open challenge, a threat of rebellion: If you harm Martin Luther, the peasantry will rise up.

When word of the poster spreads, many local prelates, including Bishop Albert, are gripped by panic. The German nobility is very aware of the danger of a peasant revolt. In most of their lands, peasants are still treated as serfs, devoid of any rights. If Charles moves against Luther, as he says he will, and the peasantry rises up in revolt, the country may soon be convulsed in all-out civil war.

Some believe that this is the very reason that Martin is able to escape from Worms under the cloak of darkness, to seek sanctuary under

Frederick's protection. The best way to ensure that nothing is done to harm him, some may have figured, is to let him get away.

But Charles V is unperturbed. He continues to work on the final communiqué as if nothing has happened, as if the empty seats around his table are still filled with attentive prince-electors. By the time the Edict of Worms is made public on May 25, declaring Luther to be a "convicted heretic" and warning anyone "not to harbor him," Martin is safely hidden in Wartburg Castle at Eisenach.

He has escaped the emperor's wrath, at least for the time being.

The question is, What should he do next? Since he is forbidden to publish any books or give any sermons, how can he possibly advance the movement he has started and continue to inspire his growing number of followers?

LIKE JOHN ON THE ISLAND OF PATMOS, Martin turns to hymn writing, and for a good reason. His Ninety-Five Theses have not been enough to nurture the cause he has begun. He doesn't only want to reach people's minds; he also wants to touch their hearts, their souls, their very being. He knows that in Saxony, his Lutheran movement is growing by leaps and bounds—as a truly Lutheran Church, no longer beholden to Rome. But every church needs a worship service. Every church needs rituals, a liturgy that comforts people and brings them closer to God. Readings from Scripture or sermons from clergy do not suffice. To lift the hearts and souls of the congregation, a church needs music.

Martin loves music, has always loved it, from an early age. As a boy he sang in a choir and learned to play the flute. He is a skillful singer, and, according to those who know him, he can hold his own on the lute, accompanying his songs.

"Music," Martin would say, "is a fair and lovely gift of God, which has often wakened and moved me to the joy of preaching." He has little patience for reformers who detest any form of art or music in liturgy. "Music drives away the Devil and makes people happy," he wrote; "they forget thereby all wrath, unchastity, arrogance, and the like. After theology, I would give music the highest place, and the highest honor."

Of course, much of the church music at this time is Gregorian plainsong. The polyphonic motets of the Renaissance, and their wonderful four-voice harmony, are still largely limited to the great courts of Burgundy, France, and England. In the countryside, it's different: all that the people hear in church is the mesmerizing monotone of Gregorian chants, usually performed by the choir.

Martin believes he can liberate music for worship. All of the congregation, not just the choir, should be swept up in this "marvelous creation of God"—and not only in churches, but also in schools, at work, and at home. To sing is to confess with heart, soul and body. It is *prayer, set to music.* "My heart bubbles up and overflows when I hear music," he would say. He wants worshippers to experience the same thing.

And so Martin begins to compose musical prayers, or *hymns.* He is not a trained composer—according to the medieval curriculum, music is a serious business, taught in conjunction with mathematics—but what he lacks in theory and experience he makes up with his exquisite sense of tone, lyrics, and melody.

Thus is born the Luther missal of hymns. The first edition is published in 1524. It contains eight hymns, four of them by Martin's hand. With his talent unleashed, he continues to fire off songs for virtually every event in the liturgical year: Advent, Christmas, Epiphany, and Easter. For inspiration, Martin turns to the Gospels, or the Psalms— many of which, it is believed, were written and composed by King David himself.

In 1527, he's at it again, and for good reason. Saxony is once again beset by turmoil. The Lutheran movement is spreading apace over large swaths of northern Europe, but at a cost. The threat of a pan-European war continues to grow. Charles V has given the princes of the German states, all 300 of them, an ultimatum: Declare yourself for either the Catholic Church or the Lutheran heresy. When the princes respond, the emperor is stunned. A clear majority has chosen to abandon Rome and create a new, indigenous church in their lands, based on the Lutheran model. With his power over the German imperial estates now slipping away, the emperor realizes that war is inevitable.

To make matters worse, Saxony suffers from an outbreak of bubonic plague. Many people pack their bags and flee Wittenberg, but Martin decides to stay, to minister to the people as best he can and brave the dangers of the plague. In the midst of these perilous times, he comes across Psalm 46, "God is our refuge and strength." He is struck by the force of these words: *Gott is unsere Zuversicht und Stärke.* This is what his congregation, in their hour of need, needs to hear.

He takes his pen, and writes:

> *Ein' feste Burg ist unser Gott,*
> *Ein gute Wehr und Waffen;*
> *Er hilft uns frei aus aller Not,*
> *Die uns jetzt hat betroffen.*

> A solid fortress is our God,
> A strong defense and weapon;
> He liberates us from all peril
> that has afflicted us at this time.*

As his quill flies over the paper, a new type of hymn emerges: a militant hymn, equally suited for liturgy as for battle, defiantly projecting a God who will protect and guide the Reformed Church against the forces of the

---

* *A literal translation by the author.*

By that time, several composers had stumbled on the hymn as well and discovered the rich texture of its rhythm and melody—as well as its considerable prestige. Not only Dietrich Buxtehude but also Johann Pachelbel—he of the famous Canon in D—poured their energies into transposing the hymn into an orchestral setting. But it was Johann Sebastian Bach who would produce the most memorable transcription in his choral cantata BWV 80, "Ein feste Burg ist unser Gott." As far as musicologists can determine, it was probably composed near the end of the 1730s for Reformation Day, celebrated on October 31. Scored for four soloists, a choir, and chamber orchestra, the chorale is, in the words of one critic, "perhaps the greatest motet chorus ever written by Bach." In the centuries to come, Felix Mendelssohn, Giocomo Meyerbeer, Richard Wagner, and even the French Impressionist Claude Debussy would weave melodic material from the hymn into their compositions.

But then came an interesting twist. In 1966, the hymn suddenly appeared in the New St. Joseph Sunday Missal and Hymnal—a Catholic collection of church hymns. An embarrassing error? Not at all. The sheer popularity of the song in churches throughout North America finally convinced the publisher to include this most Protestant song in a Catholic songbook.

Today "A Mighty Fortress" is sung in worship halls on either side of the Reformation by Christians of every confession. The battle hymn of the Protestant movement has become the great ecumenical equalizer, unifying all Christians by the sheer power of its music and lyrics: "A mighty fortress is our God, a bulwark never failing." Recently, during Sunday service at St. Monica's Catholic Church in Santa Monica, California, I browsed through the missal and there it was: "A Mighty Fortress," by Martin Luther.

Would Martin have been pleased? I believe he would have. If there is one thing about Luther that we know beyond a doubt, it is that he believed in the transformative power of music, its ability to move people's hearts and bend their mind to God. "The noble art of music is the greatest treasure in the world," he wrote, "for it controls our hearts, minds and spirits."

And why should that art be limited to confessional boundaries, the legacy of so much bloodshed some 500 years ago?

Rembrandt Peale's portrait of George Washington shows him as a quintessential man of the Enlightenment.

CHAPTER 6

GEORGE WASHINGTON'S PRAYER

I now make it my earnest prayer
that God would have you
and the State over which you preside,
in his holy protection,
that he would incline the hearts of the citizens
to cultivate a spirit of subordination
and obedience to government,
to entertain a brotherly affection and love for one another,
(and) for their fellow citizens of the United States at large.

VALLEY FORGE, PENNSYLVANIA
January 1778

Slowly, with a practiced hand, General Washington guides his horse through the fields, its plodding hooves muffled by a thick layer of snow. A stiff wind pulls at his hat, disturbing the branches in the trees above him, but he doesn't notice it. He's bundled up against the cold, wearing one of the scarves that Martha has sent him, atop his horse, which quietly lumbers along, seemingly inured to the bite of a Pennsylvania winter.

The general always knew it was foolhardy to take on the largest power on Earth—a power, moreover, with more ships under sail than he would ever see in his life, and with the men to fill them. He knew all about their military prowess, these red-coated hosts of horse and foot who had fought across Europe and Asia, and had the scars to prove it. He always knew that the British king, George III, would be a daunting foe, an enemy with ways and means to dwarf anything that the 13 Colonies could put in the field, but what was the alternative? "Our cruel and unrelenting enemy," he told his army just last August, "leaves us only the choice of brave resistance, or the most abject submission." That's why he'd accepted the command without hesitation, though not without some misgivings.

"I am embarked on a wide ocean, boundless in its prospect," he wrote to his brother, John Augustine, shortly after his appointment as commander in chief of the Continental Army, "and from whence, perhaps, no safe harbor can be found."

Today, after two years of war, his feelings haven't changed, the sense that this conflict can still go either way. And he is not the only one. There are voices in the Colonies even now that argue that the idea of making war against Great Britain is pure madness. England is a nation of more than 11 million souls, they point out; the population of its American colonies, fewer than 900,000.

And yet, he reminds himself, the Continental Army has not done too poorly these past two years. It was successful in evicting the English from their base in Boston, and it struck terror in their hearts with a daring raid across the Delaware River, bagging a healthy number of Hessian conscripts in the process. Barely a week later, he gave Cornwallis, commander of the British forces, a fine bloody nose when his forces tried to exact revenge but were driven from the field.

But that was then, January 1777. Now, one year later, the enemy's vast superiority of men and matériel has begun to tell. Just last September, British General Howe was able to invade Pennsylvania and capture the capital of the Continental Congress, Philadelphia, much to the embarrassment of the delegates. He, Washington, made a valiant attempt to relieve the city by attacking from the northwest, through a borough known as Germantown, but much to his regret, he failed to carry the day. That's when he realized that the idea of any further offensives in the depth of winter would be futile and decided to encamp here, amid the rolling hills of Pennsylvania farmland, in a place called Valley Forge.

A sudden sound: the metal click of a musket pulled to full cock, and a dark figure blocking his path.

"Halt," the picket says, but in that instant he recognizes the silhouette by the silvery light of the moon: the long face, the wide shoulders, the large frame sitting comfortably in the saddle—the very image of strength and poise that so impressed Congress on the day he was elected as commander in chief.

"Oh, General Washington, *sorrr*," the man mumbles and yanks off his hat, "sorry, *sorr*," and quickly steps aside as Washington rides right past him without so much as another glance. Perhaps he hasn't even noticed him. The general is too deeply absorbed in his thoughts, the horse carrying him where it will.

The truth of the matter is, and this he dare not reveal to anyone but himself, that his men are fought out. Done with. And shorn of everything that a soldier, by rights, should have on his person: proper breeches, a shirt, stockings, shoes. A proper hat and a greatcoat against the biting wind. Proper food, not like the pulped bone and fat that his cooks try to pass off as meat. And having a dry place to sleep, with a fire to ward off frostbite.

A general should give his soldiers all that, he thinks; certainly if he expects them to fight, and fight well, against far superior forces. The problem is, he has nothing to give.

"My brave fellows, you have done all I asked you to do, and more than can be reasonably expected," he told them just a few weeks ago, "but your country is at stake, your wives, your houses, and all that you hold dear. You have worn yourselves out with fatigues and hardships, but we know not how to spare you."

And his brave fellows, well, they did rally to his words, just as he hoped. They reenlisted, against all odds, for no man wants to be seen as a coward, a shirker, no matter how much his heart yearns to be back with his family.

But short-lived those sentiments were indeed. Many souls must have regretted their impetuousness, for only two days after he settled them at Valley Forge, he very nearly had a rebellion on his hands. Word had come from his pickets a British patrol was loafing about in a wood not too far from here, ripe for the pickings. He immediately issued orders to get the men in readiness, to create a raiding party on the quick, only to be told that such was impossible. "To my great mortification," he later wrote to Congress, "I was not only informed, but convinced that the men were unable to stir on account of provision." And, he added, "a dangerous mutiny" was only with difficulty suppressed, thanks to the spirited response from his officers.

And then he underlined the raw truth: "This army *must* inevitably be reduced to one or other of these three things: starve—dissolve—or disperse." He wasn't usually given to histrionics or hyperbole, but he had just read a report from his quartermaster warning him that 3,000 of his 12,000 troops were "unfit for duty by reason of their being barefoot and otherwise naked." How could he expect his men to fight half-naked in the depth of winter, against a far superior foe?

A SMALL ANIMAL SCURRIES AWAY UNDERFOOT, momentarily startling Washington's horse. His eyes follow it as it plunges in the undergrowth, leaving a trail of tiny feet in the snow. How amazing, he wonders, that these creatures can live in this cold. How do they forage? How do they protect themselves from sleet and snow? His men, even his sturdy Virginians, can't do that. Soldiers need warm clothes and proper barracks to survive a January in Pennsylvania, with cots and stoves and chimneys. Not the drafty huts that, in desperation, they have built for themselves with whatever material they can get their hands on: trees, brush, boulders, mud—even picket fences pulled from farmhouses nearby.

By now the delegates of the Continental Congress, stationed in York, should be fully aware of his condition. His officers have made sure of that. "There is a danger that the famine will break up the army," Jedediah Huntington has written in one letter. "Many of the troops are destitute of meat," James Mitchell Varnum has warned in another; "horses are dying for want of forage."

Alas, so far the missives have not had the desired effect. If anything, they have worked against him: one congressional faction is now calling for his removal. They say, Why not give Horatio Gates the supreme command? After all, *he* scored a big victory, at the Battle of Saratoga last October, while Washington was flailing about in Germantown, to little effect.

He sighs deeply, shifting in the saddle. In truth, it's not the fault of Congress. Not all of it, anyway; he knows that. There are storage depots all along the eastern seaboard piled high with clothing, provisions, and ammunition, but there isn't enough transport to carry them to Valley Forge. And even if there was, the heavy wagons can't get through, not when rain and wet snow have turned the roads into quagmires. Relief will come, but only in a trickle; and until then, he has to find a way to keep his men alive and his army in being.

What infuriates him, more than anything else, is that not more than 14 miles from here, the British Army is comfortably ensconced in villages and farmhouses, and even the lowest grenadier is enjoying a hot supper by day and a dry bed of feathers at night. That, in fact, is very much part of the problem. The local farmers prefer to barter with the British, who pay in hard coin. All that he, Washington, can offer them is printed Continental notes of dubious value, backed by neither silver nor gold. *Is there anything that can be done to restore the credit of our currency?* he wonders. *Its depreciation is now so bad that a wagonload of it is not enough to purchase a wagonload of provisions!*

Still stewing on the problems that bedevil his mind, he enters a clearing—and suddenly reins in his horse. He doesn't know why. It feels as if he has entered a different space, as if some unseen hand has stilled him in his tracks. He sits quietly in the saddle, looking at the warm breath from his horse in the moonlight, when suddenly the wind shifts and brings the scent of . . . what? Rotten leaves? He sniffs, and his heart stops. It is a foul smell, the smell of open latrines in his camp, several miles away. He knows what comes next. Before long, these pits will produce the pestilence that every army in winter quarters fears: dysentery, then typhus, then death. "We now have upward of 5,000 sick in our hospitals," his surgeon general, Benjamin Rush, told him just the other day. He knows it is a death sentence.

And then, before he can stop himself it, he is off his horse, has doffed his hat, and is kneeling in the soft snow, his knees touching the wet moss underneath. He crosses himself, raises his head, and looks up at the stars that are spread like jewels across black velvet.

And George Washington begins to pray. He pleads with the Almighty to save the brave and loyal men that are the Continental Army. He begs

God for a spell of sun or a hard frost, whatever it takes to make the roads solid and allow the convoys to get through. He inveighs the Divine, the Author of the Universe, to look kindly upon the colonies in their noble battle for freedom. He asks for grace, for compassion, for mercy. He prays that he might yet be victorious.

He kneels for a long time, oblivious to the cold and the snow, alone in his solitude, or so he thinks. But he is not. Isaac Potts, who owns much property in this land, including the house that Washington uses as his headquarters, is passing by this very grove when he hears a sound. "It was the voice of one speaking much in earnest," he would later remember. And when he comes closer, he sees a natural bower of ancient oaks and the commander in chief of the American armies in its midst, at prayer, on his knees.

"And there he remained," Potts would later say, "until, having ended his devotions, he rose; and, with a countenance of angelic serenity, retired to headquarters."

Isaac Potts is so moved that he rushes home to his wife, and upon entering the parlor calls out, "Sarah! My dear Sarah! All's well! All's well!"

"What! What is the matter?" she asks.

"George Washington," Isaac exclaims; "he will yet prevail!"

"Why? What do you mean?"

"You know that I always thought that the sword and the Gospel were utterly inconsistent?" he asks, a Quaker through and through.

His wife nods.

"And that no man can be a soldier and a Christian at the same time? Well, George Washington has this day convinced me of my mistake."

He sits down to catch his breath. "If George Washington be not a man of God," he adds, his voice calmer now, "I am greatly deceived—and still more shall I be deceived, if God do not, through him, work out a great salvation for America."

Isaac Potts is right. God does bring a great salvation.

IN THE WEEKS AND MONTHS THAT FOLLOW, Washington's fortunes slowly change for the better. Convoys begin to arrive, while foraging parties succeed in bringing in additional provisions. They are still wholly inadequate, but they bolster the men's morale and stem the flow of defections. The army's quartermasters, mostly political appointees, are replaced with professional men. The Conway cabal, the faction that's been plotting to oust him as commander, is silenced.

Then, on February 23, 1778, a Prussian officer named Friedrich von Steuben arrives, determined to kick the Continental Army into something that resembles a disciplined Prussian force. Better yet, the handful of French officers who were embedded in Washington's army during the attack on Germantown have made their way back to France, where they persuade King Louis XVI to ally himself with the American cause, against the British.

In March, the British forces withdraw from Philadelphia in order to consolidate their forces in New York City. But in July, a small American raiding party overruns the British-held fort at Stony Point, killing 63 redcoats and taking another 543 prisoner, for the loss of only 15 Americans killed. This stupendous victory is the tonic, the shot in the arm that the Continental Army needs.

The next two years still see much bloodshed, particularly in the South. But after the combined forces of France and the Continent defeat the British fleet at Chesapeake Bay and lay siege to the English garrison at Yorktown, Cornwallis has had enough. On October 17, 1781, the English commander asks for a parlay under flag of truce and offers his surrender. Seven thousand English troops are led to captivity. When back in Britain the news is reported to Prime Minister Frederick North, the statesman reels as if hit by a bullet in the chest. "My God!" he gasps. "It's all over!"

On September 3, 1783, the Treaty of Paris is signed by the belligerents, ending the Revolutionary War and establishing the United States as a free republic among the family of nations.

George Washington's prayer has been heard.

Three months later, the general prepares to retire to the quiet life of a country gentleman at Mount Vernon. But he feels he cannot leave without taking his pen and writing a farewell letter to the governors of the newly created American states. As he reflects on the high human toll of the war, he decides to end the letter with a prayer. He doesn't quote from the Bible or the Book of Common Prayer; he writes the prayer himself, in his own words, from the heart. Perhaps it is an echo of the words he prayed five years earlier as he knelt in the snow during the dark days of Valley Forge.

"I now make it my earnest prayer," he writes, "that God would have you and the State over which you preside, in his holy protection;" and adds:

> *He would most graciously be pleased to dispose us all*
> *to do Justice, to love mercy, and to demean ourselves*
> *that charity, humility and pacific temper of mind,*
> *which are the characteristics of the Divine Author*
> *of our blessed Religion,*
> *and without a humble imitation of whose example*
> *in these things, we can never hope to be a happy Nation.*

It is, as one author later would write, "one of the most heartfelt and moving set of remarks he would ever make."

Of course, Washington's happy thoughts of retirement would come to naught when, six years after he wrote the prayer, he was elected to be the first president of the United States. Eyewitnesses later reported that after Washington recited the oath of office, he spontaneously added the words, "so help me God." A number of historians, including scholars at the Library of Congress, have argued that there is no documentation for that claim.

Nevertheless, the custom continues to this day.

TODAY, THE STORY OF WASHINGTON'S PRAYER at Valley Forge has become a beloved episode in the history of the War of Independence, firmly embedded in the nation's consciousness. And yet its origins are rather obscure. The story was first reported by the author Mason Locke Weems, better known as Parson Weems, who in 1808 wrote a biography of Washington that described Isaac Potts's eyewitness account in detail. Another source is an autobiographical work by the Rev. Nathaniel Randolph Snowden, who claimed to be "a close friend" of the Potts family. Unfortunately, Potts himself died in 1803, so the story could never be verified.

That did not prevent Henry Woodman from including Washington's prayerful moment in his *History of Valley Forge,* published in 1850, though he did add that "how far this account is correct I am not prepared to say. But I have heard the circumstances related, and the spot was pointed out to me several years before I saw the account published." Woodman was referring to his father, a veteran of the Revolutionary War and of Valley Forge, who would frequently take his son on a tour of the old campsite and regale him with stories of camp life.

From there, the legend of the Valley Forge prayer entered the popular press, a New York magazine called the *Aldine Press.* In this rather fictionalized version, poor Potts was excised from history, replaced by two more prominent witnesses: the French Marquis de Lafayette and Gen. Peter Muhlenberg. While riding to Valley Forge, or so this story goes, they come across a barn where they see "the Father of his country kneeling, on some of the hay thrown down from above for later supply to the horses—the cloak cast back from his noble figure, his hat lying beside him, his hands clasped and raised to Heaven."

As the two officers silently withdraw, leaving their commanding general wholly absorbed in his devotion, Muhlenberg mumbles something to the effect that prayer is a sign of weakness; that's why, he opined, Washington thought it best to do it in secret.

Lafayette gently reproaches him. "I am not of your faith, general, or of the commander's as you know," he replies; "but all faith meets together, here. Duty is noble; prayer is yet nobler."

As the story became more widespread, it inspired a number of patriotic images, starting with a lithograph by the popular printing firm of Currier & Ives. This was followed by an engraving by the artist John McRae in 1866, as well as a painting by the artist Paul Weber and a bas-relief in Federal Hall in New York City. The legend continued in the 20th century, when the Valley Forge Prayer served as the cover story of the *Saturday Evening Post* of February 23, 1935, with an illustration by J. C. Leyendecker that would later be reissued as a stamp.

But the image that most Americans are familiar with is the painting "The Prayer at Valley Forge" by American artist Arnold Friberg. It was painted quite recently, in 1975, for the celebration of the U.S. Bicentennial. Friberg said that his aim was "to pay tribute to the tall and heavy-burdened man who held our struggling nation together."

But here is a fundamental question: Is the story authentic? Did George Washington truly kneel in a forest near Valley Forge to beseech God to save his army? And if he did, were his words reflected in the prayer he would write, years later, for the newly formed American states? Simply, put, is Isaac Potts's story history or legend?

A number of historians have concluded that the story may be a pious myth. When in 1918 the Valley Forge Park Commission was petitioned to create a memorial on the spot where Washington reportedly kneeled in prayer, it launched into a thorough investigation. Having scoured the Library of Congress and other repositories for Revolutionary War records, the commission concluded that "in none of these was found a single paragraph that will substantiate the tradition of the Prayer at Valley Forge." In a 1995 book, Lorrett Treese, a historian and archivist at Bryn Mawr

College, argued that Isaac Potts was not even in Valley Forge at the time, but in Pottsgrove, Pennsylvania. No one, however, has ever found documentation to refute the legend of Washington's prayer.

The issue continues to be debated to this day. In many ways, it has become an argument over the question whether George Washington was religious, with Christian writers arguing that he was and many secular historians claiming that he wasn't.

Peter Lillback, author of *George Washington's Sacred Fire,* asserts that America's first commander in chief was "an orthodox, Trinity-affirming believer in Jesus Christ." To back up his claim, he has found that in Washington's oeuvre of letters and written orders, the term *Providence* appears 26 times, and the word *God* is used as many as 16 times. Historian Fred Anderson, however, argues that Washington's sense of Providence was that of a "benevolent, as well as an omnipotent, omnipresent, omniscient being," but that it was "hardly the kind of warm and loving God embraced by the evangelical Protestants."

The problem with this discussion, as we saw in the story of Abraham, is that it brings a 21st-century frame of mind to an 18th-century question. Religion, and religious observance, was practiced differently by the 18th-century American gentry than by the deeply polarized society of today, with a largely conservative Christian constituency on the one hand and a thoroughly secularized society on the other.

In Washington's day, spiritual observance was a matter of course rather than choice. Religion permeated all levels of society, from the lowest farmer and worker to the highest nobility, as indeed had been the case in England and the other European nations from where the colonists originally hailed. A country gentleman was therefore expected to lead his community in religious rites regardless of his personal feelings on the matter of faith.

Having been baptized into the Church of England—which, until 1776, was the state religion of Virginia—Washington took scrupulous care of his responsibilities, such as endowing several pews in local churches and serving as a member of the vestry (the lay council), as a man of his position was expected to do. But in his private life, Washington may have felt differently. His personal diaries suggest that he did not regularly attend Sunday services, preferring to spend the day writing letters, foxhunting, or conducting business.

Paul Leicester Ford, who conducted a detailed analysis of Washington's diaries in 1760, found that he went to church only 16 times that year. During the First Continental Congress in Philadelphia, Washington attended church services three out of seven Sundays, but was careful to pick an Anglican, Quaker, and Catholic service in order to please all constituencies.

Inwardly, Washington's feelings toward religion may have been influenced by the ideals of the Enlightenment, which is true for many of America's Founding Fathers. This movement had its origins in the terrible destruction wrought by the Thirty Years' War, an extended religious conflict between the Protestant and Catholic princes of Europe that lasted from 1618 to 1648.

Among the leading intellectuals of the time, the war's sheer violence and destruction led to a deep skepticism about the ideals of Christianity. If the purpose of the Christian faith was to foster love and compassion, they asked, then how could Christians commit such wholesale slaughter? The French philosopher Voltaire (1694–1778) put it most succinctly: "Of all religions, the Christian should inspire the most tolerance. And yet, until now, Christians have been the most intolerant of men."

The result was a movement in which scientists, philosophers, and humanists searched for other principles to govern human ethics, and they found it in reason, the objective, reasoning mind. Though limited to a small group of elite thinkers, the Enlightenment would strongly resonate with Benjamin Franklin and Thomas Jefferson. Many of the tenets of the American Constitution, for example, were inspired by the treatise *De l'Esprit des Loix* (The Spirit of Laws) by the French savant Montesquieu, as well as the social ethics of the Scottish philosopher Francis Hutcheson. According to a study by Scott Cook and William Klay, Washington's letters clearly reveal a familiarity with Hutcheson as well as Enlightenment figures such as John Locke, George Turnbull, and Adam Smith.

The Enlightenment also produced Deism, which held that God did exist and probably created the universe, but that he did not intervene in human affairs—thus invalidating the purpose of prayer. Instead, as Deists such as Matthew Tindal argued, God gave human beings the gift of reason and free will precisely so that they could be in charge of their own destiny and try to live moral lives. From the Deist perspective, this explained why there was so much violence, tragedy, and evil in the world, despite God's innate goodness. It also challenged humanity to try to create order in the chaos, guided by rational thought, on its own terms.

Washington's references to "Providence," "Author," and "Divine Being" rather than "God" strongly suggest an influence of the Deist vocabulary. That does not necessarily make him a Deist instead of a Christian, as some have argued. The 18th century did not have much use for such labels, in contrast to our modern world. Instead, the truth is somewhere in between. Paul Boller captures that notion when he writes, "Washington's reliance upon a Grand Designer along Deist lines was as deep-seated and meaningful for his life as, say, Ralph Waldo Emerson's serene confidence in a Universal Spirit, permeating the ever shifting appearances of the everyday world."

What this means is that in Washington's 18th-century intellectual milieu, Christian ritual and doctrine were less important than the essential question of what exactly God expected from his Creation. If there was such a thing as a Divine Being, how could it be prevailed on to bless the American people in their great quest for liberty?

For Washington, there was no question that this Divine Being played a key role in the successful conclusion of the War of Independence. "The hand of Providence has been so conspicuous in all this," Washington wrote in a private letter after his reprieve from the dark days of Valley Forge, "that he must be worse than an infidel that lacks faith, and more than wicked, that has not gratitude enough to acknowledge his obligations."

The lovely story of Washington's prayer at Valley Forge may very well be the stuff of legend, but Washington's conviction that his great victory sprang from divine Providence, as attested by his prayer to the newly created states, can never be in doubt.

An iconic image from the Battle of Broodseinde brought home the hopelessness of World War I.

CHAPTER 7

THE PRAYER OF ST. FRANCIS

T

Lord, make me an instrument of your peace.

Where there is hatred, let me sow love.

Where there is injury, let me offer pardon.

Where there is discord, let me create harmony.

Where there is falsehood, let me offer truth.

Where there is doubt, let me inspire faith.

Where there is despair, let me offer hope.

Where there is shadow, let me bring your light.

Where there is sadness, let me bring joy.

L'Eglise de la Madeleine
Paris, France
1915

The Marquis Stanislas de la Rochethulon wearily climbs the 28 steps of the Church of the Madeleine, takes off his hat, and enters the cavernous church. At the entrance to the nave, he pauses briefly to dip his hand in a font of holy water—for the marquis, a comforting ritual. He has faithfully observed it all his life—even during the tumultuous events of these last four decades. Of course, he is too young to remember the Franco-Prussian War of 1870, that terrible conflict that ended France's *Deuxième Empire,* but his father most certainly did. His father is the Marquis Emmanuel-Marie-Stanislas, the officer who faithfully served Emperor Napoléon III during his long reign and even found a way to emerge from the war as a hero of sorts.

Unfortunately, the same cannot be said for his class—the old French aristocracy, with noble families that go back as far as the ancien régime of the Bourbon dynasty. No, as the marquis often reminds himself, the aristocracy has not fared well in the latest body politic that the French have foisted on themselves. The *Troisième Republique* it is called, the Third Republic, an idiotic appellation, as if the scourge of republicanism is something that warrants serialization.

But he must be fair. The republic has not done too poorly these past 40 years. It recovered from the Franco-Prussian War with a speed that took even the victors, the newly minted German Empire, by surprise. And then, much to the envy of the gentlemen in Berlin, Paris went on to produce the most glorious epoch of the century: the belle epoque! Oh, the music, the literature, the cabarets, the Opéra! Today, all the world comes to worship at the feet of Marcel Proust, Jules Massenet, Sergei Diaghilev, or Claude Monet. True, he doesn't quite understand these Impressionists and their strange obsession with blobs of paint; he prefers the art of the empire, and the fine nudes of

Bouguereau. But the important thing is, Paris is once again the center of art, music, and fashion, as it was during the glory days of the monarchy.

It is strange, though, he thinks, that all of this wonderful creativity is taking place without any credit to the patronage that served as its wellspring: the French nobility. For centuries, it was French aristocrats who commissioned the fine paintings and sculptures that now fill the halls of the Louvre, or the lovely châteaus that dot the French countryside. Alas, today, it is the nouveaux riches, these industrial barons flaunting their wealth, who occupy the best loges in the Opéra, and buy everything off the walls of the annual Salon before the paint has even had a chance to dry.

It is called *progress;* he understands that. Steam turbines, mechanization, electricity, the railways—all these inventions have changed the world beyond recognition. What took human hands weeks or months to create can now be done by machines in a matter of minutes, isn't that what they say? Human communication, which previously traveled at the speed of a horse, now flies in the span of seconds, thanks to the telephone and telegraph. There is, quite literally, nothing that humanity cannot achieve, be it in engineering, chemistry, technology, or the arts. Everyone thinks that the world stands at the pinnacle of its achievement, that things can only get better.

Well, he, Marquis Stanislas de la Rochethulon, begs to differ. He does not share the optimism of the Victorian era. Perhaps it takes the fine, discerning mind of an aristocrat to see that. The marquis has also seen the reverse coin, the dark side of mechanization. He has followed, with considerable dismay, the development of new weapons of mass destruction: artillery that can fire shells the size of an omnibus to targets beyond the horizon, for example, or this other satanic invention, the Maxim *machine* gun, which can spit bullets at the rate of 600 rounds a minute. What if, the marquis had often wondered, it actually came to blows in Europe? What if the tensions between France and Germany erupted into an all-out war and these hellish machines were actually put to use? It would be a slaughter of unimaginable proportions, a bloodbath such as the world has never seen before.

But what can a nobleman like the marquis do about it? Not much, not in a republic certainly, but he can try to do his part. He knows his bully pulpit is small, largely limited to the modest following of his Anglo-French society, the Souvenir Normand, but it is a start, isn't it? One has to set an example.

And Souvenir Normand is an appropriate platform, for its sole purpose has been to bolster close ties between France and England—longtime enemies now reconciled at last. Souvenir Normand has been true to its mission: to promote universal peace and harmony. Three years ago, for example, as the clouds of war began to gather over Europe, the marquis decided to organize a large "pacifist banquet" in the city of Grenoble, in the south of France. And what a grand affair it was! An important event meant to make the world sit up and take notice. Representatives from all nationalities were invited. Speeches were given, and toasts were offered to the solidarity of European nations. After all, did not the close commercial ties among England, France, and Germany make war an economic impossibility? Did not the familial bonds among the royal houses of Britain, Germany, and Russia, all children of Queen Victoria, offer assurance that any political conflict would be solved by diplomatic means?

Thus, the oratory flowed, as did the wine, until the small hours of the morning. Afterward, the delegates—especially those from Austria and Germany—expressed their deep satisfaction, particularly with the fine French cuisine. But that did not prevent the outbreak of the Great War, just three years later, in August 1914.

WHICH IS WHY THE MARQUIS IS climbing the stairs of the Madeleine, the parish church of the nobility's favored arrondissement, for Sunday Mass. It is in times such as these, with the nation once again at war, that he truly finds solace in his faith. The Mass has not yet begun, and while he waits for the bell to sound and the congregation to rise, he leafs through a Catholic magazine that someone has left near his personal pew. It is called *Les Annales de Notre-Dame de la Paix, The Journal of Our Lady of Peace,* an appropriate source of reading in these difficult times. As the marquis flips through the pages with his gloved fingers, his eye is caught by a prayer, printed halfway down the page. It is, the editor acknowledges, a prayer that was originally published in 1912 in another Catholic magazine, *La Clochette, The Little Bell,* published by a certain Father Esther [*sic*] Bouquerel. Of course, neither *Les Annales* nor *La Clochette* harbors any great literary ambitions other than to offer articles of a spiritually uplifting nature. But this particular prayer is something special. According to the editor, it deserves to be reprinted.

The marquis begins to read it, and as he does, he feels the hair stand up on his neck. It is, quite simply, the most beautiful poem he has ever read. Notwithstanding its deceptively casual title, "A Beautiful Prayer to Say During Mass," it is a deeply moving expression of humility and grace. And how appropriate, the marquis thinks, because here he is, reading this little gem while waiting for Mass to begin! And how lovely, the antiphonic meter of its verses! In exquisite French, it beseeches God to "make me an instrument of your peace:"

> *Seigneur, faites de moi un instrument de votre paix.*
> *Là où il y a de la haine, que je mette l'amour.*
> *Là où il y a l'offense, que je mette le pardon.*
> *Là où il y a la discorde, que je mette l'union.*
> *Là où il y a l'erreur, que je mette la vérité.*
> *Là où il y a le doute, que je mette la foi.*
> *Là où il y a le désespoir, que je mette l'espérance.*
> *Là où il y a les ténèbres, que je mette votre lumière.*
> *Là où il y a la tristesse, que je mette la joie.*

> Lord, make me an instrument of your peace.
> Where there is hatred, let me sow love.
> Where there is injury, let me offer pardon.
> Where there is discord, let me create harmony.

Where there is falsehood, let me offer truth.
Where there is doubt, let me inspire faith.
Where there is despair, let me offer hope.
Where there is shadow, let me bring your light.
Where there is sadness, let me bring joy.*

As soon as Mass ends, the marquis rushes home, the small magazine folded under his arm. There, he reads the pamphlet from cover to cover, desperately trying to find out who wrote it, but no author is identified. The editor of *Les Annales* is Father Louis Boissey, but when queried, the priest admits that he doesn't know the author either. All Father Boissey knows is that he copied the prayer—with permission, he hastens to add—from a parish bulletin, this leaflet called "La Clochette." Perhaps the prayer was composed by its publisher, Father Bouquerel? Not an implausible suggestion. But, truth be told, who cares who wrote it? What matters is that here, in nine simple verses, is all the anguish, the agony and despair of a nation at war, captured in the euphonic rhythm of a prayer, an urgent plea to God.

The marquis considers what to do with it. If he, a scion of a French noble house, is so moved by it, would not the leaders of the warring nations feel the same way? Can one conceive of the possibility, no matter how small, that this innocent little prayer has the power to touch the hearts of the belligerents? That it can inspire the warlords to end this horrible conflict and seek a peaceful solution to their quarrel? If there is such a chance, then clearly it is incumbent on him, Stanislas de la Rochethulon, to make it happen, to see to it that the prayer is widely read across Europe.

But this raises another question: How to do such a thing? In another era, a marquis would have simply ordered the commons to read it, but alas, those times are no more. Who can do so instead? Which person can publish this

---

* *A literal translation by the author.*

prayer to the world at large and inspire the warring leaders to take it seriously?

For the marquis, there is only one answer, and that is the pope. As it happens, Giacomo Paolo della Chiesa was elected Pope Benedict XV just weeks after the outbreak of the Great War and is as shocked by the carnage as everyone else. That's why he made the decision, right after his election, to declare the Vatican's neutrality in the conflict, not only because both sides have large Catholic constituencies but also because he wants to act as an honest broker, an impartial negotiator. Not everyone is happy with that decision. France, for example, is deeply dismayed, for everyone knows that it has staunchly defended the papacy for centuries and hoped to have the pope on its side.

But Benedict has made good on his pledge to serve as a neutral arbiter. In December 1914, he called on the belligerents to observe a Christmas truce as a prelude to negotiations. The fact that his plea was ignored does not stop him from proposing all sorts of other peace initiatives, though unfortunately they have had little impact on the hostilities. The German Hohenzollern regime, staunchly Protestant, is deeply suspicious of the Vatican, and the French politician Georges Clemenceau, who soon will serve as France's prime minister, has called the Vatican decidedly "anti-French." What few realize, however, is that by inserting himself so fully into a secular conflict between nations, Benedict XV has quietly revolutionized the papal see, and indeed the role of the papacy altogether, as a key figure in world affairs.

This also explains why a letter from the French nobleman Marquis de la Rochethulon is avidly read and eventually forwarded to the personal attention of the pope. As Benedict's advisers explain, the marquis has enclosed a small but beautiful French prayer and suggests that the Vatican publish it in an effort to promote peace. Benedict is intrigued. He is a man who understands the power of literature and poetry. Before entering the priesthood, he earned a doctorate in law, and as archbishop of Bologna, he insisted on adding science and classical literature to the curriculum of the local seminaries. What's more, the pope himself has tried to use the power of prayer to bring the warring nations to the peace table. Just before receiving the note from the marquis, he issued a pastoral letter that was carried by newspapers around the world, including the United States. "The form of the prayer for peace announced by the pope for the Catholics of America to be said next Sunday is made public in Chicago archdiocese by Archbishop Quigley," the *Chicago Tribune* reported on March 14, 1915. It went on to print the prayer in full, beginning with the opening line, "Dismayed at the horrors of war which is bringing ruin to peoples and nations, we turn, O Jesus, to thy most loving heart as our last hope."

Unfortunately, the prayer did not have the impact that the pope had hoped for. The war still rages on and in fact is showing every sign of escalating, of becoming a global conflict. That is why Benedict is grateful to the marquis for giving him an opportunity to try once more. He directs one of his prelates, Cardinal Gasparri, to thank the Frenchman.

And so the Second Act begins. On January 20, 1916, the "Beautiful Prayer"—now translated in Italian—is carried prominently on the front page of the Vatican newspaper, *L'Osservatore Romano,* under the title *La Preghiera di Souvenir Normand per la Pace,* "The Prayer of Souvenir Normand for Peace."

The foreign press in Rome takes notice of it, and many correspondents duly transmit the text to their editors abroad—where, unfortunately, it is promptly spiked because there is far more important news to report. For example, Montenegro has just capitulated after a furious Austro-Hungarian offensive. The island of Corfu has been occupied. And in Turkey, the Gallipoli campaign has ended in an ignominious defeat for the Allies.

AND SO THE STORY OF THE BEAUTIFUL PRAYER might have ended here, by quietly fading from the pages of history. But, remarkably, that's not the case, because the worst part of the war is still to come. After the Second Battle of the Aisne in April 1917, where French generals have once again flung hundreds of thousands of French soldiers to their deaths, the *poilus,* the common soldiers, have had enough. They mutiny. They refuse to take one more step, not until the "idiots" in the French High Command come up with a better plan than to send the infantry into senseless, frontal attacks. They have a point: Since 1914, nearly *one million* French soldiers have been killed, and yet the front lines have hardly budged. Defeatism and desperation set in. True, on April 6, 1917, the United States declares war and comes to the aid of the Allies, but everyone knows it will take at least a year or more before American troops can make their presence felt.

This is when a priest in Reims, Father Étienne Benoît, rediscovers the prayer. He decides to reprint it—not in a parish bulletin but on a small devotional card. Such religious cards have become all the rage in Catholic countries. First developed by Aloys Senefelder, the inventor of the lithographic press, the cards allow the faithful to gaze at the pious image of a saint as they whisper their devotions. Thousands of soldiers also carry these cards into battle or pin them to the wall of their dugouts in the trenches.

Father Benoît hopes—nay, *believes*—that the prayer can rekindle the faith of a dispirited nation. And as it happens, he is a member of the Franciscan Order. Therefore, the question of which saint should be printed on the card's reverse side is easily settled: It should be a picture of St. Francis.

And thus begins the Third Act of Father Bouquerel's "Beautiful Prayer," this time under the title *Prière pour la Paix*, or "Prayer for Peace." That St. Francis is printed on the reverse is simply a happy accident, but that does not stop those who use the card from referring to it as "The Prayer of St. Francis." In fact, for those who know the exploits of St. Francis, the prayer's text seems wholly in character. After all, St. Francis of Assisi devoted himself to the poor, the sick, and the downtrodden, even to victims of the dreaded leprosy disease, just as Jesus himself had done. His reputation for a simple lifestyle, matched by a joyful embrace of animals and nature, has made him one of the most endearing figures in the Catholic tradition—and not only in Catholic circles. When in 1927 the French Protestant organization Les Chevaliers du Prince de la Paix (The Knights of the Prince of Peace) decides to reprint the prayer, the Knights also identifies it as the "Prière de St. Francis," and it is under this title that it is carried into the English-speaking world.

By then, the Great War had come to an end, at the 11th hour on November 11, 1918, and Europe has been changed beyond all recognition. A large swath of destruction still runs from the Swiss border to the Atlantic coast. In the battle zones, not only on the Western Front but also in the East, thousands of towns and villages are in ruins. More than 17 million people are dead, with another 20 million wounded, making it the deadliest conflict in history up to this point. Everyone is sick and tired of war. Around the world, people of all persuasions and confessions vow to abjure war as an instrument of policy. The League of Nations is formed to ensure that such a calamity can never happen again. Pacifism reigns supreme.

And here the Fourth Act begins. In 1936, an American Disciples of Christ minister named Kirby Page includes the Prayer of St. Francis in his book *Living Courageously.* It is not his first book by far. A fierce pacifist and "social evangelist," Page has written a great number of books, one of which, *Jesus or Christianity: A Study in Contrasts,* raised some hackles in 1929. Christianity, he argues, "has accumulated so many alien and hostile elements as to make it a different religion from the simple faith of its founder." This explains, he says, why Jesus' deeply pacifist message has become so distorted over time. But the Prayer of St. Francis can help us to recover that message. It can lead us on the path of peace.

Unfortunately, these lofty ideals come to naught when, three years after the publication of *Living Courageously,* German dictator Adolf Hitler invades Poland, igniting the outbreak of World War II. Suddenly the Prayer of St. Francis is once again on everyone's lips. The archbishop of New York, Francis Cardinal Spellman, is particularly taken with it and orders millions of copies printed as devotional cards. Once again, many of these cards find their way into the kits of American sons and daughters heading for battle, including those who will soon find themselves defending a small town called Bastogne in the Ardennes forest, in Belgium.

And thus, a little prayer for peace, written by a French priest in 1912, enters the mainstream of American public life.

T

AND, REMARKABLY, THAT IS WHERE IT REMAINED, even after World War II came to an end in 1945. When in 1946 the U.S. Senate wanted to mark the end of the hostilities with a prayer, Albert Hawkes, senator of New Jersey, chose the Prayer of St. Francis. It seemed a fitting conclusion to the most destructive conflict in human history.

Thirty-three years later, Margaret Thatcher stood on the doorstep of 10 Downing Street, just hours after she became the first woman in that kingdom's thousand-year history to be named prime minister. She decided to mark the moment by reciting from the prayer. In that same year, 1979, Mother Teresa of Calcutta accepted the Nobel Peace Prize in Oslo, and as part of her speech, also read from the Prayer of St. Francis. Her reading would make a deep impression on a man from South Africa named Desmond Tutu, who himself would win the Nobel Peace Prize in 1984.

In 1995, Pope John Paul II arrived in New York to address the United Nations, and President Bill Clinton welcomed him by quoting from the Prayer of St. Francis. Eleven years later, Nancy Pelosi read the prayer as she became the first woman to hold the office of Speaker of the U.S. House of Representatives.

Today, Father Bouquerel's little prayer continues to inspire people around the world. It has been featured in Hollywood movies and television shows, in popular books and songs, at rock concerts and important national events. The pop singer Sarah McLachlan, the British composer John Rutter, and the Irish singer Sinéad O'Connor are just a few who have set the prayer to music.

And when in 1997 the world stopped to lay a beloved princess to rest, it was the words of the Prayer of St. Francis, sung as a hymn, that brought a moment of comfort to the hundreds of mourners in Westminster Abbey, and to the two billion viewers who witnessed Diana's funeral from around the globe.

A lonely soldier shivers in the snow near Bastogne.

SUPREME HEADQUARTERS OF THE
ALLIED EXPEDITIONARY FORCES (SHAEF)
Versailles, France
December 15, 1944

O N THE EVENING OF DECEMBER 15, all is quiet on the Western Front. The weather forecast shows more rain, wet snow, and low cloud for several days, but the Supreme Headquarters of the Allied Expeditionary Forces (SHAEF) is not concerned. A more pressing matter, especially for Gen. Omar Bradley, commander of U.S. land forces in the west, is the urgent need for replacements. Ever since it crossed the German border and plunged into the dreaded Hürtgen Forest, the U.S. Army has suffered an average of 2,000 casualties a day—a number approaching the butcher bill of World War I. The miserable weather has further decimated the ranks with more than 50,000 cases of trench foot. Gen. George Patton Jr., commander of Third Army, is also bombarding SHAEF with requests for reinforcements, for he claims that his divisions are short of 11,000 men.

Fortunately, things are blessedly quiet at Gen. Troy Middleton's headquarters of VIII Corps, nestled in the picturesque town of Bastogne in the heart of the Belgian Ardennes. Here, too, the men are looking forward to Christmas, just ten days away, though some are fretting whether Christmas packages from home will get through the supply bottlenecks in time.

In fact, these bottlenecks are symptomatic of a bigger problem. Though no one at SHAEF is ready to admit it, the American juggernaut has run out of steam. The momentum that has propelled the Allied forces from Normandy toward Paris has stalled. Omar Bradley's divisions are mired in the dark and gloom of the Hürtgen Forest. Bernard Montgomery's bold airborne assault on Arnhem—an attempt to outflank German defenses and capture the strategic Ruhr area—has failed after German forces push the British forces back from the Rhine River.

CHAPTER 8

THE PRAYER FOR BASTOGNE

Almighty and most merciful Father,
we humbly beseech Thee, of Thy great goodness,
to restrain these immoderate rains
with which we have had to contend.
Grant us fair weather for Battle.
Graciously hearken to us as soldiers who call upon Thee that,
armed with Thy power, we may advance from victory to victory,
and crush the oppression and wickedness of our enemies
and establish Thy justice among men and nations.

But the German defenses on the threshold of *das Vaterland* are not the only reason that the Allied thrust is stalling. The truth is that the American and British armies are outrunning their lines of supply—a serious problem, when a single mechanized division can consume as much as 100,000 pounds of fuel and 500 tons of matériel *each day*. As early as August 31, 1944, the tanks of George Patton's Third Army have begun to run out of gas.

The issue with supply, the officers at SHAEF will tell you, has to do with ports. Even though the Belgian city of Antwerp, the most logical supply point for the Allied thrust into Europe, has been liberated, it was not available for shipping until just two weeks before. The reason is that its approaches were not only mined but also under constant fire from German batteries on the island of Walcheren, in western Holland. That meant that all the ammunition, fuel, provisions, and reinforcements had to be trucked all the way from the original D-Day ports on the Atlantic coast, a distance of more than 400 miles.

Still, SHAEF, located in palatial splendor in Versailles, is unperturbed. Since the giddy days of July and August 1944, when all of France fell to Allied might, a certain insouciance has settled in at headquarters. There is the unspoken belief that the Germans are whipped, that the fall of Hitler is merely a matter of time. After all, while the British and American armies ate up the miles in the west, the Soviet steamroller in the east was doing its part: pushing as far as Poland, demolishing one German division after another. Dwight Eisenhower, the Supreme Commander of Allied forces, has even placed bets with his quarrelsome subordinate, Field Marshal Montgomery, that the war will be over by Christmas.

Yet the pause in the Allied thrust is disturbing. It certainly confounds the opposition, particularly Feldmarschall Gerd von Rundstedt, commander in chief of German forces in the west. Neither he nor his generals can figure out what is going on. Since reconnaissance sorties by the Luftwaffe are all but impossible given the overwhelming Allied air supremacy, German estimates of Allied movement are often wildly inaccurate.

That doesn't mean that Rundstedt isn't grateful for the respite. He most certainly is, for it has allowed him to organize Germany's western defenses as best he can. But deep in his heart, he knows that the vaunted "West Wall" that Joseph Goebbels, the minister of propaganda, crows about in his radio speeches has more psychological than military value—certainly given the unfathomable resources in armor, artillery, and airpower that the Allies can bring to bear.

So what is stopping them? Why have the Russians halted at the Vistula River? Why are the Western Allies wasting their time with small probing attacks along an impossibly broad front?

ADOLF HITLER THINKS HE KNOWS the answer. Ever since he survived an assassination attempt at his Wolfschanze, or "Wolf's Lair," headquarters in July, he is convinced that his actions are guided by Providence, that God has saved him so that he can save the German people. In fact, as the führer often reminds his generals, he predicted that this would happen. For him, the respite on the Western Front is a clear sign that the Allied armies have exhausted themselves, at least temporarily (an assessment that is not far from the truth). Therefore, the time has come for the German armies to take the initiative and launch a daring offensive.

This, he says, is the moment to stake everything on the roll of the dice. He knows he cannot stop the Soviet steamroller in the east; the Russian armies are simply too vast. Therefore, the decisive battle must come in the west. By marshaling all of his remaining resources, Hitler believes he will have enough firepower for one bold counterstroke. He is convinced that this will sow confusion among his enemies and split them, perhaps even defeat them. "Never in history was there a coalition such as that of our enemies," he tells his generals. "Ultra-capitalist states on the one hand; ultra-Marxist states on the other." Such an unnatural and conflicted alliance is bound to break. "If now we can deliver a few more heavy blows," the führer declares, "then at any moment this artificially bolstered common front may suddenly collapse with a gigantic clap of thunder."

To deliver such "heavy blows," Hitler has picked the same region that once witnessed one of the most glorious German feats of the war: the spectacular panzer breakthrough through the Belgian Ardennes forest in May 1940. This daring thrust cleverly bypassed the French Maginot line and precipitated France's defeat. Allied experts thought that the forest was too dense and impenetrable for a tank division, but Hitler surprised them. Now, the führer wants to repeat this miracle, just when the American and British forces least expect it.

There is one important difference, however. The German army is a mere shadow of the formidable force that had hurled itself against Holland, Belgium, and France four years ago. Against the 96 Allied divisions now in the field and another 10 divisions en route from Great Britain, Nazi Germany can put up only 25 divisions, with another 5 in reserve. Most of these are woefully understrength. What's more, the Luftwaffe's fighters and bombers that played such a key role in the victory of 1940 have been thoroughly decimated.

To deal with these disadvantages, Hitler has given a lot of thought to the conditions under which the attack, deceptively code-named Wacht am Rhein ("Watch on the Rhine") should be launched. One, they must have the benefit of complete surprise to negate the numerical superiority of the Allies. Two, the weather forecast should prescribe low cloud for several days, thus denying the Americans the use of their airpower. And three, the assault must be spearheaded by armored forces going hell bent for leather, just as in 1940.

The offensive will deploy three prongs of attack in order to split the Americans from their British allies. The ultimate objective is the port of Antwerp, but possibly not even Hitler believes his panzer divisions can range that far. His real objective is psychological: to stun the Allied forces with the shock and awe of an overwhelming assault, swing public opinion

in the United States against the war, and force the Americans to the negotiating table.

On paper, it all makes perfect sense. But Hitler must first scrape together
a force large enough to deal such a debilitating blow. From September
onward, OKW (Oberkommando der Wehrmacht, the Supreme Command
of the German Army) begins to systematically comb its occupied territories
for anything that can be used in the attack: artillery pieces, mortars, assault
guns, trucks, personnel carriers, even motorcycles. Almost all of the factory
output of new tanks through November, including the formidable Panther
and King Tiger tanks, is allocated to the west instead of the Eastern Front,
where such armor is desperately needed. The draft age is lowered to 16 and
raised to 60 in order to bring the divisions up the strength, at least on paper.
The coming battle will be fought by children and old men, side by side
with veterans culled from around the Nazi empire.

From early December onward, almost all train traffic in Germany is
diverted to get the men and their matériel to the jump-off points. Since
the Allies control the skies, much of this movement takes place by night,
to avoid the dreaded Jabos (or Jagdbomber, as the Germans call American
fighter-bombers) and detection by Allied reconnaissance. The element of
surprise is essential; without it, the great offensive, now renamed Herbstnebel ("Autumn Fog") will not succeed.

The intelligence officers at SHAEF, comfortably ensconced in the
Trianon Palace Hotel in Versailles, are oblivious to it all. The Allied decep-
tion plan for D-Day, which persuaded the Germans into thinking that
the invasion will come at the Pas de Calais rather than Normandy, was a
ringing success. But no one has the foresight to think that the Germans
can turn the tables on the Allies and pull off a similar feat.

This is reinforced by the belief that whatever the German command
can come up with, the Allies will know about it soon enough. Early in the
war, cryptographers at Bletchley Park in England deciphered the Enigma
machine with which much of German military traffic is encoded. By the

end of 1944, U.S. intelligence has become so reliant on "Ultra" traffic (as Enigma decrypts are called) that if something doesn't show up in these transcripts, it simply doesn't exist. No one suspects that in the interest of security, Hitler has commanded that all orders for Herbstnebel are to be transmitted over landlines or via messenger rather than over the ether. Nothing, absolutely nothing, will be allowed to imperil Germany's last great offensive of the war.

BACK AT GEN. TROY MIDDLETON's headquarters of VIII Corps in Bastogne, night has fallen and the weather is as miserable as before. Most of the senior officers are actually hors de combat, out of action, since they've left on holiday passes to enjoy the fleshpots of Brussels and Paris. To boost the morale of those who remain behind, the staff decides to throw a small party commemorating the anniversary of their arrival in England.

But as the evening wears on, strange messages begin to trickle in. Forward troops report hearing the distinctive clank and whir of tank treads on asphalt less than a mile from where they are shivering in their foxholes. No one is overly concerned. Clearly the Germans are simply strengthening their defenses. After all, every intelligence officer from SHAEF on down is inculcated with the belief that the German army is too depleted to attempt any aggressive action. Once such an idea is invested in the human mind, it is very difficult to countermand it, to imagine the opposite.

And yet the American defenses have already suffered a reversal, before a single shot has even been fired. The three veteran U.S. divisions that have been guarding the 85-mile front in this area, known as the Losheim Gap in the Schnee Eifel, have just been replaced with two exhausted divisions pulled from the bloody battles in the Hürtgen. The third replacement division is in even worse shape. The 106th is a collection of young, green recruits who have just disembarked and have yet to see a shot fired in anger. Middleton is worried about it and has sent a note to General Bradley, warning him that the line is "too thinly held."

"Don't worry, Tony," Bradley replies soothingly; "they won't come through here."

Unfortunately, that's exactly what the Germans intend to do. On the morning of December 16, a Saturday, the German guns finally speak. At 5:30 a.m., a withering fire from more than 1,600 tubes strikes American forward positions across an 80-mile front, obliterating almost everything in their path. Shortly after, three separate German armies spring forward to begin their three-pronged thrust: Sixth Panzer Army led by SS General Sepp Dietrich, taking the northern route toward Antwerp; Seventh Army under Erich Brandenberger, pushing toward the south in support; and the central thrust toward Brussels, led by the tank hero of 1940, Hasso von Manteuffel, leading the Fifth Panzer Army. The soldiers march into battle with a message from Rundstedt still ringing in their ears. "Soldiers of the Western Front, your great hour has arrived," it declares; "we gamble everything! You carry with you the holy obligation to give everything, and achieve things beyond human capacity for our Fatherland and our Führer!"

Among the American defenders, surprise is total. Most commanders refuse to believe the frantic reports that forward positions are being overrun. As fate would have it, Bradley himself is incommunicado, having left by car for a meeting with Eisenhower in Versailles, since the low cloud has made flying impossible. Even when reports of the German breakthrough finally work their way up the chain to Eisenhower, shortly after Bradley's arrival, both generals are skeptical. It is no more than "a spoiling attack," or so they think. What's more, Eisenhower is in no mood for doom; he has just received word from Washington that President Roosevelt has nominated him for a fifth star. This will place him on an equal footing with his subordinate Montgomery, a British field marshal. Not for nothing will historians later refer to this conflict, known as the Battle of the Bulge, as "the greatest American intelligence failure after Pearl Harbor."

And a dangerous "bulge," American slang for an enemy salient, it will become. General Troy Middleton, commander of VIII Corps, realizes this before anyone else, because he happens to be sitting in Manteuffel's bull's-eye: the Belgian city of Bastogne. Since the Ardennes are covered with craggy hills and densely packed forests, tanks and other mechanized equipment can move only on roads. That makes Bastogne a key objective, because no fewer than seven roads radiate to and from this ancient trading town. That's why Manteuffel has identified Bastogne—and a smaller place, St. Vith—as key objectives of the initial assault. "Just a glance at the map would be sufficient for anyone without military training to understand that Bastogne was vital for the offensive," German general Fritz Bayerlein would say later. In sum, whoever controls Bastogne, controls the fate of Germany's last throw of the dice.

Middleton is not kept in the dark about the direction of the German assault for long. Later that day, papers are found on a dead German officer with orders for the 116th Panzer Division to capture both Belgian towns in the next 24 hours. Middleton is stunned. He knows that he has to hold on to these towns at all cost if he is to prevent the German deluge from overwhelming the American line.

Late in the evening of December 16, SHAEF is finally waking up to the danger. "I think you had better send Middleton some help," Eisenhower tells Bradley, and releases two divisions: the 101st and the 82nd. They are the legendary airborne divisions from D-Day, but both were severely mauled during Operation Market Garden, the ill-fated attempt to capture Arnhem Bridge. When the orders arrive, they are enjoying some badly needed rest near Reims, in France. Cursing under their breath, the weary troops of the 101st, the Screaming Eagles, begin to make their way to Bastogne.

There is only one problem: The 101st is effectively leaderless. Its commanding officer, Gen. Maxwell Taylor, is in Washington, D.C., and its assistant commander, Gerald J. Higgins, is in England. Neither officer could conceive of something as outlandish as a German offensive in the dead of winter, certainly not in the most inhospitable terrain on the Western Front. That leaves the division in charge of the next senior officer in line: a short and avuncular man named Anthony McAuliffe, who happens to be a brigadier general in charge of the division's artillery. As authors Leo Barron and Don Cygan put it, "For years, McAuliffe had wanted a division command, and now he had one"—though not quite under the circumstances he had in mind.

Worse, as soon as McAuliffe arrives in Bastogne, he's told by Middleton that VIII Corps headquarters is pulling out. He and his staff are relocating to the city of Neufchâteau, some 16 miles to the west. For all intents and purposes, McAuliffe is on his own. The artillery chief knows better than to complain. He sighs, sets up a command post in the Hôtel de Commerce, and begins to organize his defenses.

For the next 48 hours, Herbstnebel unfolds in all of its terrifying fury, though not quite as Hitler has hoped. The northern pincer attack by the German Sixth Army runs into determined resistance from the American 2nd and 99th Infantry Divisions. Worse, one unit of the Sixth Army, led by an unscrupulous SS fanatic named Joachim "Blowtorch" Peiper, is blocked by miles of German military traffic. When it does finally jump off around 4 p.m., Kampfgruppe Peiper makes better progress than others, seizing a fuel depot at Büllingen before running into determined American resistance on the Elsenborn Ridge, the gateway to the Meuse River. Desperately trying to find a detour, Peiper turns southeast and at some time after noon on the next day finds himself between the towns of Malmédy and Ligneuville. Here, he stumbles onto the 285th Field Artillery Observation Battalion and quickly captures a company of some 150 American soldiers.

As Peiper charges westward, his officers take their American captives to a snowy field, break out their machine guns, and ruthlessly mow them down. Some 84 are killed, but others survive and are able to make their way to American lines. As soon as news of the Malmédy massacre spreads, many American soldiers make a solemn vow: No SS soldiers will be taken alive.

By December 19, the northern assault has run out of steam. Even Gruppe Peiper has come to a halt near the village of Trois Ponts, or "Three Bridges," since each crossing has been blown up by American engineers. In response, Hitler and Rundstedt have no choice but to shift the main German effort to the center thrust, led by Manteuffel. Unfortunately, there remains one big obstacle: Bastogne is still in American hands, and without Bastogne, the lunge to Brussels and Antwerp cannot succeed.

In the coming days, the pressure on Bastogne builds to a fever pitch. Using the sheer brute force of its armored firepower, Fifth Panzer plows through the initial American defenses and surrounds two regiments of the "green" 106th Division, resulting in the loss of more than 8,000 Americans—the greatest defeat of American arms in the West. The German armored host then races ahead, determined to complete the encirclement of Bastogne. The weary paratroopers of the 101st Airborne, exhausted from their long trip from Reims, are able to get just inside the perimeter before the door is slammed shut by German tanks cutting the last road into town.

Completely surrounded, Bastogne is now truly on its own. It will either stand and fight, or perish in the effort. McAuliffe knows that surrender is not an option. To surrender the city is to give the Nazi forces a free pass into Belgium's interior and the heart of the Allied armies, just as Hitler has intended.

But what do they have that can withstand the fury of a German panzer army? Bastogne has not been reinforced. It does not have the necessary supplies to withstand a long siege. McAuliffe has quickly deployed three artillery battalions at strategic points around the city, but his stock of artillery shells is running low, as are his food supplies. He has no cold weather gear or medical supplies. What's more, the paratroopers of the 101st, though undoubtedly brave, are armed with little more than mortars, bazookas, and rifles. They are outnumbered five to one, and the bad weather means that resupply by air is out of the question.

How are they going to stop a host of panzer tanks? How is their puny, hardscrabble force, holed up in a small Belgian town, going to stop an army of 4,500 Germans in their tracks?

THAT SAME DAY, DECEMBER 19, Eisenhower summons his senior commanders to a crisis meeting in the French city of Verdun, a fitting choice, perhaps, because Verdun will forever be associated with one of the bloodiest battles during World War I. And the Ardennes Offensive is very much beginning to look like a major battle. "All of us, without exception, were astonished" by the fury of Herbstnebel, a chastened Eisenhower has just cabled his superior, Gen. George Marshall, in Washington.

Not surprisingly, the mood inside the meeting room is very different from the one that prevailed just three days earlier. Every general has had plenty of time to ponder the consequences of the intelligence failure and the cocksure attitude that blinded them to Hitler's intentions.

But Eisenhower will have none of it. "The present situation is to be regarded as one of opportunity for us and not disaster," he announces as soon as he walks into the meeting. The commanders, who were expecting a tongue lashing, perk up. "There will be only cheerful faces at this conference table," Eisenhower adds with his trademark grin.

In principle, Ike is not wrong. By pushing virtually all of his remaining assets into a bulge deep behind American lines, Rundstedt has exposed his flanks—perhaps fatally. Here is indeed a great opportunity: to cut off his line of supply at the border and destroy what remains of the German army in the West while it is out in the open rather than behind the defenses of the West Wall.

"Hell," George Patton says, "let's have the guts to let the bastards go all the way to Paris. Then, we'll really cut 'em off and chew 'em up."

Eisenhower demurs. To launch such a counteroffensive would require a massive concentration of forces in an area where American troops are very thin on the ground. After all, there are now nearly 25 German divisions running amok in eastern Belgium. How to stop them? Who has the necessary strength?

Montgomery's British forces are too far north. That leaves Eisenhower with only one option: Patton's Third Army. Patton, sitting at the table with a determined expression on his face, has come to the same conclusion, so when Eisenhower finally turns to him, Patton is prepared.

"When will you be able to attack, George?" Ike asks, expecting the worst. To turn an army of 300,000 men around and move it up north is a huge task that under normal circumstances would require a week, if not more.

"The morning of the 21st," Patton says, without missing a beat. "With three divisions." In other words, *in two days.*

Around the table, the generals smirk and shake their heads. *That's Patton for you,* they think, *always shooting off his mouth.*

"Don't be fatuous, George," Eisenhower replies. "If you go that early, you won't have all three divisions ready and you'll go piecemeal. You will start on the 22nd."

Patton shrugs, says okay, if that's what you want. What he doesn't tell Ike is that he has anticipated this request and has already ordered his staff to begin planning the move to the Ardennes. Right after the Verdun meeting breaks up, Patton's Fourth Armored, as well as the 26th and 80th Infantry Divisions, receive their orders. They will turn to the north and race like hell to save Bastogne, just like the U.S. cavalry in a Hollywood Western, flying to the rescue.

MEANWHILE, IN BASTOGNE, THE SITUATION has become desperate. German artillery shells plow into the city with depressing frequency. Probing attacks by German tanks nearly succeed in overrunning the American positions southwest of Bastogne before they're beaten back by a make-shift force. Annoyed, XLVII Panzer Corps commander General von Lüttwitz switches to the southwest side, which is defended by only a single airborne brigade. Among the American defenders, ammunition is running dangerously low and food stocks are all but depleted, save for sacks of doughnut flour that have been discovered in one of the cellars. The cooks hastily produce mounds of pancakes, but McAuliffe knows that this will not last.

Lüttwitz also has troubles of his own. Everyone knows that Patton is coming; therefore, he has to capture the city now, without delay, or heads will roll. Lüttwitz then decides on an interesting gambit. He knows the situation in Bastogne is desperate, so why not offer them an honorable way out? It would save precious German fuel, manpower, and, above all, time. He quickly dictates a note and sends it under a flag of truce to Bastogne, where it is promptly forwarded to McAuliffe.

"The fortune of war is changing," the note begins, as if the Americans need to be told.

There is only one possibility to save the encircled U.S.A. troops from total annihilation: that is the honorable surrender of the encircled town. In order to think it over a term of two hours will be granted beginning with the presentation of this note.

If this proposal should be rejected, one German Artillery Corps and six heavy A.A. Battalions are ready to annihilate the U.S.A. troops in and near Bastogne. The order for firing will be given immediately after this two hours term.

All the serious civilian losses caused by this artillery fire would not correspond with the well-known American humanity.

The German Commander

McAuliffe reads the note, folds it, says "Nuts," and leaves the room to check on one of his units. When he returns an hour or so later, a staff officer reminds him that the German delegation is still waiting for an answer. McAuliffe scratches his head, wondering what he should say, how he should phrase his reply.

"I thought your initial reaction was hard to beat, General," the staffer says.

McAuliffe laughs. "All right then. Go ahead."

A few minutes later, the German officers are formally presented with McAuliffe's response. The officer opens the note and reads:

```
To the German Commander.


N-U-T-S!


The American Commander
```

The Germans are mystified. "What does it mean, 'nuts'?" they ask. "Is the reply negative or affirmative?"

"Oh, it is *definitely* not affirmative," the American officer explains. "It means, 'go to hell.'"

And with that, the German officers are sent on their way.

But the satisfied looks at Bastogne headquarters do not last. Everyone knows that Lüttwitz's response will not be long in coming. It arrives that night: a devastating attack by German bombers. Taking advantage of the poor weather, Ju-88 night fighter-bombers skim low over the tall firs of the Eifel forest and drop their bombs on Bastogne with devastating accuracy. Meanwhile, XLVII Panzer Corps breaks through American defenses in the west and pushes within striking range of Bastogne's center.

The dawn of December 22 brings even more snow, wind, and cold. The defenders have reached their nadir. Food supplies are all but gone.

Devoid of winter clothing, the troops shiver in their foxholes, frostbite nipping at their exposed skin. The dead lie frozen stiff. Overhead, the sky is still covered with low cloud, eliminating any chance of reinforcements by air. The situation is desperate.

Where is Patton? Where is the promised cavalry, coming to Bastogne's rescue?

That afternoon, McAuliffe receives a coded message from Patton: "Xmas eve present coming up. Hold on." But in fact, Patton's spearhead is still many miles from Bastogne, delayed by skirmishes as well as the atrocious weather. His tanks skid and slip on the icy uphill roads or run into ditches in thick fog. His men, particularly the troops huddling in open trucks, are exhausted from the cold and lack of sleep. Still, Patton drives them on without letup. "Drive like hell," he keeps urging his tank commanders; "we have an opportunity of winning the war."

Privately, Patton fumes at the impossible roads, the impossible weather, and the impossible odds. He does not know that the Germans are intercepting all of his radio transmissions, which enables them to throw up one perfectly sited ambush after another. Patton vows revenge. "If those Hun bastards want war in the raw," he promises his staff, "then that's the way we'll give it to them."

If only Bastogne can hang on that long. If only the weather would clear so that they can fly in supplies and reinforcements. Does God not know what is at stake? Has he not heard the prayer? The prayer that he, Patton, earlier ordered his chaplains to distribute across the Third Army, to ask for the Almighty's blessing?

THE IDEA CAME TO HIM ON DECEMBER 14, a few days before the start of the Battle of the Bulge. Colonel Paul Harkins, who served as Patton's deputy chief, was there, and later recorded it in his book, *War as I Knew It*, based on the general's diaries. A slightly different version would later be published by Patton's chief chaplain, Msgr. James O'Neill, in a 1948 edition of *Military Chaplain* magazine. As Harkins described it, Patton summoned O'Neill into his office and said, "Chaplain, I want you to publish a prayer for good weather."

"Sir," O'Neill replied, "it's going to take a pretty thick rug for that kind of praying."

"I don't care if it takes a flying carpet!" Patton barked. "I want the praying done."

A few minutes later, Harkins and the padre stood outside, and O'Neill was trying to figure out what to do. "Whew, that's a tough one," he said. "What do you think he wants?"

A prayer, Harkins told him, just as the general said: *Right now.*

O'Neill was nonplussed. A prayer for good *weather?* No one had ever asked him that before. But an hour or so later, he marched back into Patton's office.

"Well?" said Patton.

Wordlessly, O'Neill handed him a card on which he had typed the following prayer:

Almighty and most merciful Father,
we humbly beseech Thee, of Thy great goodness,
to restrain these immoderate rains with which we have
had to contend.
Grant us fair weather for Battle.
Graciously hearken to us as soldiers who call upon Thee that,
armed with Thy power, we may advance from victory to victory,
and crush the oppression and wickedness of our enemies
and establish Thy justice among men and nations.

Patton read the prayer carefully, then gave it back to O'Neill.

"Have 250,000 copies printed and see to it that every man in the Third Army gets one," he ordered.

O'Neill was stunned. He knew that Harkins had talked to an Army engineer, who said that the field topographical office could probably print whatever prayer they came up with. But this wasn't exactly an official prayer—just something that he'd hastily scribbled on a piece of paper, out of the blue.

But as he would later recall, "I said nothing but the usual, 'Very well, sir!' " expecting to be dismissed. Instead, Patton rose from his desk, walked to the window, and stared out. He was, O'Neill remembered, "dressed stunningly, as usual, and his six-foot-two powerfully built physique made an unforgettable silhouette against the great window."

"Chaplain," he asked, "how much praying is being done in the Third Army?"

O'Neill paused. "Well, sir," he confessed, "I don't believe that much praying is going on." In the heat of battle, yes, of course. But when they're not engaged, the troops "just sit and wait for things to happen."

Patton nodded. "Between the plan and the operation, there is always an unknown," he said. "That unknown spells defeat or victory, success or failure. Some people call that getting the breaks; I call it God. God has his part, or margin in everything. That's where prayer comes in."

O'Neill agreed. In the end, the prayer was distributed to more than 300,000 soldiers throughout the Third Army, not only by their chaplains but also by their immediate superiors. Patton issued it as an order. "At this stage of the operations," his note read, "I would call upon the chaplains and the men of the Third United States Army to focus their attention on the importance of prayer." *Pray everywhere,* the order continued. Pray when driving. Pray when fighting. And especially, *pray for good weather*.

But, did the prayer work? Did it have its intended effect?

As the morning of December 23 dawns over the men huddling in their snowy foxholes in and around Bastogne, the soldiers look up and see something miraculous. Despite a forecast that has promised more doom and gloom, they find themselves squinting into the sun. The sky above is a vast dome of deep blue that makes the snowy fields around them sparkle like diamonds. Though it is still cold, the men feel the warmth of the sun on their skin, and their spirits rise.

Then, at 9:30 a.m., comes the sound that they have longed to hear: the distinctive, deep-throated throb of Pratt & Whitney engines. A small flight of C-47s, venerable Dakotas, appears on the horizon and skims low over the ridges in their final approach to Bastogne. Out tumbles a small platoon of airborne pathfinders, who land without mishap in the snowy fields and quickly make their way to the command post. Everything happens so fast that the Germans are almost as surprised as the Americans, and they forget to fire their antiaircraft batteries.

The pathfinders quickly rig up a provisional antenna and spin the dials on their radios. They don't have a minute to lose, for right behind them comes a massive phalanx of 240 C-47s from Ninth Troop Carrier Command. Each plane is packed to the hilt with supplies and urgently in need of directions of where to put them. Fortunately, McAuliffe's staff has already marked out suitable drop zones.

At noon, the armada roars over Bastogne, blotting out the sun with silvery wings. Hundreds of packages drift downward: red parachutes carrying rounds of ammunition, green parachutes denoting food, and blue chutes bringing water and other desperately needed items. The American GIs run around and whoop with joy as if it is Christmas morning. By now the German flak is alerted, and multiple batteries begin firing at the transports, but the pilots rigorously continue on course, deftly banking across the drop zones as part of some unseen choreography, even as the flak shells come up and find their victims.

No sooner have the C-47s spilled their cargo and left than their minders—a wing of angry Thunderbolts from the 514th Fighter Squadron—leave their station and dive into the attack. Screaming low over the German lines, they rake their cannon across the 26th Volksgrenadier

Division, poised for the assault, sowing death and destruction in their wake. One American soldier who witnesses the deadly ballet turns to his officer and says, "We'll beat the Krauts now, sir."

At exactly the same time, noon, Patton's spearheads reach the village of Chaumont, just seven miles south of Bastogne. A fierce clash ensues around the village, which delays the American advance by another 36 hours, at the cost of 11 Sherman tanks. But on December 26, Patton's Fourth Armored Division punches through the German defenses at the village of Assenois and races ahead to break the siege of Bastogne. Shortly after 5 p.m., the first tank battalions clatter into the city. As one of the battalion commanders, Lt. Col. Creighton Abrams, dismounts from his tank, General McAuliffe is waiting to shake his hand. "It's good to see you, Colonel," McAuliffe says with typical understatement.

It would be another month before Chaplain O'Neill sees Patton again, in Luxembourg City. "He stood directly in front of me," O'Neill later recalled, "and smiled, saying, 'Well, padre, our prayers worked. I knew they would.' Then he cracked me on the side of my steel helmet with his riding crop. That was his way of saying, 'Well done.'"

THE BATTLE OF THE BULGE, OR THE ARDENNES OFFENSIVE as it is called in Europe, was the biggest battle on the Western Front during World War II. In a single month, U.S. forces sustained 77,726 casualties, followed by another 69,000 in January; more than 27,500 of these were killed in action. These numbers do not include the 3,000 Belgian civilians who were killed or wounded during the battle by German or American shells and bombs.

"The Battle in the Ardennes was unlike any seen before in American history, nor like any to be seen again," Rick Atkinson wrote. Even when one factors in the war in the Pacific, one out of every ten U.S. combat casualties in World War II took place in the Ardennes. Yet the Battle of the Bulge is often overlooked in the public eye. Modern TV specials tend to favor the more celebrated exploits of World War II, such as the invasion of D-Day, the liberation of Paris, or the fall of Berlin.

If Hitler's principal aim was merely to sow confusion among the Allied ranks, then Herbstnebel was certainly a success. Even after the siege of Bastogne was lifted, fierce fighting continued in the Ardennes and eastern Belgium, draining American manpower and supplies at an alarming rate. Not until January 15 did Hitler finally accept that the jig was up. He had thrown the dice, and he had lost. Without another word, he left his forward headquarters, the Adlerhorst in Hesse, and boarded his personal train for the return trip to Berlin.

As Eisenhower had foreseen and Patton had urged, Herbstnebel presented a unique opportunity to tie off the bulge and destroy Rundstedt's forces while they were still exposed, in the open, rather than behind the relative safety of the West Wall. It could have been a repeat of the Falaise Pocket in Normandy, where in August 1944, tens of thousands of German troops were trapped and destroyed. But this did not happen. Some historians blame the poor condition of the roads, while others point to ill feeling among Allied generals, particularly Omar Bradley and his British counterpart, Bernard Montgomery. During an ill-advised press conference on January 6, 1945, Montgomery claimed credit for stopping the Ardennes Offensive—even though British forces had hardly been involved. And so, about two-thirds of Rundstedt's forces were able to slip from the Allies' grasp and make it back to Germany, where they would fight another day.

For all these reasons, the Battle of the Bulge was truly a turning point in World War II. The Allies realized that Hitler was not yet beaten; he could still put powerful forces in the field, and much hard fighting lay ahead before Nazi Germany could be defeated. And although the Bulge may have been a missed opportunity, it was in many ways the war's cataclysmic engagement in the West. For the first time, American and German soldiers clashed in close proximity to one another without benefit of air support, with forces that were roughly matched, and on terrain and in weather that dealt equal disadvantages to both sides. That American arms prevailed in the end is due to the tenacity and heroism of men like Tony McAuliffe, the Screaming Eagles of the 101st, Patton's Fourth Armored, and all the other soldiers at Bastogne who stayed in the fight when the chances of a reprieve were close to nil.

Like other prayers that changed the course of history, the Prayer for Bastogne has become the stuff of legend. The same is true for the way it came about. There is, in fact, quite a different account of how the prayer was written. In 1960, O'Neill's executive officer, a chaplain named George Metcalf, published a *third* version of the Patton Prayer; some historians believe it is perhaps the most authoritative.

Metcalf worked very closely with O'Neill and, as author Michael Keane suggests, "developed a warm and admiring relationship with his new boss," even though O'Neill was Catholic and Metcalf was Episcopalian. So most likely, his account was not motivated by any negative feelings toward his superior; he simply wanted to set the record straight.

In this version, it is Metcalf who answers the call from Patton. As it happens, it is still early, around eight o'clock in the morning, just a few days from Christmas, and Americans troops are battling German forces all over the Ardennes.

"Do you have any prayers for fair weather?" Patton asks without preamble. He explains that the low overcast is preventing Allied aircraft from dropping badly needed supplies in Bastogne. Metcalf replies that he and O'Neill will get on it right away.

And so they do. In effect, they split the work: both will scour their Missals, Catholic and Episcopal, and see if they can find something suitable. And, says Metcalf, in short order he came up with a prayer for Victory from his Missal, and I found an Anglican petition for Fair Weather from the American Book of Common Prayer. Chaplain O'Neill then directed me to combine the two, made a few changes himself, and took the final draft to General Patton.

Keane, who has researched both sources, concludes that this must be accurate; the first sentence, *Almighty and most merciful Father, we humbly beseech Thee, of Thy great goodness, to restrain these immoderate rains,* is clearly lifted from a prayer in the 1928 edition of the Book of Common Prayer. Since it is from an Anglican source, it is unlikely that O'Neill would have found the prayer himself. Thus, the Prayer for Bastogne is actually an ecumenical effort of sorts, a joint prayer for good battle weather, irrespective of confessional boundaries. Fitting, perhaps, for an army in which chaplains from almost every denomination worked side by side to offer succor to the troops regardless of religious affiliation.

Did the prayer have its intended effect? Whether it was divine intervention or the normal course of nature, Metcalf wrote, we will never know, but the fact remains that "the weather cleared and remained perfect for six days"—a very unusual development in late December in that part of Europe.

Patton had no doubts on the matter whatsoever. He summoned the assistant chaplain to his office and said, "God damn! Look at the weather. That O'Neill sure did some potent praying. Get him up here. I want to pin a medal on him."

And he did. The next day, Chaplain James O'Neill was awarded the Bronze Star.

Mohandas Gandhi is unquestionably the 20th century's foremost paragon of peace.

CHAPTER 9

GANDHI'S PRAYER FOR PEACE

I offer you peace.

I offer you love.

I offer you friendship.

I see your beauty.

I hear your need.

I feel your feelings.

My wisdom flows from the highest source.

I salute that source in you.

Let us work together.

For unity and peace.

BIRLA HOUSE, NEW DELHI
Republic of India
January 1948

The Mahatma smooths his simple, homespun *khadi* and sits down, cross-legged, on his cot in the garden, ready for his breakfast. The repast, as usual, is simple and vegetarian: boiled greens, including boiled spinach mixed with goat curds; a handful of chopped apples and orange slices; and a cup of goat's milk. Like many other Hindus, he abstains from cow's milk.

As the old man chews his food, his eyes take in the breathtaking beauty of the garden: flower beds overflowing with marigolds and nasturtiums, even in winter; a bright orange trumpet vine, spilling over the trellis that flanks his cot; and the quiet murmur of a brook, framed by maroon-colored petunias and glazed brickwork. If he is embarrassed by the splendor of this house, built by his longtime supporter, the millionaire Seth Birla, he does not show it—even though it is a world apart from Delhi's shantytown dwellings where he has stayed in years past.

Back then, he made a point of living among the Untouchables, ostracized by the Indian caste system—in this case, the *Bhangis,* or street sweepers of the city. But now, the idea of staying anywhere in the Bhangi slums is out of the question. Many of Delhi's shantytowns have been overrun by Hindu refugees, fleeing the fighting in the provinces. Like a dark cloud, a palpable pall hangs over the city, as if Delhi is a big fuse waiting to explode. India has been independent for only four months, but much of the country is already in flames.

The Mahatma—an honorific meaning "Great Soul," bestowed on him in 1915 by his devotees—calmly continues to chew his food, taking time to savor each morsel as he puts it in his mouth. A witness, photographer Margaret Bourke-White, is amazed that "he takes two hours to eat that breakfast." Only Mohandas Gandhi knows the reason. He has already decided that this simple breakfast will be his last. There will be no other.

And so he purposefully savors each bite, as if storing away its taste for the time when he will lie on his cot, slowly starving himself to death.

He has suffered long fasts before, usually in protest, as a way of forcing people to see the error of their ways. Before 1947, those people were the British; now, sadly, the target of his wrath are the people of India themselves.

Ever since he arrived in India from South Africa in 1915, he had made it his life's mission to oust the British from this ancient land and return the power to its native population. But getting the British to "quit India," as he often put it, was one thing. Getting the country's diverse ethnic and religious groups—Hindus, Muslims, Sikhs—to live in harmony, well, that was quite another. His whole life had been devoted to fusing the future Indian nation into one independent entity, not despite the disparity of its religious beliefs but precisely *because of it*. It was faith in the Divine— whomever one held that to be, whether Rama, Allah, or God—that bound the people together, that wove them as strands in the multicolored tapestry that was India. But now, Muslims and Hindus are tearing that fabric asunder. Now, Indians are killing and maiming each other in bloody riots that, by some estimates, have already left nearly half a million people dead.

He always knew this would happen. That's why he fought, tooth and nail, against the idea of partitioning the British Raj into two separate limbs: a Hindu India and a Muslim Pakistan. That idea had originated with Mohammad Ali Jinnah, like Gandhi a British-trained lawyer who had long served in the Indian National Congress, the main political movement that strove for Indian independence. But unlike Gandhi, Jinnah had no faith in *satyagraha,* Gandhi's strategy of nonviolent protest, after it was embraced in 1920 by the Congress Party. Instead, Jinnah believed in action. And so he formed his own party, the Muslim League.

By the early 1940s, when Britain, hard-pressed in its struggle against Nazi Germany and Imperial Japan, indicated that it would be ready to give India its freedom after the war, many Muslims began to defect from Congress to the league. Their fear was that they would become an oppressed minority in a Hindu-majority nation. And with much of the Congress leadership imprisoned by the British, including Gandhi, the political initiative shifted to the Muslim League. For Jinnah, there was only one way for the Muslims of the Raj to achieve their destiny: to become a nation onto their own.

To ITS CREDIT, BRITAIN VALIANTLY TRIED TO come up with a different solution, one that would satisfy all parties, including Gandhi. Though the Mahatma had never filled a formal political role, he was undoubtedly the soul, the moral drive, the raison d'être of India's struggle for independence. No solution for the Indian question could succeed, or so it was thought, unless it had the blessing and support of the barefoot, half-naked man with his cheap wire-rimmed glasses.

And so His Majesty's Government dispatched a three-man mission to India, consisting of three members of the cabinet, to try to sort things out. They arrived on March 24, 1946, and set about their task, which included the obligatory pilgrimage to the slum dwelling in the Bhangi Colony, where Gandhi insisted on receiving all his visitors, including ministers and diplomats.

Two months later, on May 16, the Cabinet Mission presented its plan. It was a rather complicated plan, to say the least, and that probably doomed it from the start. There would be a federal government, known as the Union, based in Delhi, which would embrace everything that was the British Raj. But its authority, such as it was, would be limited to matters of defense, foreign policy, and communications. That meant that the real power lay in its component parts, the provinces. Here, the ministers envisioned two groupings: one predominantly Hindu, the other mostly Muslim. Of course, that in itself was a questionable concept, because even in Hindu-majority regions like the Punjab, there were very large and ancient Muslim communities. And if that wasn't enough, there was also a third tier of other regions, the princely states—regions governed by semiautonomous maharajas—that might, or might not, be willing to join one region or the other, under terms to be agreed on. And if that didn't work out, each province would be free to leave in a year or so if it felt the urge.

The plan was a castle built of sand, and though it was unlikely to work, most officials felt it was the only thing that all parties could agree to. Knowing full well what the alternative would be, Gandhi hastened to add his support. "My conviction abides," he said, "that it is the best document the British government could have produced under the circumstances." But the proposal ran into trouble when the British viceroy of India, Field Marshal Archibald Wavell, tried to put together an interim government composed of Congress and League delegates. On June 26, the plan was unceremoniously shelved, and the Cabinet Mission returned to Britain.

Relations between the two Indian parties then went from bad to worse. When Wavell invited Jawaharlal Nehru, head of the majority Congress Party, to form an interim government, Jinnah erupted in fury and declared August 16, 1946, a Direct Action Day. His declaration lit the fuse of widespread riots between Hindus and Muslims, starting in the city of Calcutta. For one long week, later known as the Week of Long Knives, the streets of Calcutta ran with blood, leaving more than 5,000 people dead and 100,000 people homeless. As one of the Muslim League leaders put it, "The aim of our 'Direct Action' is to paralyze Nehru's Government." In this, they most certainly succeeded.

In the weeks and months to come, the orgy of violence spread from Calcutta into Bengal province, one of the most diverse regions in India. Rampaging Muslims set fire to Hindu houses and temples, raping women and slaughtering men as they went. Deeply distressed by the escalating terror, Gandhi insisted on traveling to Noakhali, deep in the Bengal, and staying there until, as he said, "the Hindus and Muslims learnt to live together in peace and harmony."

The Hindu communities, however, weren't about to take the Muslim violence lying down. October 25, 1946, was declared to be Noakhali Day, a day of Hindu retaliation for the blood-drenched Direct Action Day. Vast crowds of Hindus vented their wrath on Muslim homes and mosques, resulting in the killing of more than 4,000 Muslims.

Gandhi was despondent. "The bad act of one party is no justification for a similar act by the opposing party," he wrote. Nevertheless, Gandhi refused any form of intervention by British forces in order to restore law and order. "Hindus and Muslims must realize that if India is to be an independent nation, one or both must deliberately cease to look to British authority for protection," he wrote in his weekly journal, *Harijan*. "Whoever wants to drink the ozone of freedom must steel himself against seeking military or police aid. He or they must ever rely upon their own strong arms or what is infinitely better, their strong mind and will, which are independent of arms, their own or others." It was a collective form of satyagraha, pushed to its extreme.

Shortly after, Gandhi arrived in Noakhali, a remote area in the water-logged delta of the Ganges and Brahmaputra Rivers. He strenuously tried to stop the violence. It was, he confessed, the darkest day in his life. Had his life's mission, to make religious harmony the cornerstone of the new India, been in vain? A lot of others began to feel that way. "How can you account for the growing political violence among your own people?" Gandhi was asked, time and again, in letters and telegrams from around the globe. "Does your message of nonviolence still hold good for the world?"

A difficult question. Gandhi was almost too disheartened to reply. "I must confess my bankruptcy, though not that of non-violence," he wrote. "Failure of my technique of non-violence causes no loss of faith in [non-violence] itself."

What's more, he was old. Now 77 years of age, he began to feel that his end was near. "This Noakhali chapter may perhaps be my last," he wrote to one of the Congress leaders, his former disciple Vallabhbhai Patel. "My non-violence is being tested here in a way it has never been tested before."

But unbeknown to him, Gandhi was being tested in other ways as well. Up to this point, no substantive discussion about the future of India had taken place without his involvement. He was the *Bapu*, the father of the nation; no major decision could ever be taken without Mahatma having his say. But with the outbreak of nationwide riots and with Gandhi deep in the Bengal, far from Delhi, events began to slip from his grasp.

It was Patel, a Congress leader second only to Nehru, who first argued that Jinnah's plan for partition might be the best solution. The violence had become too extreme, the wounds too deep, to ever imagine that Hindu and Muslim could live in the same nation. Perhaps it was for the best, Patel reasoned. Perhaps that's what destiny had intended for postcolonial India all along.

This is when a new British viceroy appeared on the scene. Wavell, a British general who had been cashiered from his North African command after his failure to break the siege of Tobruk, was too exhausted by the infighting to be of much further use. He was replaced by Louis Lord Mountbatten, a dashing and vigorous commander known for his buccaneering exploits with British commandos during World War II and a great-grandson of Queen Victoria. He had ended the war as Supreme Commander of Allied Forces in Asia, which in the eyes of the new British prime minister, Clement Attlee, made him a perfect candidate to negotiate Britain's exit from India.

Mountbatten did not disappoint. After his arrival in March 1947, he promptly sat down with all key leaders, including Nehru and Jinnah, knowing full well, as he said later, that "if it could be said that any single man held the future of India in the palm of his hand in 1947, that man was Mohammad Ali Jinnah."

The new viceroy then made a show of inviting Gandhi as well. Newly returned from Bihar, Gandhi was grandly received in the viceroy's palace, and for an hour or so, Mountbatten listened politely to what the Mahatma had to say. But the die had been cast without Gandhi and indeed without any consideration to his lifelong struggle to keep India intact. Gandhi knew it too, and launched one last and desperate gambit to keep India together. What if, he suggested, the viceroy offered Jinnah, the Muslim leader, the choice to replace *Pandit* Nehru ("scholar Nehru") as the head of the provisional government? Would that not persuade him to stay? Would that not compel him to maintain India as a nation of both Muslims and Hindus?

Mmm, said Mountbatten, certainly "a bold and imaginative idea," and he promised to submit it to his council—where, inevitably, it was rejected out of hand. The viceroy, the council warned, "should not allow himself to be drawn into negotiation with the Mahatma," but rather, "should only listen to his advice." Translation: Gandhi had ceased to be a credible negotiating partner. His ideas belonged to the past. What's more, his inflexibility made him unsuitable to Britain's now strenuous quest to get out of India fast, before the place went up in flames.

On May 1, all parties formally agreed to the partition of India, which somehow had become known as the "Mountbatten Plan."

Gandhi was inconsolable. "My life's work seems to be over," he wrote sorrowfully. "I hope God will spare me further humiliation. Let it not be said that Gandhi was a party to India's vivisection."

MOUNTBATTEN, WITH THE WIND IN HIS SAILS, now moved with all possible speed to wrap things up. Back in London, Prime Minister Attlee had decided to move the official date of India's independence forward, from August 1948 to August 1947. That left the viceroy of India with mere weeks—*weeks!*—to sort out the tremendous problems posed in the act of severing a nation, including its armed forces, police units, railways, postal services, tax collection agencies, communications networks, and thousands of other government functions. Just the question of how India's assets should be divided required the attention of some 50 separate committees.

On Independence Day, August 15, Gandhi was in Calcutta, urging those who had moved into abandoned Muslim homes to respect their property until their owners could safely return. Everyone hoped that his

presence in the city would restrain the Hindu majority from
another rampage. While the nation erupted in independence cele
Gandhi sat alone in his temporary abode, spinning, fasting, and

Meanwhile, a great migration had begun. Muslims as well as Sik
to be left "in a nation hostile to their faith," packed up their belon
began the long trek to the territories soon to be known as Pakist
Hindus in Pakistani provinces were moving in the opposite direct
torians have calculated that in the Punjab alone, some 15 millio
were displaced, the vast majority on foot. Mountbatten, flying
Punjab, saw "something of the stupendous scale" of the upheaval. "
brief bird's-eye view must have revealed nearly half a million refuge
roads," he wrote. Inevitably, the huge mass movements led to renewe

But where all else had failed, Gandhi continued to believe in th
of prayer to stop the mayhem. "Prayer," he said, "is the only n
bringing about orderliness and peace and repose in our daily a
had to appear before Him in all one's weakness, empty-handed
spirit of full surrender, and then He enabled you to stand before
world and protects you from all harm."

As soon as he was back in Delhi, he reinstituted daily prayer m
Over the past decades, these meetings had attracted hundreds, eve
sands, in all parts of India. During one such session, he read a pra
perfectly captured his yearning for peace and reconciliation—cor
without which, in his mind, India would never realize its destiny

I offer you peace.
I offer you love.
I offer you friendship.
I see your beauty.
I hear your need.
I feel your feelings.
My wisdom flows from the highest source.

I salute that source in you.
Let us work together.
For unity and peace.

To underscore this idea of "working together for unity and peace," it was his habit to read from scripture—not just Hindu texts, but also from the Quran, the holy book of Islam, as well as the Bible and other sacred texts. Doing so, Gandhi believed, would stress the unifying power of prayer across all religions, regardless of their individual doctrines. "I do not believe in the exclusive divinity of the Vedas [Hindu scriptures]," he once said. "I believe the Bible and the Quran to be as much divinely inspired as the Vedas."

But not everyone was happy with these attempts at ecumenical harmony. A week after he returned to Delhi, he journeyed to the slums of the Bhangi Colony to meet with an extremist group known as Rashtriya Swayamsevak Sangh (RSS). It was widely known that the RSS had instigated much of the Hindu violence against Muslims, but Gandhi was unperturbed. He believed he could reason with these people and "find common ground, as one Indian patriot speaking to another in the cause of civil peace." But as soon as he started the prayer meeting and tried to read a verse from the Quran, a group of Hindus began to shout *Gandhi murdabad!* "Death to Gandhi!" Later, during a visit to a refugee camp near the fort of Purana Qila, he was besieged by an angry mob of Muslims who demanded to be taken to Pakistan.

New Delhi had become a tinder keg. One out of every four people in the city was a refugee. Mosques were burned down and Muslim residents driven from their homes and shops. A military curfew was imposed, but every dawn still revealed fresh corpses on the street.

With tensions at an all-time high, the Mahatma was persuaded to move his evening prayer meetings to the walled garden of the Birla House, where security personnel could keep an eye on visitors. Given that only a limited number of people could cram into the garden, All-India Radio began to

broadcast a 15-minute excerpt from Gandhi's prayers every night, like clockwork, in an effort to calm the city.

Thus, for the last four months of his life, Gandhi's prayer of peace once again reached out to his people in a last-ditch effort to restore the sense of solidarity that had bound Indians together under the British yoke.

Here, at Birla House, he celebrated his 78th birthday on October 2, 1947, but the moment brought little joy. "Ever since I came to India I have made it my profession to work for communal harmony," he said. "Today, we seem to have become enemies. We assert that there can never be an honest Muslim. A Muslim always remains a worthless fellow." Some 137 mosques had been damaged in Delhi, and others had been turned into Hindu temples. "In such a situation," he asked, "what place do I have in India, and what is the point of my being here?"

And then, just as everyone thought it couldn't get any worse, it did. The two newly formed states, brothers of the former British Raj, moved into a state of war. The reason, once again, was a dispute over land. In this case, the princely state of Kashmir.

Kashmir was a Muslim state ruled by a Hindu maharaja who had not yet decided which side he should join. A group of Muslim militia decided to make the choice for him. They pushed into Kashmir, thereby creating the perfect pretext for Pakistani troops to invade and "restore order." Alarmed, the maharaja turned to India for help. On October 29, 1947, Indian troops moved in to stop the Pakistani invasion and formally accept Kashmir's accession to India.

While all this was going on, India's interior minister, Vallabhbhai Patel, blocked a transfer of 500 million rupees to Islamabad. This was Pakistan's legitimate share of the Indian treasury left by the British. But Patel feared that Jinnah, now Pakistan's governor-general, would use the money to buy arms to fight Indian troops.

The war fanned the flames of religious hatred throughout India, and especially in Delhi. Patel made matters worse when he publicly scolded thousands of Muslim refugees, accusing them of disloyalty. "Why did you not open your mouths on the Kashmir issue?" he said. "Why did you not condemn the action of Pakistan?" And then he followed up with a threat: "I want to tell you very frankly that you cannot ride two horses. Select one horse. Those who want to go to Pakistan can go there."

"Do or die"—that had been the Mahatma's motto from the very beginning of his struggle to liberate India. But now, as he addressed the crowds in the garden of Birla House, he felt his moment in history slipping away. India was hurtling deeper into the abyss. What could he do? What action could he take? He knew he had lost control over his disciples who now ran the country—but perhaps he could still regain his captaincy over his people.

THE MAHATMA CALMLY FINISHES HIS BREAKFAST and gets up from his cot. He slips the watch off his wrist and places it on a chair; he no longer has any need of it. Either he will bring peace to India or die in the attempt. "I will end this fast when I am convinced that the various communities have resumed their friendly relations," he says, "not because of pressure from outside, but of their own free will."

Some of his women followers begin to cry, including his personal physician, a devoted woman known as Sushila. She knows perfectly well what a fast will do to a 78-year-old man, already reduced to mere skin and bones. Gandhi sees her weeping and goes to her.

"What do you expect me to do?" he says softly. "Because the whole world has gone mad shall I go mad also? No, I shall go mad only for God."

With that, the Mahatma begins the last fast of his life, in the only way he knows how: with prayers, inspired by the three great religions of his homeland. Together with the women and those who stand near, he recites a sura from the Quran, then sings one of his favorite Anglican hymns: Isaac Watts's "When I Survey the Wondrous Cross on Which the Prince of Glory Died." There follows an excerpt from the Bhagavad-Gita, one of the stories from the Hindu epic *Mahabharata;* and his beloved Hindu song, "Ram Dhun." "Chief of the house of Raghu, Lord Rama," he sings in his croaked, high-pitched voice; "O beloved, praise Sita and Rama, God and Allah are your names, show your mercy to everyone, O Lord."

When all is said and done, he thanks everyone courteously, curls up on his cot, and goes to sleep.

By then, the news that Gandhi has started a fast, this time to the bitter end, is racing through the city, the nation, and eventually the world. That night, and on the nights that follow, he continues to lead his visitors in prayer meetings, pleading for peace. The first few days he is carried into the garden, but when he becomes too weak to sit up, a microphone is placed next to the cot where he lies. From there, he continues to pray with the crowd, regardless of whether one is caste or Untouchable, Hindu or Muslim, Sikh or Christian. "Prayer is nothing else but an intense longing of the heart," he once said. "You may express yourself through the lips; you may express yourself in the private closet or in the public; but to be genuine, the expression must come from the deepest recesses of the heart."

Only then will prayer have the "power to melt mountains of misery." Only then shall his people find the strength and the love to become a unified nation once more.

As HIS FAST WEARS ON AND THE ORGANS IN HIS BODY start to fail, the warring factions begin to feel the pressure. Margaret Bourke-White later wrote that it wasn't just the Hindu-Muslim enmity that was on trial; it was he, the Mahatma himself. "His whole philosophy of nonviolence is at stake," she wrote as she pondered the frail figure lying motionless on his cot. "He could not survive another Calcutta carnage, another Punjab. He is afraid that everything he stands for in the eyes of the world may prove a myth."

Both Patel and Nehru are shocked and dismayed by the fast. Patel is particularly upset, for he feels that the fast is directed against him because of his strident anti-Muslim rhetoric and his refusal to release the funds to Pakistan. It is not far from the truth. On January 14, the two leaders meet at Gandhi's bedside and strenuously try to convince the Mahatma to end his fast, even offering to release the funds to Pakistan. But neither Patel nor Nehru is able to satisfy all conditions that Gandhi insists on, including the complete rehabilitation of Muslim life in India.

But then—slowly, imperceptibly—the tide begins to change. On January 15, alarmed by the news that Gandhi's health is in rapid decline, a spontaneous procession of thousands of people marches down the streets of New Delhi, extolling Hindu-Muslim unity. The next day, a group of Muslim and Sikh refugees report that Hindu violence has abated. They urge Gandhi to end the fast, but he demurs. "Whatever you do, should ring true," he whispers. "I want solid work."

Mountbatten, now serving as India's governor-general, hastens to pay his respects as well. "Ah," the Mahatma says with a wan smile, when he sees the tall Englishman at his bedside, "I see that it takes a fast to bring you to me."

Inexorably, the momentum continues to build. All of India, both Muslim and Hindu, begins to realize that Gandhiji—the *ji* a diminutive expressing affection and respect—is truly on the verge of death. A telegram arrives from refugees in Karachi who have been driven from their homes in Delhi. Is it safe for them to return? Will the Hindu population allow them to go back? One of Gandhi's followers races into the city. By the end of the day, more than a thousand Hindu refugees have signed a declaration that, yes, they will vacate the Muslim homes they have occupied so that the original owners may return.

Meanwhile, telegrams keep pouring in, even from leaders in Pakistan, expressing their love and support. But for Gandhi, it is still not enough. "He was," Bourke-White observed, "pitting all the physical strength he had left in his thin wiry body against the spirit of hate consuming his country."

A Central Peace Committee is formed. Its 130 members are sworn to restore peace and amity in the city. Convoys of trucks drive through New Delhi with placards that read, "Mahatmaji's life is more precious than ours!"

and students chant, "We will die before Mahatma dies!" Ten thousand people, on bicycle and on foot, meet in Urdu Park and march down to Birla House as a demonstration of love and religious comity. It takes all night for them to pass through the gates of Birla House. Prime Minister Pandit Nehru joins them and speaks, saying that "if we want to be free, we must free each other first. This is what Gandhiji taught us." And still it isn't enough.

Later that night, doctors issue a prognosis that Gandhi's kidneys are failing and that he may not have more than 24 hours to live.

The next day is January 18, 1948. With Gandhi's life in the balance, the Congress Party is able to push through a resolution in Parliament that guarantees all Muslim property throughout the land; safeguards Muslim pilgrimages, shrines, and feast days; and invites all Muslim refugees back to India. The document is signed by representatives from all religions: Hindus, Muslims, Sikhs, Christians, Jews, and even the RSS.

A hundred-man delegation brings the document to Gandhi's bedside later that day. Even the Pakistani ambassador to India, the High Commissioner Zahid Hussain, appears in Birla House to pledge his support. Patel assures him that India will release Pakistan's share of the Raj treasury. The head of the Delhi police chimes in to say that the situation on Delhi's street is back to normal.

Gandhi lies on his cot, deep in thought. At long last he clears his throat and whispers, "I will break the fast. God's will is done. All of you may well be a witness to it."

As soon as he says it, a happy cry goes up from the house. Women begin to sing, laugh, and weep for joy. Bourke-White, who is standing outside, pushes through the crowd and jumps on the table in Gandhi's room to take a photograph. There is the Mahatma, lying on his mattress on the floor, clutching one of the telegrams stacked around him, a smile on his face.

He is once again the captain of his people. For a brief moment, he has united the nation once more.

IN THE DECADES SINCE, GANDHI'S NAME HAS BECOME synonymous with nonviolent resistance. Though he was not the first to formulate the principle (Gandhi himself credited Plato, Ruskin, Thoreau, and Tolstoy as key influences), he was the first to apply it on a wide scale, not only in the political but also in the economic, ethical, and spiritual spheres. His example inspired countless leaders of the postwar era, including anti-apartheid activist Nelson Mandela, who would become South Africa's first black president, and Martin Luther King Jr., who once wrote that "Christ gave us the goals and Mahatma Gandhi the tactics." Today, Gandhi's satyagraha continues to ricochet from the Occupy Wall Street protests in the United States to the Umbrella Movement in Hong Kong, while Aung San Suu Kyi, the Burmese activist, cites the Mahatma as her model for nonviolent activism.

From a strictly political perspective, Gandhi's role in the creation of modern India was certainly decisive, even if the India that emerged from the British Empire was not what he had hoped. The religious friction that prompted the partition into a Hindu and a Muslim state continues to this day. Now armed with nuclear weapons, India and Pakistan often remain at loggerheads, with Kashmir often serving as a major flash point. Despite recent attempts to lower the tension between the two states, their rivalry has been exacerbated by the fact that India is becoming a major economic power, whereas Pakistan is not. Today, India's economy is not the self-sufficient, village-based economy that Gandhi favored; it has become a major economic colossus. And the growing schism between rich and poor is alarming: Though India's 2015 gross domestic product is estimated to be worth $2.03 trillion, the average take-home pay of its 1.2 billion people is still only $1,364 per year.

In sharp contrast to Gandhi's emphasis on nonviolence and the peaceful resolution of conflict, India is also becoming a major military power, partly in response to China's growing territorial assertiveness. Its standing army of two million is one of the largest in South Asia. Therefore, it is probably fair to say that the impact of Gandhi's teachings, and particularly his prayer for peace, was felt on a more global scale than in India itself. Rather than a model of Indian statecraft, as Nehru would become, Gandhi is today revered as an icon of nonviolent protest and religious tolerance.

Gandhi did not live to witness India's stunning growth. Just 12 days after ending his fast, he was walking to his usual garden spot to lead a prayer meeting when he was shot by a Hindu nationalist. The assassin was furious over Gandhi's support for Muslim Indians, particularly his insistence that Pakistan's share of the Raj treasury should be remitted.

As the three bullets entered his chest, Gandhi mumbled "*Hē Ram!*— Oh, God!" and sank to his knees. He was dead before his assistants were able to rush him back inside Birla House.

"The light has gone out of our lives," Prime Minister Nehru said on All-India Radio later that night. "Our beloved leader, *Bapu* as we called him, the father of the nation, is no more . . . The light has gone out, I said, and yet I was wrong. The light that has illuminated this country for these many years will illuminate this country for many more years, and a thousand years later that light will still be seen in this country. The world will see it, and it will give solace to innumerable hearts."

Pandit Nehru was right. Ever since, Gandhi's shining light, and his prayer for peace, has consoled thousands of hearts, and continues to do so in our day.

Mother Teresa never wavered from her unflinching devotion to the poor.

CHAPTER 10

MOTHER TERESA'S DAILY PRAYER

Jesus, my patient, how sweet it is to serve you.
Lord, give me this seeing faith,
then my work will never be monotonous.
I will ever find joy in humouring the fancies
and gratifying the wishes of all poor sufferers.
O beloved sick, how doubly dear you are to me,
when you personify Christ;
and what a privilege is mine to be allowed
to tend to you.

EN ROUTE FROM CALCUTTA TO DARJEELING
India
September 10, 1946

A train is slowly weaving its way through the patchwork of cotton fields in West Bengal. It is in no particular hurry. The journey from Calcutta to the Himalaya can take anywhere from 22 to 26 hours, and that's on a good day.

The heat is oppressive, this close to the monsoon season, which explains why the smoke from the engine doesn't quite rise in the heavy air but curls around the train like a blanket, forcing its passengers to choose between unbearable heat and the stink of smoke and soot wafting through the windows.

As is the policy of the Great Indian Peninsula Railway (GIPR), the coaches are organized in three classes, but up close it's hard to tell the difference. The war has ravaged much of the GIPR's rolling stock. Most of its best engines and coaches have been shipped abroad, to places like Burma and Iraq, to better ferry troops to the fields of battle. As a result, the train that slowly crawls through the Bengali plains is an odd assortment of dilapidated cars and threadbare furnishings—perhaps not unlike the British Empire itself.

The third class is located at the rear of the train. As usual, its hard wooden benches are overflowing with all sorts of humanity: stoic farmers with hens in wicker baskets; perspiring mothers, fanning themselves while clutching their babies; young soldiers on leave, fresh from the Hindu-Muslim clashes in the cities. Any space that is not occupied by a human being is stacked with provisions that fill the fetid air with the most pungent aromas imaginable.

Already, the train has made considerable progress. After leaving Calcutta, it worked its way northward, stopping at Burdwan and Bolpur before crossing the bridge over Mayurakshi River for its long run to Pakur.

In another five hours, it will sharply bend to the right, toward Farakka, where, God willing, a rusting span will carry the train across the Ganges River. Most of the passengers will not be aware of it, for they will be asleep, lulled by the soporific cadence of wheels thudding over the old meter-gauge track.

A 36-year-old woman, dressed in the habit of a nun, is not one of those. She is awake, though her hair under her cap is matted and her eyes are ringed with a shadow of fatigue. With her dark East European complexion, so unlike the white skin of her fellow sisters, one could easily take her for a Bengali native. But such is far from the truth, for the woman is actually Albanian, a native of Skopje, from a land known as Yugoslavia.

She is also very ill. At this moment she is running a fever, which is why she leans her head against the dirty glass of the window, hoping for a breath of fresh air. Eventually she too closes her eyes, as if she is ready to fall asleep. But such sweet oblivion still eludes her, for deep inside, she is heartbroken, and close to despair.

It was the Sisters of Loreto, with whom she lives in a convent in Calcutta, who urged her to make this journey. *You must go to the cool forests and pastures of the Punjab,* they told her. *You must rest. And, perchance, find peace in whatever God has planned for you.*

Of course, it didn't start out this way. There was a time when the idea of serving as a missionary in this strange land was all she could think about. She still remembers how, as a blushing 18-year-old postulate, she was overcome with excitement at seeing this exotic land for the first time. "With a joy I cannot ascribe," she wrote, "we touched the soil of Bengal for the first time." Upon her arrival, a great Mass was offered to thank God for bringing her safely from Ireland, where she had trained to be a nun. "Pray for us a great deal," she wrote to her family back home, "that we may become good and courageous missionaries."

But as it turned out, that's not what her religious order had in mind for her. Almost immediately upon her arrival, she was whisked off to Darjeeling, a delightful city in the north where the Sisters of Loreto managed a school complex for the wealthy expatriate community. In hindsight, it was truly an enviable appointment. Ever since the British discovered its mild, almost alpine-like climate at an altitude of nearly 7,000 feet, Darjeeling had become India's oasis, a land of tea plantations and cherry trees in blossom.

And so it was that for the first two years of her career as a nun, the young Albanian girl did not live among the filth and poverty of Calcutta, as many believe, but among the tropical gentility of the British Raj at the peak of its wealth. She was no stranger to wealth. As the third child of a successful Albanian entrepreneur, Nikollë Bojaxhiu, little Anjezë Gonxhe (Agnes Rose in English) had grown up in an affluent and cosmopolitan household filled with servants and tutors. Though both of her parents were Albanian, the family had moved to Skopje, then part of the Ottoman *vilayet,* or district of Kosovo, so that Nikollë could better tap into the fast-developing business connections within the Turkish Ottoman Empire. What he didn't realize is that by doing so, he had unwittingly placed his family in one of the flash points of the 20th century. In 1912, when Agnes was just two years old, Skopje was annexed by the brash Kingdom of Serbia during the Third Balkan War. Two years later, that same Kingdom of Serbia precipitated the outbreak of World War I by training a Bosnian nationalist to assassinate the heir of the Austrian Habsburg Empire.

Nikollë did quite well during the Great War, becoming stupendously rich in the trade of all sorts of goods that armies need in times of war. But the clouds were already gathering. While the Muslim majority of Albania had been largely tolerant of Catholics like Nikollë and his wife, Dranafile (or Drana), sentiments were very different in Serbia. The kingdom was staunchly Eastern Orthodox and resented and repressed its Catholic minority. Shortly after the annexation of 1912, many Catholic families had been evicted from their homes. There were even reports that some mothers and their daughters had been raped while their fathers were forced to watch before being killed themselves. The persecution escalated after the end of World War I.

The religious enmity between Orthodox and Catholics made a deep impression on little Agnes. *Why,* she may have wondered, *do the Serbs hate us so if we all profess to believe in Jesus, Prince of Peace?*

Nikollë did not understand it either and decided to become active in a political movement that clamored for Kosovo's secession in order to be integrated with Albania. Inevitably this activity brought him to the attention of the authorities. Serbia was now part of a new body politic, an odd assortment of ethnicities eventually known as the Kingdom of Yugoslavia, and the last thing its rulers needed was the headache of a rebellious province. In 1919, Nikollë returned from a demonstration in Belgrade, the capital, complaining of severe stomach pains. Within 48 hours, he was dead. There were strong suspicions that he was poisoned, most likely by the Yugoslav secret police.

Nikollë's death destroyed the domestic tranquility of the Bojaxhiu household. His wife, Drana, plunged into a deep depression. We can only imagine the impact of these developments on nine-year-old Agnes. What saved the family, perhaps, were its close ties to the local Catholic parish of the Sacred Heart, where Agnes and her sister, Aga, sang in the choir.

As the years progressed, the wounds healed and Drana found ways to support her family, albeit in a much more modest lifestyle. These were happy years, Agnes would later recall. Her brother, Lazar, left Skopje to become an officer in the Albanian army. After Albania's annexation by fascist Italy, he went to Rome to join Mussolini's government. Agnes too thought she had found her calling. At age 12 she announced her desire to become a nun. "It was not a vision," she said later; "it was a personal matter."

Father Jambrekovic, a Croat priest who was appointed to Agnes's parish in 1925, took the young girl under his wing. A Jesuit by training, Jambrekovic told her all about the Jesuits and their commitment to educate the young around the world. As it happened, that also included India, where the Jesuits ran a number of missions in places like Calcutta. The more Agnes listened to his stories, the more she decided that that's where she wanted to go as well, and work as a missionary.

There were some who questioned the wisdom of this decision. Agnes's health was precarious, as everyone who knew her could attest. She had a deep, bronchial cough that one of her doctors believed could be the onset of tuberculosis. In addition, she was born with a clubfoot and suffered from malaria, which sometimes produced a high fever that made her delirious. Such symptoms did not bode well for someone planning to live in a tropical climate—least of all in a city where midday temperatures in the shade reached 110 degrees and disease was rampant. But Agnes was not to be dissuaded. She felt a calling to go to India, and to India she would go.

Father Jambrekovic knew that the Jesuits of Calcutta worked closely with the religious women of the Institute of the Blessed Virgin Mary. This order, founded in 1609, shared the Jesuit passion for educating the young. Since its founder, the Englishwoman Mary Ward, used to pray at the Virgin Mary shrine of Loreto, Italy, the women were also known as the Sisters of Loreto. The idea struck a chord in Agnes.

"I wanted to be a missionary," she told the BBC journalist Malcolm Muggeridge many years later. "At that time some missionaries had gone to India from Yugoslavia. They told me the Loreto nuns were doing work in Calcutta and other places. I offered myself to go out to the Bengal Mission."

ON SEPTEMBER 26, 1928, SHORTLY AFTER turning 18, Agnes embraced her mother and sister and began the long journey to the Irish convent where she would receive her principal training. She would never see her relatives again. It was as if Agnes had firmly closed the door on a youth filled with trauma and heartbreak. From now on, she would devote herself entirely to her calling as a young religious woman.

Her training was short, and five months after her arrival in Darjeeling she officially became a novice, or novitiate, preparing for a future in a monastery. To signal this, Agnes began wearing the long black habit of her order. She also adopted a new name that, by custom, was derived from a Catholic saint. She chose Thérèse of Lisieux, a 19th-century French nun also known as Thérèse of the Child Jesus, who only four years earlier had been canonized by Pope Pius XI. Like Agnes, Thérèse had been a sickly child, suffering from tuberculosis. Upon her canonization, she was recognized as the saint of illnesses and missions. This resonated with Agnes, since it captured the challenges that she herself would be facing. Unfortunately, another sister had also chosen the name Theresa. Agnes then decided to adopt the Spanish spelling: Teresa.

For the next eight years, Teresa devoted herself to her teaching career. Her pupils were a world apart from the children whom she would later work with in Calcutta. In Darjeeling, the children all hailed from India's elite, including British administrators or affluent Indian families. Even after she was transferred in 1931 to the Sisters of Mary convent in Calcutta, she continued to serve a mostly well-heeled group of children while living in a modern and comfortable convent in the upscale Entally neighborhood. The complex, which still exists, was a sprawling enclave framed with pilasters and lovely green shutters, separated from the outside world by high, whitewashed walls.

Although she was sequestered behind these walls like any other nun, she soon got a glimpse what life was like on the other side through her contact with the so-called Bengali Sisters. These religious women also managed a school within the compound, but it served quite a different population, mostly orphans or abandoned children. Teresa took a liking to the Bengali Sisters. She particularly admired their cotton dress, an Indian draped garment known as a sari, which was a lot more comfortable than the thick woolen habits that the Loreto Sisters were forced to wear.

In 1937, the same year that Teresa took her vows and officially became a nun, she was promoted to the post of principal of St. Mary School. Soon after, she also succeeded Mother Cénacle, a Mauritian nun, as mother superior of the Entally convent. This was rather unusual for one so young, especially a young woman who had no higher education than high school. Perhaps Sister Teresa had made a genuine impression on her superiors with her dedication and gift for organization.

Naturally, the newly minted Mother Teresa was over the moon. "This is a new life," she exulted in one of her few letters to her mother, Drana. "Our center here is very fine. I am a teacher and I love the work. I am also Head of the whole school, and everybody wishes me well."

BEYOND THE WALLS OF ST. MARY'S, the world was rapidly spiraling out of control. For a long time, Calcutta had been one of the loveliest urban centers of the British Raj. Originally an agglomeration of three Bengali villages, the British had chosen the area in 1771 to become the headquarters of the East India Company, the commercial entity that ruled India as a corporate fiefdom. By the middle of the 19th century, Calcutta had grown into two districts: the White Town to the south, filled with elegant white buildings for the British expatriate community, and Black Town to the north, reserved for the largely Indian population. Most of these Indians, however, were upper-caste Hindus who served in the colonial administration and formed a well-to-do bourgeois community of their own. Indeed, much of the city's growing prosperity was due to the opium trade, for which Calcutta served as a crucial collection point.

But the social climate changed after Calcutta began to nurture a budding Indian independence movement. The growing political unrest prompted the colonial government to move the capital to Delhi, taking much of British trade and patronage with it. In 1937, the same year that Teresa was appointed headmistress, a massive earthquake in the Bihar region brought hundreds of thousands of displaced villagers to Calcutta. Within weeks, the quaint alleys and byways of the city were reduced to a slum netherworld of unimaginable poverty. The outbreak of World War II aggravated the situation by forcing millions of refugees from British dominions now occupied by Japan to flee to Calcutta, given its prominent location in the lower Ganges Delta, close to the Indian Ocean.

By then, the war had also affected the convent of the Sisters of Loreto. The British military decided to turn their complex into a military head-quarters, which forced Mother Teresa to move to a new location on Convent Road. It disrupted their quiet, sequestered life and compelled them to confront the city and its desperate cycle of daily survival. Every morning, hundreds of poor and displaced people banged on the door of the convent, begging for food and shelter. Mother Teresa had her hands full just trying to keep the school and convent operating, despite food shortages and the periodic bombardment by Japanese warplanes.

Life became even more precarious after the great Bengal Famine of 1943 drove thousands of additional peasant families into the starving city. Each day brought more babies on Mother Teresa's doorstep, abandoned by their mothers. And yet against all odds, she managed to keep the convent going, determined not to allow any interruption in the daily classes.

Conventional lore holds that this is when Mother Teresa began to question her mission, surrounded as she was by so much abject poverty and despair. But a witness, a Belgian priest named Father Celeste who said Mass for the Loreto Sisters, said that this was not the case. "Some accounts have tried to make a connection between Mother Teresa's life behind convent walls and the poverty and communal killing in Calcutta in those days," he said later, "but these accounts are completely wrong, only a hypothesis."

This "communal killing" escalated after the end of the war. Mohandas Gandhi, the *Bapu* of the nation, had long fought for Indian independence through a strategy of nonviolent protest, but his long imprisonment by the British had allowed the more militant Muslim League to seize the initiative. The League's demand for a separate Muslim state, to be known as Pakistan, led to massive clashes between Indian Hindus and Muslims, particularly in Calcutta. More than four million refugees poured into the already overcrowded city, creating three thousand new slums. As the city's sewage system collapsed, the streets became open sewers filled with offal and human refuse, creating a medieval world of unspeakable poverty and disease. Life expectancy in Calcutta dropped to the lowest rate in the world, with more than 90 percent of the people suffering from either dysentery or malnutrition.

Inside their convent, the Sisters of Loreto were to some extent inured from these appalling conditions. Mother Teresa tried to distract her school-children by keeping them focused on their schoolwork. When the shortage of teachers threatened the cancellation of some of the classes, she jumped in and taught them herself. When there was no food to feed them, Teresa would go and scrounge for provisions. "Mother told us, 'I am going out. Children, you stay in the chapel and pray,'" one pupil would remember later. "And then, by 4 p.m., the store room was full of different kinds of vegetables and food."

And yet the greatest shock was yet to come. Shortly after the Muslim League's Direct Action Day led to massacres throughout the Bengal, Mother Teresa received a terse note from the abbess of the Sisters of Loreto. It informed her, in no uncertain terms, that she was removed from her position as school principal. Worse, she was terminated as mother superior of the Entally convent. No reason was given.

In a moment, Teresa's world collapsed. All through the upheaval of the last few years, she had struggled valiantly to sustain the convent and the 300 children in her care. And now, when by rights she should have received some recognition for her work, she was summarily dismissed, demoted to the status of an ordinary nun. As *Sister* Teresa. It was a devastating experience.

Why did the Loreto Order remove her from her post? It was not as if a younger replacement was waiting in the wings, for her successor was the same mother superior she'd replaced back in 1937—Mother Cénacle, already much advanced in age. Author Paul Williams suggests that Teresa lacked the requisite academic credentials to serve as the principal of a prominent high school. After all, he writes, "she knew little of art and literature, let alone the intricacies of scholastic theology." That sentiment is echoed by Father Celeste, whose impression of Teresa at that time was that she was "a very simple nun, very devout but not particularly remarkable." But why did she not receive credit for the superhuman effort of keeping the convent and the school in operation through the tremendous upheaval of World War II? Was the abbess blind to the conditions in India? Or was the dismissal the result of internal politics? Was Mother Teresa too much of a maverick, a woman too beholden to unconventional methods? Did the abbess feel that she had "gone native"?

Kathryn Spink suggests another motive: that the dismissal was prompted by concern for Teresa's health. "We were careful of her," a fellow sister, Marie Thérèse, remembered later. "I don't know whether she realized it, but we were. When it came to the work and the running around, our Superiors took extra care with her." Her struggle with bronchitis and the ever present threat of tuberculosis was well known. Perhaps the abbess thought that by discharging her from a stressful job, she was doing Teresa a kindness.

But the opposite was the case. The loss of her position, with its myriad of responsibilities, provoked the very stress that the order may have wanted to prevent. Teresa's bronchial symptoms returned with a vengeance. She was ordered to take a rest every afternoon for three hours, but it made little difference.

Father Celeste, a keen observer, noticed the change in her right away. "I have seen her upset at the death of a sister," he recalled later, referring to the death of her older sister, Aga, "but I have never seen her cry. But then, there were tears in her eyes. It was very hard for her to be in bed and not to do the work."

With the loss of her position Teresa was robbed of her purpose, her mission in life. Her sense of self had been shattered. She had nothing to look forward to other than the humiliation of returning to the simple life of an ordinary, obedient nun. Today, we might have diagnosed her condition as one of acute depression. But it manifested itself in an acute deterioration of her health.

In the end, it was decided that she take her annual leave and return to Darjeeling, the very station where she had begun her career, in the hope that the cool air would help restore her health.

AND SO IT IS THAT SHE FINDS HERSELF on a ramshackle train to Jalpaiguri, rattling along at a steady pace as the passengers around her sleep.

This is the moment when she has her vision—out of the blue, when she least expects it. In her feverish and slightly delirious state, she experiences an epiphany, not unlike the way other saints have experienced divine whispers in centuries past. "I was sure it was God's voice," she would say later. "I was certain he was calling me." Moreover, the voice that spoke to her was direct, explicit, unambiguous. "I was to leave the convent," Teresa said, "and help the poor while living among them." It was that simple.

Actually, not that simple. There are religious orders devoted to service, to social work among the poor, but the convent of the Sisters of Loreto is not one of them. This is a closed congregation that keeps its nuns sequestered from all worldly concerns. To do what the voice told her was tantamount to breaking her vows.

And yet by the time Teresa's train enters the Batasia Loop for the final run to Darjeeling, she has made up her mind. With the Kanchenjunga range towering high above her, she resolves to do what the voice has told her. "It was an order," she would say later; "to fail it would have been to break the faith."

Needless to say, her superiors are shocked, dismayed, when she tells them of her intentions to leave. They are even more astonished when she tells them that she wants to create a new community of sisters—one that, in her words, "will work for the poorest of the poor in the slums, in a spirit of poverty and cheerfulness," just as Jesus had ministered to the poor and destitute of Galilee. And she fully expects to manage all this without any form of ecclesiastical or institutional support. "The work," Father Celeste would later remember, "was to be among the *abandoned*—those with nobody, the very poorest."

There now began the long and tortuous process by which a nun, once committed to her vows, tries to extricate herself from that pledge—a path far from easy. What's more, Teresa's motive is unprecedented, even bewildering. Here is a nun determined to leave her convent—in order to start a new congregation! For heaven's sake, *why*, Archbishop Ferdinand Périer wants to know. There are already congregations that serve the poor of Calcutta, such as the Sisters of Charity and the Daughters of St. Anne. Why doesn't Sister Teresa simply request a transfer to any of these orders?

"Because," Father Celeste tells him in an effort to plead her case, "it is the will of God."

"What?!" the archbishop bristles. "You say this is the will of God, just like that? I am a bishop, and *I* don't profess to know what is the will of God!"

But Teresa is not to be dissuaded. And then, surprisingly, there arrives a letter of support from a very unexpected quarter: the abbess in Ireland. Perhaps the Mother General, Gertrude Kennedy, now regrets Teresa's dismissal from her original post. Or perhaps, as some authors have suggested, she wants to distance herself from a situation that might become a distraction.

Whatever the case may be, the abbess writes a letter that explicitly authorizes Teresa to go *over the heads of her superiors in India* and make a direct appeal to the pope. This, too, is unprecedented—to allow a nun to bypass all of the ecclesiastical layers that the Church has placed on her is unheard of. If Teresa's call has indeed been divinely inspired, then surely that same divine hand continues to work in mysterious ways.

The reply from the Vatican, which she receives on April 20, 1948, is even more astonishing: Teresa's wish is to be granted. She can leave the convent to organize a new group of religious sisters—not as sequestered nuns but as women who will live among the poor in order to serve the poor.

THUS BEGINS THE EXTRAORDINARY STORY of Mother Teresa among the most destitute people of our modern world. Given her passion for teaching, she starts with a small school in a middle-class neighborhood of Motijhil, followed by the creation of a small dispensary. She relies on begging to finance her operations. One day, she spends an entire day on the floor of a pharmacy, reciting her rosary in quiet protest until the pharmacist capitulates and gives her the medicines that her charges need. This school is followed by a second, with a dispensary, in the Tiljara district.

Mother Teresa then turns her mind to forming a proper congregation of sisters and teachers that will operate these facilities. She begins to recruit candidates from among her former students—pupils she taught while serving as principal of the St. Mary School. Many respond to her call, and readily accept a lifestyle as a religious. "We lived as nuns, but we had not yet been recognized as a separate congregation," one of the first recruits would remember later. "The archbishop had yet to approve our way, and there was no constitution yet. But we were convinced that approval would come."

All sisters are told to adopt the signature habit that Mother Teresa wears: an Indian white sari with blue ornamental bands, symbol of Indian widowhood. These young women in their white saris soon become a familiar sight, not only in the neighborhoods where they teach but also in the nearby slums where they try to care for the sick.

Meanwhile, Father Celeste is charged with drawing up the new order's constitution. The organization is to be devoted to "the helpless, such as abandoned infants and children, or lepers and dying destitutes," he writes. And most important, the order's mission is not meant as social work but as a "charity for Christ in the poor."

This is a theme that Mother Teresa stresses throughout her subsequent career. To care for the downtrodden, she would say, is to care for Jesus. To do so is an act of compassion rather than social responsibility; it is an act of love. This idea is captured in one of her many prayers, one of which would eventually become the daily prayer of her new order, the Missionary Sisters of Charity. The prayer, she said, serves as a daily reminder to all her followers that the purpose of their efforts was to "see Jesus in every person who is sick":

> *Jesus, my patient, how sweet it is to serve you.*
> *Lord, give me this seeing faith,*
> *then my work will never be monotonous.*
> *I will ever find joy in humouring the fancies*
> *and gratifying the wishes of all poor sufferers.*
> *O beloved sick, how doubly dear you are to me,*
> *when you personify Christ;*
> *and what a privilege is mine to be allowed to*
> *tend to you.*

Sometime in March 1953, the new congregation sets up its Mother House in a cluster of two homes on 54A Lower Circular Road in Calcutta. Their principal source of income is begging, as before—not for themselves but for the poor they are dedicated to serve. "Mother gave us a love for begging from door to door," one of the sisters would remember.

But the living are not the only ones who are desperately in need of charity; the dying are yearning for comfort as well. In fact, the rate of people dying in the street, untended by any of the city's medical services, has become an acute source of embarrassment for Calcutta, and indeed for the newly formed Republic of India altogether. One day, a report appears in the local newspapers about a malnourished boy of 14 who has been left to die on the sidewalk. One of the people who sees him lying there runs to a phone and calls an ambulance. But when the boy arrives at a nearby hospital, the staff refuses to accept him because he is obviously too poor to pay for the treatment. Shockingly, the child is driven back to the gutter where he was found and placed there to die. The story produces a storm of outrage, not only in India but also around the world.

This may explain the reason that Calcutta is suddenly eager to approve Mother Teresa's pending application for a "house" for the dying. The only problem is that city officials really don't have a house to give her. Or if they do, they aren't particularly keen to hand it over to a Western woman, and a Christian besides. And so, in the end, Mother Teresa is offered the use of some pilgrim dormitories attached to the Temple of Kali.

Kali, literally "the black one," fulfills an important role in the Hindu pantheon of gods. She is the goddess of change and death; of time before the creation of light. To this day, many elderly people who feel the approach of death are brought to the Kali temple to pray. Thus, the idea of creating a hospice for the dying at this prominent Hindu temple is certainly appropriate, as Mother Teresa well knows. "This is a very famous Hindu temple," she would later explain to an interviewer, "and people used to come there to worship and rest; so I thought that this would be the best place for our people to be able to rest before they went to heaven."

The sisters immediately set to work to convert the dirty and shabby dormitory facilities into what would be known as Nirmal Hriday, the "place of the Immaculate Heart." Soon the place is filled with dying men, women, and children. Many are in a terrible state, with limbs or open wounds chewed by dogs or rats. Everyone is cleaned, fed, and made comfortable. In Mother Teresa's words, they who have lived like animals will now die like angels.

Not everyone is pleased with this initiative from a Christian woman, so close to a sacred Hindu shrine. Rumors begin to spread that the dying are forcefully baptized as Catholics in order to receive treatment. The Sisters are jeered; death threats are issued. One day, when a riotous crowd starts to throw stones into the dormitories, Mother Teresa rushes outside and loudly declares, "Kill me if you want to, but do not disturb those inside. Let them die in peace."

Eventually the priests from the Kali temple lodge a formal protest with the police. A motion is introduced into the city legislature, ordering the transfer of Nirmal Hriday to another location. Mother Teresa vigorously protests, arguing that every dying person is afforded the last rites according to their faith: Hindus are washed in the water of the Ganges, and suras from the Quran are read for Muslims. Only those who can be positively identified as Christian are given Christian ministrations. All to no avail.

Mother Teresa then takes a different tack. She invites the city officials to come and see for themselves and determine whether the accusations are true. The city takes her up on her offer. A delegation is formed, to be led by the distinguished Dr. Ahmad, a Muslim physician who serves as Calcutta's chief medical officer.

When the appointed day arrived arrives, the delegation is courteously received and ushered into the dormitory. "We wish to see Mother Teresa," they state ponderously. Certainly, the sister replies, and ushers them to one of the pallets where Mother Teresa is sitting. But she is too absorbed to acknowledge the visitors. Using a fine set of tweezers, with the tip of her tongue between her lips, she is carefully picking maggots out of the open wound of a beggar's face. Appalled, the officials recoil from the sight.

They turn around, and wherever they look, they see more of the same: countless human wrecks, lying on their pallets, waiting patiently to die a dignified death.

A few moments later, a visibly shaken Dr. Ahmad emerges from the hospice to face the crowd that has gathered outside. He clears his throat and declares, "Yes, I will send this woman away."

Loud cheers from the crowd.

"But," Dr. Ahmad continues, "only after you have persuaded *your* mothers and sisters to come here and do the work that she is doing." He pauses and adds, "This woman is a saint."

Thus it falls to a Muslim, and a doctor, to be the first to suggest that Mother Teresa's work might be that of a modern saint.

IN THE DECADES TO COME, MOTHER TERESA'S Missionary Sisters of Charity organization, or "MC" as she herself referred to it, would grow to more than 4,000 sisters running schools, orphanages, hospices, and charity centers in Asia, Africa, Europe, and the United States. In each of these facilities, the day starts with the Daily Prayer that Mother Teresa composed herself, to remind her staff of the presence of Jesus in every person they serve. In 1984, her operations were expanded with an organization for priests and religious men, known as the Missionaries of Charity Fathers. As of 2007, these groups claimed a membership of 450 brothers and 5,000 sisters operating in 600 missions, schools, and shelters, spread over 120 countries.

At the same time, Mother Teresa became a major celebrity—an icon of selfless compassion in a selfish and materialistic world. Long extolled in the Indian press, she was "discovered" by European journalists in the 1970s after her interview with BBC reporter Malcolm Muggeridge, and her fame grew rapidly from there. In 1979, she was awarded the Nobel Peace Prize, and six years later she was given the Presidential Medal of Freedom by Ronald Reagan during a ceremony at the White House. In 1999, she ranked first in a Gallup poll of the most admired people of the 20th century.

And yet, in some ways, Mother Teresa remains a mystery. Part of the reason, as Gëzim Alpion of the University of Birmingham wrote, is that "a complete biography of Mother Teresa has yet to be written," because "even the best of her authorized and unauthorized biographies tend to offer only a partial picture of her life." In fact, the literature on Mother Teresa is polarized into two camps: devoted hagiographies on the one hand, extolling Mother Teresa as a "modern saint," and fiercely critical articles and books on the other, attempting to puncture her presumed sheen of sainthood.

Some of her critics, for example, point to the fact that Mother Teresa was not very discriminating when it came to accepting money from shady characters, eager to bask in the glory of her saintly persona, such as François "Papa Doc" Duvalier, the ruthless dictator of Haiti, or the disgraced British tycoon Robert Maxwell. In her lifetime, Mother Teresa shrugged off such criticism, arguing that it didn't matter where the money came from as long as it was put to good use.

Other critics deplore the fact that Mother Teresa strenuously fought attempts by the Indian government to make contraceptives available to the poor, even though overpopulation is the main source of the intense poverty that she fought her entire life. Her deep faith and commitment to Catholic doctrine would not permit any consideration of family planning aids, even though such could have served as a way out for much of India's poor. Indeed, a recent projection suggests that by 2022, India will bypass China as the most populous nation in the world.

More recently, some have asked why Mother Teresa did not allow strong analgesics or opiates to lessen the suffering of those dying in her care. On this subject, others have come to her defense, pointing out that until very recently, pain relief was a rather controversial notion in India, and that "palliative care training has been available only since 1997."

Of course, neither saintly hagiographies nor hostile narratives can provide a true portrait of this exceptional woman, who single-handedly turned the eyes of a weary postwar world to the plight of the poor and dispossessed. That is Mother Teresa's great achievement, as is her insistence that such a commitment should be an all-consuming gift to God, without regard for oneself. But it is also true that many aspects of her story have yet to be explored to the fullest. One such insight, which has only recently come to light, is rather startling in itself.

Soon after Mother Teresa's death in 1997, the Vatican initiated the first steps toward canonization, the process by which the Catholic Church declares someone to be a saint. Part of this procedure is a thorough investigation of the subject using both published and unpublished sources. In the course of this research, the postulator, or lead investigator, Brian Kolodiejchuk, uncovered notes and letters that showed that—notwithstanding her extraordinary dedication to her mission—Mother Teresa had lost faith in God herself. In the words of the Reverend Kolodiejchuk, for much of the 50 years of her missionary activity Mother Teresa "felt no presence of God whatsoever." In one of her private notes, she writes hauntingly, "Where is my faith? Even deep down . . . there is nothing but emptiness and darkness."

Of course, it is only natural for human beings to experience doubt, and clergy are not immune from such feelings. But in the case of Mother Teresa, the sense of loss and abandonment ran particularly deep. "When I try to raise my thoughts to Heaven," she wrote, "there is such convicting emptiness that those very thoughts return like sharp knives and hurt my very soul."

For many of us, these misgivings make Mother Teresa an even more remarkable figure. To labor so unremittingly against such impossible odds, without the comfort and inspiration that set her on her course to begin with, must have been a heavy burden. And yet this frail and unassuming woman carried on with her mission, regardless.

Mother Teresa may not be a saint in the conventional sense of the word or the type of saint that Church tradition expects her to be. But that she was one of the most exceptional women of our modern times is beyond question. Perhaps, then, that is the true legacy of Mother Teresa: how a very human figure found the strength to transcend her doubts and change the world in ways that are still with us today.

Hindu women pray at the Tirta Empul water temple in Bali, Indonesia.

EPILOGUE

Is there such a thing as a Divine Being? And if so, does this being take an active interest in our affairs? Better put, is there a way for us to tap into that divine presence and perhaps find a strength far beyond our human potential?

This collection of stories, from Abraham to Gandhi and Mother Teresa, would suggest that the answer is yes. Each of these stories reveals that at different stages in the evolution of humanity, certain men and women have had a spiritual experience that empowered them to do truly extraordinary things.

But that's not the only thing these short stories tell us. What I think is so interesting is that they show that the Divine—whatever we may call him: Yahweh, God, Allah, Rama—did not limit his revelation to one particular group or faith alone. For many of us, that may seem obvious, but in practice it's not. To this day, most of our religions—Catholic, Protestant, Jewish, Sunni, Shia, Sufi, Hindu—steadfastly maintain that they are the *only* true way to God and that all others are, well, let's say, *misguided*. The most extreme example is the scourge of Islamist terrorism, which is challenging the very foundation of our pluralistic societies. But what these violent fundamentalists do not realize is that when they kill men or women because they are Shia or Sunni, Christian or Jewish, they violate the very core of their own faith.

All of the world's foundational texts, not only the Quran but also Hebrew Scripture, the Bhagavad-Gita, and the Sutras, argue that *God is the Creator of us all.* By murdering innocent men and women, these terrorists destroy the very creations of the Divine they claim to worship. God is omnipotent and infallible—but humankind most certainly is not. Faith may be divinely inspired, but religion is most certainly the work of human minds. It is not God but human beings who create the divisions that torment our modern world as never before.

Almost all of the people featured in this book understood that. Just as Abraham was the forefather of three monotheistic traditions, trusting them to behave like brothers and sisters, so too did Constantine the Great allow the people in the Roman Empire to worship God in their own way, whatever suited their culture and custom.

In the 21st century, that lesson is largely forgotten. It is we human beings who build walls around our religious expressions and call them perfect and exclusive. But of course, that is a folly. No human being has the copyright on God. We are all creatures of Divine love. Why, then, should God limit his grace to only a small number of us? Do we not love our own children with equal intensity, regardless of their individual flaws and foibles? Would we restrict that love to only one child and deny it to others? Of course not. So why do we think that God would be any different?

This is exactly why Jesus insists, time and again, that love for one's neighbor is the governing principle of the Kingdom of God. That is why the strains of a hymn like "A Mighty Fortress" or the words of the Prayer of St. Francis can move our hearts regardless of what faith tradition we belong to. And that is why George Washington beseeched the newly independent states "to do justice, to love mercy, and demean ourselves with charity," irrespective of our individual beliefs.

The yearning for spirituality is universal. As the great American theologian Thomas Merton once wrote, "The things on the surface are nothing. What is deep is the Real. We are creatures of Love."

Significantly, Merton spoke these words in Calcutta because Gandhi taught the same thing. "For me," Gandhi said, "the different religions are beautiful flowers from the same garden, branches of the same majestic tree. Therefore they are equally true, though their reception and interpretation through human instruments are equally imperfect."

Gandhi wrote these words in 1937 for his journal *Harijan,* and I think he hit the nail on the head. While God is perfect, we as humans are not. While God's love is infinite, ours most certainly isn't. God's message may be consistent, but our interpretation of that message is not, skewed as it is by our culture, our customs, and our political aspirations.

So if we want to defeat the ideology of extreme fundamentalism, we must begin here. We must accept that even though we were raised Jewish or Christian, there is much beauty and truth to be found in the Quran, the *Mahabharata,* or the Buddhist Sutras. We must recognize the moral superiority of spiritual pluralism and the great civic virtue of religious tolerance. Only then can we truly open our hearts to the possibility of God in all of his infinite dimensions.

"What does it matter that we take different roads, so long as we reach the same goal?" Gandhi once asked. And if we deny that possibility, if we deny others the freedom to experience God in their own way, then we deny the purpose of why God put us on Earth to begin with. The root of the word *rachman,* "mercy," is the same in Arabic as in Hebrew. So why is it so difficult to practice it?

"Let us work together," Gandhi said in his prayer. "For unity and peace."

ACKNOWLEDGMENTS

Writing *Ten Prayers That Changed the World* was a most challenging but also deeply rewarding experience. As a historian, I have been fascinated by the intersection of history, narrative, and spirituality for many years, though it was Lisa Thomas, head of National Geographic's Book Division, who first suggested the concept for this book. Once again, I am deeply grateful for her strong and unerring support throughout its long genesis. In the same breath I must also thank my wonderful editor, Barbara Payne, on this, our fifth book, together. Many thanks to the designer, Nicole Miller; photo editors, Susan Blair and Patrick Bagley; and my eagle-eyed copy editor, Beverly Miller.

Any historian foolish enough to embark on a quest across 4,000 years will incur a debt to a wide range of authors and scholars. I have tried to recognize their contributions in the *Notes* as well as the *Further Reading* section of this book.

I thank my doctoral students at Fielding Graduate University who assisted me in my research, including Amanpreet Gohal, Patrick McNabb, Millicent Mocodean, and Ethan Snyder. Many thanks also to artist Jesse Martino for creating the icons for each chapter, inspired by historical precedent.

Thanks are due to my agent, Peter Miller, and his staff at Global Lion Intellectual Property Management. And finally, I must express my deepest gratitude to my wonderful wife, Cathie, who will always be my muse, my fiercest critic, and my best friend.

JEAN-PIERRE ISBOUTS

NOTES

ABRAHAM'S PLEA

"Abraham's Plea"

Abraham is the progenitor of Judaism, Christianity, and Islam, the three main monotheistic religions today. What's more, the first reference to "prayer" in the Bible occurs in Genesis, in the story of Abraham and Abimelech: "For he [is] a prophet, and he shall pray for you" (Genesis 20:7). It therefore seems entirely appropriate to open this book with the story of Abraham. As noted in this chapter, the historicity of the figure of Abraham has been questioned by scholars. Some believe he is a composite figure from several different oral traditions, which were then harmonized during the early Kingdom of Israel. Nevertheless, clues in the Abraham stories may point to a specific historical context, such as Terah's departure from Ur for Harran (assuming that Genesis is referring to Ur of Sumer), the famine in Canaan, and a major cataclysmic event in the Dead Sea region, the putative location of Sodom and Gomorrah. Some scholars have associated this with a major earthquake between 2100 and 1900 B.C.E. On this basis, I believe that the Abraham story is set near the end of the reign of King Ibbi-Sin (1963–1940 B.C.E.), the last ruler of Ur during the Neo-Sumerian period, when Amorite invasions led to a profound destabilization of the region, and much of the population was forced to flee.

"His father, Terah, was a merchant. What could he possibly expect from life?"

The idea that Terah was a merchant is suggested by his putative contacts with Harran, one of the farthest outposts of the Sumerian trade network near the end of the third millennium B.C.E.

"He constructed stations for the great gods."

The Sumerian creation epic has come to us in the form of Akkadian tablets dating from the first millennium B.C.E. However, since it contains many characters from the familiar cast of Sumerian gods, including Enki, Enlil, and Ea, it is likely that the epic is much older, dating to the Old Babylonian period (second millennium B.C.E) or even the late Sumerian period itself. See James B. Pritchard, *The Ancient Near East* (Princeton University Press, 1973), vol. 1, pp. 35-36.

"And then, one day, his brother Haran died."
Based on the verse from Genesis: "Terah was the father of Abram, Nahor, and Haran; and Haran was the father of Lot. Haran died before his father Terah in the land of his birth, in Ur of the Chaldeans (Genesis 11:27-28).

"Terah and his family were already far to the north."
Based on the verse from Genesis: "Terah took his son Abram and his grandson Lot son of Haran, and his daughter-in-law Sarai, his son Abram's wife, and they went out together from Ur of the Chaldeans to go into the land of Canaan; but when they came to Haran, they settled there" (Genesis 11:31).

"The family had slogged north along the Euphrates River."
To reach his destination, Terah probably took the principal trade route between Ur and the Mediterranean that ran along the Euphrates. For many centuries, this had been the main artery of trade between Mesopotamia and the Egyptian empire. A steady flow of gold, silver, and obsidian went one way, and textiles, cereals, and other agricultural products went the other. The route went up to Harran (in today's southern Turkey), then turned south toward Canaan and the Egyptian border.

"One night he went into his tent, lay down on his roll, and never rose again."
See Genesis: "The days of Terah were two hundred five years; and Terah died in Harran" (Genesis 11:32).

"The encounter with God took place at dawn."
Genesis refers to God as El. Cuneiform tablets discovered in 1929 among the ruins of the ancient city of Ugarit, near Tell Ras Shamra, Syria, refer to a divinity named El as the supreme head of the pantheon of gods, father of creation.

"Go now from your country and your kindred and your father's house."
Genesis 12:1.

"I will make of you a great nation, and I will bless you, and make your name great."
Genesis 12:2.

"And embarked on their journey to a land that God would show him."
Genesis says: "Abram took his wife Sarai and his brother's son Lot, and all the possessions that they had gathered, and the persons whom they had acquired in Harran; and they set forth to go to the land of Canaan" (Genesis 12:5). This is the starting point for the great narrative arc of the Pentateuch and the Deuteronomistic history—the story of how across the span of hundreds of years, from the fields of Harran to the walls of Jericho, God's promise will be fulfilled.

"At Shechem, in a holy place marked by an oak tree."
Genesis says: "Abram passed through the land to the place at Shechem, to the oak of Moreh" (Genesis 12:6). Modern excavations have revealed that ancient Shechem was located at Tell Balata, southeast of the city known today as Nablus, across the hills of Gerizim and Eval. Here, Abraham paused to build an altar to God. A large temple platform is still visible today, but it dates from the 13th century B.C.E. and is most likely dedicated to Baal, the preeminent fertility god of Canaan.

"To your offspring I will give this land."
Genesis 12:6. The word *Canaan* was already current in Mesopotamia as early as the 16th century B.C.E. The reference *eres-kena'an* (land of Canaan) appears in a cuneiform inscription dedicated to the ruler of Alalakh, Idri-mi, discovered by British archaeologist Leonard Woolley in the late 1930s.

"His flocks struggled to find any edible shrub in these highlands."
The Canaan of Abraham's time was a sparsely populated place with just a narrow strip of lush valleys surrounded by hill country. Most of the urban settlements were located closer to the coast, but because of Canaanite hostility, Abraham was forced to dwell in the hills, moving from Hazor (just north of the Sea of Galilee) to Shechem (the Egyptian Sekmem) in the heart of the Samarian Mountains.

"A famine spread across the land."
See Genesis: "Now there was a famine in the land. So Abram went down

to Egypt to reside there as an alien, for the famine was severe in the land" (Genesis 12:10).

"And then his confusion had turned to *fear*."

Genesis describes this rather shocking development as follows: "When he was about to enter Egypt, he said to his wife Sarai, 'I know well that you are a woman beautiful in appearance; and when the Egyptians see you, they will say, "This is his wife"; then they will kill me, but they will let you live' " (Genesis 12:11-12).

"Say you are my sister, so that it may go well with me because of you, and that my life may be spared on your account."

Genesis 12:12.

"It got worse when Pharaoh began to deliver all sorts of 'gifts.' "

Genesis says: "And for her sake [Pharaoh] dealt well with Abram; and he had sheep, oxen, male donkeys, male and female slaves, female donkeys, and camels (Genesis 12:16).

"He prayed to God."

As noted above, the first reference to "prayer" in the Bible occurs in Genesis, in the story of Abraham and Abimelech (Genesis 20:7).

"Great plagues began to affect Pharaoh and his house."

Genesis says: "But the Lord afflicted Pharaoh and his house with great plagues because of Sarai, Abram's wife" (Genesis 12:17).

"What is this you have done to me?"

Genesis 12:18.

"Now then, here is your wife. Take her, and be gone."

Genesis 12:19.

"With his wife and all that he had."

Genesis 12:20.

"Let there be no strife between you and me."

Genesis 13:8.

"For all the land that you see I will give to you and to your offspring forever."
Genesis 13:14-15.

"She chose a girl from among the Egyptian slaves."
Genesis says: "She had an Egyptian slave-girl whose name was Hagar, and Sarai said to Abram, 'You see that the Lord has prevented me from bearing children; go in to my slave-girl; it may be that I shall obtain children by her'" (Genesis 16:1-2). This appears to have been the custom in Mesopotamian cultures. An Assyrian marriage contract from the 19th century B.C.E., for example, stipulates that if the bride cannot bear children within the first two years of marriage, she must purchase a slave woman as a "surrogate mother" to bear a child for her husband.

"I gave my slave-girl to your embrace."
Genesis 16:5.

"Your slave-girl is in your power; do to her as you please."
Genesis 16:6.

"Where have you come from?" the angel asked.
Genesis 16:8.

"I will so greatly multiply your offspring that they cannot be counted for multitude."
Genesis 16:10.

"You shall call him Ishmael, for the Lord has given heed to your affliction."
Genesis 16:11.

"You shall be the ancestor of a multitude of nations."
Genesis 17:4

"And to seal his covenant, God did two things."
This narrative, including the prophecy of a son named Isaac, is based on Genesis chapter 17. Henceforth, all male children born from Abraham's issue, starting with Ishmael, are circumcised on the eighth day after birth. In the Jewish faith, this rite of *Brit milah* has been faithfully observed ever since. But because Ishmael was also circumcised, many Muslims observe the rite of circumcision (*Khitan* in Arabic) as well.

"So shall my covenant be in your flesh."
    Genesis 17:13.

"As for Sarah your wife," he said, "I will bless her."
    Genesis 17:15-16.

"Abraham fell on his face and laughed so hard that tears rolled down his cheeks."
    Genesis 17:17.

"How great is the outcry against Sodom and Gomorrah."
    This segment, including Abraham's "bargaining session" with God, is based on Genesis 18:20-33.

"Would you indeed sweep away the righteous with the wicked?"
    Genesis 18:23.

"Far be it from you to do such a thing."
    Genesis 18:25.

"If I find at Sodom fifty righteous in the city."
    Genesis 18:26.

"Oh, do not let the Lord be angry if I speak just once more."
    Genesis 18: 32.

"For the sake of ten I will not destroy it."
    Genesis 18:32.

"Cast out this slave woman with her son."
    Genesis 21:10.

"Immolation [in Mesopotamia] was usually performed for the king."
    When excavating Ur's Royal Tombs, Sir Leonard Woolley discovered that important figures were accompanied by a number of servants, put to death at the moment of their lord's burial. Since there was no sign of fatal injuries, Woolley theorized that these servants drank poison, or a sleeping drug, before being entombed. Child sacrifice was practiced as part of the Phoenician cult

of Ba'a, known as Moloch in Canaan. The Torah, however, explicitly forbids the practice, to "give any of your children to devote them by fire to Moloch, and so profane the name of your God" (Leviticus 18:21). The message of the story in Genesis therefore may be that Abraham's God rejects such horrific practices out of hand.

"Here I am."
    Genesis 22:11.

"Do not lay your hand on the boy, for now I know that you fear God."
    Genesis 22:12.

Jesus' Prayer to Abba

"Jesus rises well before dawn, careful not to wake the others."
    The inspiration for this story is found in the Gospel of Mark: "In the morning, while it was still very dark, he got up and went out to a deserted place, and there he prayed" (Mark 1:35).

"He knew all about the multitudes who flocked to the Baptist's camp in Bethany."
    The popularity of John the Baptist is attested not only in the Gospels but also in the writings of the Jewish first-century historian Josephus, who wrote that John's followers "seemed ready to do anything he should advise." In the politically charged atmosphere of Judea, this strong language was bound to elicit some form of response, in this case from Herod Antipas.

"Augustus had kicked him off his throne and sent him into exile in Vienne."
    In the year 6 c.e., Archelaus, ethnarch of Judea and Samaria, was removed from office after a delegation from Judea had asked Augustus to intervene because of the ethnarch's misrule. But Augustus then decided to annex Judea as a Roman possession. This is why henceforth, the province would be ruled by Roman prefects, including Pontius Pilate.

"Who would 'clear his threshing floor' with his winnowing fork."
    Luke 3:17.

"A company of the tetrarch's mounted militia rode into the camp one morning."

Mark tells us that the reason for John's arrest was that he took great umbrage at Antipas's marriage to Herodias (Mark 6:18). Josephus, however, claims that Antipas intervened because he feared that John had the "power and inclination to raise a rebellion."

"He suggested they stay in Bethsaida rather than move on to Capernaum."
Matthew states that after his baptism by John, Jesus withdrew into the desert where "he fasted forty days and forty nights" (Matthew 4:2). This is a symbolic allusion, typical for Matthew, to the 40 years that Moses spent in the desert, in preparation for entry into the Promised Land. Mark merely states that "Jesus withdrew to Galilee after John had been arrested" (Mark 1:14). Bethsaida was an obvious destination. All three—Andrew, Peter, and a disciple named Philip—were natives of this town on the shores of the Sea of Galilee. What's more, Bethsaida would later figure prominently in the Gospel of Mark (Mark 8:22-26) and Luke (Luke 9:10-17) as one of the three cities that formed Jesus' ministry triangle.

"We have found the Messiah."
John 1:41.

"Jesus went in search of solitude, walking deep into the wilderness."
In my depiction, this is the time of preparation described as the 40 days in the wilderness by Matthew and Luke.

"That was the price that Galilee had paid for the vainglorious ambition of King Herod."
King Herod imposed a brutal tax regime on Galilee, designed to squeeze the farmers dry. On top of the 25 to 35 percent they were obligated to pay to the Levites, the Temple, and the Romans (as tribute), Galilean farmers were now burdened with a fourth layer of taxation, to pay for Herod's lavish courts and his vainglorious building projects. In my view, this explains the great multitudes of hungry, poor, and dispossessed people who cleave to Jesus' words.

"The Spirit of the Lord is upon me, for he has anointed me."
Luke 4:18.

"Today, this scripture has been fulfilled in your hearing."
> Luke 4:21.

"Everyone turned to their neighbors and began to talk."
> Mark says, "Many who heard him were astounded. They took offense at him" (Mark 6:2). In Luke's version, set in Nazareth, the congregation is so upset that they're ready to throw him off a cliff (Luke 4:29).

"What have you to do with us, Jesus of Nazareth?"
> Mark 1:24. The exorcism had its intended effect, says Mark, for "at once his fame began to spread throughout the surrounding region of Galilee."

"And the line in front of Peter's house became a stream of hundreds."
> "That evening, at sundown," says Mark, "they brought to him all who were sick or possessed with demons. And the whole city was gathered around the door" (Mark 1:32-33).

"Blessed are you who are poor, for yours is the Kingdom of God."
> The beatitudes presented here are taken from Luke 6:20-22. While Matthew's beatitudes emphasize the strict ethics of the Kingdom of God, Luke's are more preoccupied with issues of love, compassion, and social justice.

Some reached out to him as if to touch him and feel the power of his presence.
> Luke 6:19.

"What is the Kingdom of God like? And to what should I compare it?"
> Luke 13:18.

"It is the smallest of all the seeds, but when it has grown it is the greatest of shrubs."
> Matthew 13:31.

"As if someone scattered seed on the ground and went on to sleep."
> Mark 4:26-28.

"The earth produces of itself, first the stalk, then the head."
> Mark 4:28-29.

"Taken from the body of Ruricius Pompeianus."

Ruricius Pompeianus was the prefect of the Praetorian Guard and Maxentius's principal military commander. He was killed in 312 during the Battle of Verona, a heavy engagement between Maxentius's legions and the mainstay of Constantine's army.

"It looked as if the sun had split into three parts."

The original text by Eusebius (ca 260–ca 339), Bishop of Caesarea, apparently based on a later "interview" with Constantine, is as follows: "He said that about noon, when the day was already beginning to decline, he saw with his own eyes the trophy of a cross of light in the heavens, above the sun, and bearing the inscription, CONQUER BY THIS. He said, moreover, that he doubted within himself what the import of this apparition could be. And while he continued to ponder and reason on its meaning, night suddenly came on; then in his sleep the Christ of God appeared to him with the same sign which he had seen in the heavens, and commanded him to make a likeness of that sign which he had seen in the heavens, and to use it as a safeguard in all engagements with his enemies." Eusebius, *Vita Constantini*, 1:28-29.

"That Apollo himself once appeared to the emperor?"

According to a panegyric delivered in Gaul in 310, Constantine had experienced a vision in which Apollo, accompanied by Victoria, goddess of victory, had presented the emperor with a laurel crown marked with the Roman numeral XXX (30), indicating that he would rule for 30 years. See Paul Stephenson, *Constantine: Roman Emperor, Christian Victor,* p. 129.

"*En toutoi nika,* it read."

The Greek Ἐν τούτῳ νίκα was later translated in Latin as *in hoc signo vinces:* "In this sign, you will conquer."

"Carve a sign in the sky as clearly as if someone is drawing it with a pen on a scroll."

The original source is Lactantius (ca 250–ca 325), a later Christian adviser to Constantine, who wrote: "Constantine was directed in a dream to cause the heavenly sign to be delineated on the shields of his soldiers, and so to proceed to battle. He did as he had been commanded, and he marked on their shields the letter X, with a perpendicular line drawn through it and turned round thus at the top, being the cipher of CHRIST. Having this sign (XP), his troops stood to arms." Lactantius, *Liber de Mortibus Persecutorum*, XLIV.

"It is the *chi rho* emblem, the first two letters of the Greek word *Christos*."
Later, this symbol would become known as the *labarum*, the military standard displaying the Christogram based on the first two letters of the word Χριστός, or "Christ" in Greek: chi (Χ) and rho (ρ).

"A furious battle ensues."
Lactantius, presumably based on Constantine's eyewitness account, wrote that "the armies met, and fought with the utmost exertions of valour, and firmly maintained their ground . . . The bridge in [Maxentius's] rear was broken down. At sight of that the battle grew hotter. The hand of the Lord prevailed, and the forces of Maxentius were routed. He fled towards the broken bridge; but the multitude pressing on him, he was driven headlong into the Tiber." Lactantius, *Liber de Mortibus Persecutorum*, XLIV.

"He feels it needs to be accompanied by a *votum*, a national vow or prayer."
The text of the prayer is taken from David S. Potter, *The Roman Empire at Bay, AD 180–395* (Routledge, 2014), p. 359.

"But according to the panegyrist describing the parade, Constantine declined to do so."
To be more precise, the anonymous panegyrist does not include a reference of a visit to the Temple of Jupiter Optimus Maximus on Capitoline Hill. Nevertheless, this omission is certainly peculiar, since in many ways it served as the climax of the military parade. Several sources have therefore concluded that Constantine simply avoided going to the temple at all, so as to withhold credit for his victory from Rome's chief god.

"Constantine specifically earmarked the property of imperial guards."
"It is remarkable," Stephenson wrote, "that all of Constantine's Christian buildings in Rome were connected in some way with [the *equites*'] destruction or that of the Praetorian Guard . . . It is hard indeed not to reach the conclusion that Constantine wished to assert that his victory over the Praetorians and the horse-guard was achieved through the power of the god of the Christians." Stephenson, *Constantine*, p. 149.

"The edict has rightfully been acknowledged as a watershed."
While the edict offered free and unencumbered religious practice to Christians, it was careful to offer the same freedom to all other religions of the empire as well, including those that had also been persecuted previously. The conclusion of the edict read: "The open and free exercise of their respective religions is granted to all others, as well as to the Christians. For it befits the well-ordered state and the tranquility of our times that each individual be allowed, according to his own choice, to worship the Divinity; and we mean not to derogate aught from the honor due to any religion or its votaries." Quoted from Alexander Roberts and James Donaldson, *The Ante-Nicene Fathers* (Christian Literature Publishing, 1886), vol. 7, p. 320.

"The construction of St. Peter's Basilica took 25 years."
For a description as well as a 15th-century illustration of the original St. Peter's Basilica drawn by Domenio Tasselli, see Jean-Pierre Isbouts, *The Story of Christianity* (National Geographic, 2014), pp. 82-85.

THE VOICES OF JOAN OF ARC

"When she was 12, Jehanette was a good and sincere girl."
Larissa Juliet Taylor, *The Virgin Warrior: The Life and Death of Joan of Arc,* p. 13.

"When she heard the bell toll while in the fields, she came running to the church."
Nancy Goldstone, *The Maid and the Queen: The Secret History of Joan of Arc,* pp. 88-89.

"She would go off on her own sometimes and speak to God."
This quote, like most other eyewitness accounts, was recorded in the proceedings of Joan's posthumous nullification trial. Pierre Duparc, *Procès et nullité de la condamnation de Jeanne d'Arc* (C. Klincksieck, 1986), vol. 3, p. 265.

"These perilous times saw the rise of a number of mystics."
During the 13th century, the mystic phenomenon became broadly popular in all social classes, and particularly among women. Mechthild of Magdeburg (ca 1207–ca 1280), a member of the German beguine movement, gained fame for a number of visions that she described in her book *The Flowing Light of the Divine*. Mechthild's life was closely paralleled by that

of the 13th-century Dutch mystic Hadewig of Brabant, who described her visions as an experience in which "my heart and my veins and all my limbs trembled and quivered with eager desire, and such madness and fear beset my mind that it seemed to me . . . that I must go mad."

"One seer, Bridget of Sweden, warned the people of France."
Bridget of Sweden (1303–1373), mystic and saint, was a married woman who became the founder of the Bridgettine nuns and monks after the death of her husband. Marie of Avignon (?–1399), known as Marie Robine, lived in Avignon during the period of the Western Schism, when no fewer than three popes claimed the throne of St. Peter. She is credited with 12 visions.

"It was summer, and I was in my father's garden."
Joan added, "This Voice has always guarded me well, and I have always understood it; it instructed me to be good and to go often to Church; it told me it was necessary for me to come into France." From Joan's testimony during the Second Public Examination in Rouen on February 22, 1431. Virginia Frohlick, Saint Joan of Arc Center, www.stjoan-center.com.

"He'd wish they would drown you."
Goldstone, *The Maid and the Queen,* p. 96.

"Go to Orléans to raise the siege that the English have laid around the city."
From Joan's testimony during the Second Public Examination in Rouen on February 22, 1431.

"I am Jeanne, Jeanne d'Arc from Domrémy."
This dialogue is based on the account of an eyewitness to the first encounter between Joan and Captain Baudricourt. Goldstone, *The Maid and the Queen*, p. 100.

"Two of Baudricourt's officers, Jean de Metz and Bertrand de Poulengy."
From "The Testimony of Jean de Novelemport, Knight, known as Jean de Metz," in Duparc, *Procès et nullité de la condamnation de Jeanne d'Arc.*

"The siege of Orléans has taken a turn for the worse?"
This dialogue is based on an eyewitness account described in Margaret Oliphant, *Jeanne d'Arc: Her Life and Death* (Putnam, 1896), chap. 2.

"For this reason also, Jean de Metz has dressed Jeanne in men's clothes."
Jean de Metz testified, "I asked her if she could make this journey, dressed as she was. She replied that she would willingly take a man's dress. Then I gave her the dress and equipment of one of my men. Afterwards, the inhabitants of Vaucouleurs had a man's dress made for her, with all the necessary requisites; I also procured for her a horse at the price of about sixteen francs. Thus dressed and mounted, and furnished with a safe-conduct from the Sieur Charles, Duke de Lorraine, she went to visit the said Lord Duke." From "The Testimony of Jean de Novelemport Knight, known as Jean de Metz," in Duparc, *Procès et nullité de la condamnation de Jeanne d'Arc.*

"She never swore, and I myself was much stimulated by her voices."
Poulengy testified, "At night, Jeanne slept beside Jean de Metz and myself, fully dressed and armed. I was young then; nevertheless I never felt towards her any desire: I should never have dared to molest her, because of the great goodness which I saw in her. We were eleven days on the road, during which we had many anxieties. But Jeanne told us always that we had nothing to fear, and that, once arrived at Chinon, the noble Dauphin would show us good countenance." From "The Testimony of Bertrand de Poulengy," in Duparc, *Procès et nullité de la condamnation de Jeanne d'Arc.*

"I have come, and I have been sent by God, to bring aid to you and to the kingdom."
This dialogue is based on the eyewitness account of Raoul de Gaucourt, a courtier, and Joan's account to her confessor, Friar Jean Pasquerel. Regine Pernoud and Narue-Veronique Clin, *Joan of Arc: Her Story,* pp. 22-26.

"According to a groom of his chamber, Charles would often pray to God."
The issue of legitimacy resulted in a propaganda war between the English and the French. The English even produced a poster that traced the English pretender's lineage to the French king Louis IX, later canonized as St. Louis. The obvious implication was that Charles was not legitimate, and rather the bastard son of the Duke of Orléans by Isabeau of Bavaria, the French queen. The propaganda had its effect, certainly on Charles

himself, who begged God in his prayers to reveal whether he was legitimate. Goldstone, *The Maid and the Queen*, pp. 104, 117.

MARTIN LUTHER'S HYMN

"Of course, indulgences are nothing new."
In the early 20th century, a document that Martin Luther sent on October 31, 1517, to Archbishop Albrecht was discovered in the archives of Mainz. It details his objections to the sale of the indulgences and probably accompanied the text of his Ninety-Five Theses, which he also sent to the archbishop on this date. "Although indulgences are the very merits of Christ and of His saints and so should be treated with all reverence, they have in fact nonetheless become a shocking exercise of greed," Luther wrote. "For who actually seeks the salvation of souls through indulgences, and not instead money for his coffers? This is evident from the way indulgences are preached." From "Tractatus de indulgentiis per Doctorem Martinum ordinis s. Augustini Wittenbergae editus" [A Treatise on indulgences published by Doctor Martin of the Order of St. Augustine in Wittenberg], in F. Hermann, *Zeitschrift für Kirchengeschichte* (1907), vol. 28, pp. 370-373.

"St. Anne, help me! I will become a monk!"
This episode, and the subsequent argument between Luther and his father, Hans, is cited in Roland H. Bainton, *Here I Stand: A Life of Martin Luther,* pp. 5, 27.

"If ever a monk got to heaven through monasticism, I should have been that man."
Denis R. Janz, *The Reformation Reader* (Fortress Press, 2008), p. 84.

"His desperate search for Christ."
"I lost touch with Christ the Savior and Comforter," Martin wrote of his time in the monastery, "and made of him the jailer and hangman of my poor soul." James Kittelson, *Luther the Reformer* (Augsburg Fortress Publishing House, 1986), p. 79.

"Listen to the voices of your dear dead relatives and friends, beseeching you."
Patrick V. Reid, *Readings in Western Religious Thought: The Middle Ages Through the Reformation* (Paulist Press, 1995), p. 300.

"Look at the ghastly shedding of blood by [Pope] Julius II."
    Bainton, *Here I Stand*, p. 77.

"He issued a papal bull . . . Exsurge Domine ("Arise, O Lord")."
    Vatican decrees and papal bulls are usually referred to by their first words.
    In the case of Leo X, the first sentence read, "Arise, O Lord, and judge thy
    cause. A wild boar has invaded thy vineyard." William Roscoe Estep, *Renais-
    sance and Reformation* (Eerdmans Publishing, 1986), p. 128.

"We are desirous that you should bring the abovementioned Luther to the diet."
    The text of Charles's letter is reproduced in Bainton, *Here I Stand*, p. 167.

" 'Honorable, beloved, and devoted [Luther],' his message began."
    Heiko Augustinus Oberman and Eileen Walliser-Schwarzbart, *Luther:
    Man Between God and the Devil*, p. 35.

"I will go, even if I am too sick to stand on my feet."
    Bainton, *Here I Stand*, p. 169.

"A priest embraced him and touched his habit three times."
    Oberman and Walliser-Schwarzbart, *Luther*, p. 199.

"The fool entered with a smile on his face and kept moving his head back and forth."
    Timothy F. Lull and Derek R. Nelson, *Resilient Reformer*, p. 125.

"Do you defend them all, or do you care to reject a part?"
    One of the most detailed descriptions of von Eck's interrogation of Luther
    at Worms is found in Bainton, *Here I Stand*, pp. 177-186.

"Music is a fair and lovely gift of God, which has often wakened and moved me."
    Franklin M. Segler and Randall Bradley, *Christian Worship: Its Theology
    and Practice* (B&H Publishing Group, 2006), p. 107.

"Martin's translation of the New Testament is published in 1522, after his return
to Wittenberg."
    Martin's Bible was not the first attempt to create a German translation.
    An early version, in Gothic, was written as early as the 4th century by the
    German bishop and missionary Wulfila. The first Bibles in vernacular

German appeared in the 13th century, followed by the venerable Augsburger Bible of 1350 and the Mentel version of 1466. The difference is that these German translations were made from the Latin, or "Vulgate," edition that is the official version of the Catholic Church. Martin, however, harked back to the original version in Greek, the language used by the evangelists themselves. He followed up with a translation of the Old Testament in 1534.

" 'Ein' feste Burg' was first published in 1529."
See John Julian, *A Dictionary of Hymnology: Setting Forth the Origin and History of Christian Hymns of All Ages and All Nations* (John Murray, 1908).

" 'It was sung in the streets,' wrote Louis Benson."
Louis F. Benson, *Studies of Familia Hymns* (Westminster Press, 1903).

"The Christian battle cry during the wars against the Ottoman Empire."
John M. Merriman, *A History of Modern Europe: From the Renaissance to the Age of Napoleon*, 3rd ed. (Norton, 2009), vol. 1, p. 101.

"Perhaps the greatest motet chorus ever written by Bach."
Craig Smith, *Bach Cantata Notes: BWV 80*. Emmanuel Music, www .emmanuelmusic.org.

George Washington's Prayer

"Our cruel and unrelenting enemy leaves us only the choice of brave resistance."
George Washington's address to the Continental Army before the Battle of Long Island, August 27, 1776.

"My brave fellows, you have done all I asked you to do."
George Washington's address to the troops to reenlist in the army, December 31, 1777.

"A dangerous mutiny."
Edward G. Lengel, *General George Washington: A Military Life,* p. 269.

"Starve—dissolve—or disperse."
Stephen Brumwell, *George Washington: Gentleman Warrior,* p. 323.

"Barefoot and otherwise naked."
Brumwell, *George Washington,* p. 323.

"There is a danger that the famine will break up the army."
Brig. Gen. Jedediah Huntington to Lord Stirling, February 12, 1778, in Lengel, *General George Washington,* p. 279.

"Many of the troops are destitute of meat."
Brig. Gen. James Mitchell Varnum to Nathanael Greene, February 12, 1778, in Lengel, *General George Washington,* p. 279.

"A wagonload of it is not enough to purchase a wagonload of provisions."
From Letter to John Jay, April 23, 1779, in *The Papers of George Washington, Revolutionary War Series,* vol. 20, April 8–May 31, 1779, ed. Edward G. Lengel (University of Virginia Press, 2010), p. 177.

"Dysentery, then typhus, then death."
In the six months after Washington's arrival in Valley Forge, some 2,500 men, or roughly a quarter of the army, would die of dysentery and typhus. Brumwell, *George Washington,* p. 328.

"Sarah! My dear Sarah! All's well!"
Mason Locke Weems, *A History of the Life and Death, Virtues and Exploits of General George Washington* (Lippincott, 1808), p. 234 vv.

"That God would have you and the State over which you preside, in his holy protection."
Jared Sparks, *The Writings of George Washington* (American Stationers Co., 1838), vol. 8, p. 452.

"One of the most heartfelt and moving set of remarks he would ever make."
James P. Moore Jr., *One Nation Under God: The History of Prayer in America* (Doubleday, 2005), p. 74.

"The story was first reported by the author Mason Locke Weems."
Weems erroneously referred to Sarah as the wife of Isaac Potts, when in fact he was married to a woman named Martha at the time. Isaac would not marry Sarah until 1803, the same year he died. See *Memorial of Thomas*

Potts, Junior, Who Settled in Pennsylvania; With an Historic-Genealogical Account of his Descendants to the Eighth Generation, 1874.

"Another source is an autobiographical work by the Rev. Nathaniel Randolph Snowden."

Snowden reports Pott's account as follows: "to my astonishment I saw the great George Washington on his knees alone, with his sword on one side and his cocked hat on the other. He was at Prayer to the God of the Armies, beseeching to interpose with his Divine aid, as it was ye Crisis, & the cause of the country, of humanity & of the world." Nathaniel Randolph Snowden, "Diary and Remembrances," manuscript, Historical Society of Pennsylvania, Philadelphia.

"That did not prevent Henry Woodman from including."

Henry Woodman, *The History of Valley Forge* (Oaks, PA, 1850).

"The Father of his country kneeling."

This greatly fictionalized account appeared in the series "The Spur of Monmouth," *Aldine Press,* 1878. The story even pinpoints the date of Washington's prayerful moment: January 17, 1778.

"Isaac Potts was not even in Valley Forge at the time."

See Lorrett Treese, *Valley Forge: Making and Remaking of a National Symbol* (Penn State University Press, 1995).

"An orthodox, Trinity-affirming believer in Jesus Christ."

Peter Lillback and Jerry Newcombe, *George Washington's Sacred Fire,* p. 25.

"An omnipotent, omnipresent, omniscient being."

From Fred Anderson and Philander D. Chase, *George Washington Remembers: Reflections on the French and Indian War* (Rowman & Littlefield, 2004), p. 129.

"Paul Leicester Ford, who conducted a detailed analysis of Washington's diaries."

Paul Leicester Ford, *The True George Washington* (CreateSpace, 2015).

"Of all religions, the Christian should inspire the most tolerance."

Jean-Pierre Isbouts, *The Story of Christianity* (National Geographic, 2013), p. 273.

"Washington's letters clearly reveal a familiarity with Hutcheson."
    Scott A. Cook and William Earle Klay, "George Washington and Enlight-
    enment Ideas on Educating Future Citizens and Public Servants," *Journal
    of Public Affairs Education* 20, no. 1.

"Washington's reliance upon a Grand Designer along Deist lines."
    Paul F. Boller Jr., *George Washington and Religion* (SMU Press, 1963),
    p. 92.

"The hand of Providence has been so conspicuous in all this."
    From Letter to Brigadier-General Nelson, August 20, 1778, in Chauncey
    Ford, *Writings of George Washington* (1890), vol. 7, p. 161.

THE PRAYER OF ST. FRANCIS

"His father is the Marquis Emmanuel-Marie-Stanislas."
    See "Emmanuel-Marie-Stanislas de Noblet de la Rochethulon, Biographie
    extraite du dictionnaire des parlementaires français de 1789 à 1889,"
    http://www.assemblee-nationale.fr/.

"His Anglo-French society, the Souvenir Normand."
    For a detailed description of the activities of this society around the turn
    of the 19th century, see Laurent Quevilly, "La Renaissance du Souvenir
    Normand," http://jumieges.free.fr/Souvenir_normand.html.

"It is called . . . *The Journal of Our Lady of Peace.*"
    Most publications on the subject assume that the marquis was introduced
    to the prayer by reading the magazine *La Clochette*. Father Christophe-
    André of *l'Eglise Gallicane*, however, has shown that the prayer was also
    published in the January 1913 edition of *Les Annales de Notre-Dame de la
    Paix,* and that it is, most likely, this publication that caught the eye of the
    marquis. See http://www.gallican.org/plapaix.htm. The suggestion that
    the marquis discovered the pamphlet in the Church of the Madeleine is
    my imagination.

"Perhaps the prayer was composed by its publisher, Father Bouquerel?"
    This suggestion is made by Christian Renoux, associate professor of the
    University of Orléans, France, and the author of a book on the prayer.

Christian Renoux, *La prière pour la paix attribuée à saint François: Une énigme à résoudre* (Éditions Franciscaines, 2001).

"The form of the prayer for peace announced by the pope."
Chicago Tribune, March 14, 1915, http://archives.chicagotribune
.com/1915/03/14/page/3/article/prayer-for-peace-from-pope-benedict.

"He directs one of his prelates, Cardinal Gasparri, to thank the Frenchman."
Leonardo Boff, *The Prayer of Saint Francis: A Message of Peace for the World Today* (Orbis Books, 2001), p. 7. Boff also claims that the marquis directed the prayer "to the Sacred Heart of Jesus," a particular devotion from the late 19th century.

"The Prayer of Souvenir Normand for Peace."
The publication of the prayer in the *Osservatore Romano* included an intro-duction as follows: "Souvenir Normand has sent the Holy Father the text of some prayers for peace. We have pleasure in presenting in particular the prayer addressed to the Sacred Heart, inspired by the testament of William the Conqueror." This was an error, for the marquis had not sent the prayer as an initiative from Souvenir Normand but from himself. After the Vatican article was carried verbatim in the French newspaper *La Croix* on January 28, 1916, the marquis send a note to correct this. However, in his note, he failed to mention the fact that he had found the prayer in a Catholic pamphlet.

THE PRAYER FOR BASTOGNE

"The U.S. Army has suffered an average of 2,000 casualties a day."
These and other statistics from Rick Atkinson, *The Guns at Last Light,* pp. 408-409.

"Consume as much as 100,000 pounds of fuel."
Ibid., p. 221.

"Never in history was there a coalition such as that of our enemies."
Hitler quoted in ibid., p. 393.

"Don't worry, Tony, they won't come through here."
Quoted from William K. Goolrick and Ogden Tanner, *The Battle of the*

Bulge (Time-Life Books, 1979), p. 35. Goolrick and Tanner also show that at least one intelligence officer, Benjamin A. "Monk" Dickson, head of First Army Intelligence, suspected that something was up. The information came from a captured German soldier who said that "every means possible is being gathered for the coming all-out counteroffensive." Other indications came from an eyewitness who had observed the big buildup "from the direction of Bitburg." Remarkably, Dickson's report was dismissed.

"Soldiers of the Western Front, your great hour has arrived."
Leo Barron and Don Cygan, *No Silent Night*, p. 90.

"It was no more than 'a spoiling attack.'"
Many years later, with the benefit of hindsight, both Bradley and Eisenhower remembered these events differently, of course. "I was immediately convinced that this was no local attack," Eisenhower said. "It seemed likely to Bradley and me that they were now starting this kind of attack." Dwight D. Eisenhower, *Crusade in Europe* (Johns Hopkins University Press, 1997), p. 342.

"For years, McAuliffe had wanted a division command. Now he had one."
Barron and Cygan, p. 125.

"Bastogne was vital for the offensive."
Fritz Bayerlein, *After Action Reports of the Panzer Lehr Division Commander: From D-Day to the Ruhr* (2005), p. 75, quoted in Barron and Cygan, *No Silent Night*, p. 107.

"'All of us, without exception, were astonished' by the fury of Herbstnebel."
Quoted from Atkinson, *The Guns at Last Light*, p. 439.

"There will be only cheerful faces at this conference table."
See Alex Kershaw, *The Longest Winter: The Battle of the Bulge and the Epic Story of World War II's Most Decorated Platoon* (Da Capo Press, 2005), p. 143.

"I thought your initial reaction was hard to beat, General."
There are many accounts of how General McAuliffe arrived at his legendary "Nuts!" but Barron and Cygan's version is by far the most entertaining. Barron and Cygan, *No Silent Night*, p. 239.

"Paul Harkins, who served as Patton's deputy chief, was there."
Paul Harkins and George S. Patton Jr., *War as I Knew It* (Houghton Mifflin, 1947), pp. 185-186.

"His six-foot-two powerfully built physique made an unforgettable silhouette."
The account of this conversation and the genesis of the prayer is based on the personal recollection of the prayer's author, Msgr. James O'Neill, first published in *Review of the News,* October 6, 1971; retrieved from General Patton's Prayer, Bastogne.html.

"The pathfinders quickly rig up a provisional antenna."
Here, I am relying on Barron and Cygan, p. 125.

"We'll beat the Krauts now, sir."
Fred MacKenzie, *The Men of Bastogne* (McKay, 1968), pp. 180-182.

"A *third* version of the Patton Prayer."
George R. Metcalf, *With Cross and Shovel* (Riverside Press, 1960), pp. 176-184.

"Keane, who has researched both sources, concludes that this must be accurate."
Michael Keane, *Patton,* p. 284.

Gandhi's Prayer for Peace

"Boiled spinach mixed with goat curds."
This observation, and that of the garden, are based on Margaret Bourke-White's eyewitness account in her book *Halfway to Freedom,* pp. 30-31.

"The aim of our 'Direct Action' is to paralyze Nehru's Government."
Yogesh Chadha, *Gandhi: A Life* (John Wiley & Sons, 1997), p. 416.

"One or both must deliberately cease to look to British authority for protection."
From *Harijan,* September 15, 1946.

"I must confess my bankruptcy, though not that of non-violence."
From a message written during the prayer meeting of June 15, 1947, cited in D. G. Tendulkar, *Mahatma,* vol. 8 (India Ministry of Information and Broadcasting, 1969), pp. 22-23.

"That man was Mohammad Ali Jinnah."
  Damodar SarDesai, *India: The Definitive History* (Westview Press, 2007), p. 313.

"Afraid to be left in 'a nation hostile to their faith.'"
  Chadha, *Gandhi,* p. 437.

"Nearly half a million refugees on the roads."
  Philip Ziegler, *Mountbatten: A Biography* (Knopf, 1985), p. 435.

"I do not believe in the exclusive divinity of the Vedas."
  Young India, October 6, 1921.

"As one Indian patriot speaking to another in the cause of civil peace."
  Joseph Lelyveld, *Great Soul: Mahatma Gandhi and His Struggle with India,* p. 334.

"On October 29, 1947, Indian troops moved in to stop the Pakistani invasion." Gandhi was horrified, but when prodded, he refused to condemn India's decision to invade. Many of his supporters were shocked. Since when did the Mahatma condone violence and aggression to settle a political dispute? The reason, Gandhi said, is that Kashmir had voluntarily chosen accession to India rather than to Pakistan. But the real reason is more complex. Gandhi hoped that with the addition of another Muslim province as part of greater India, the internecine fighting would subside, and India could finally restore itself as a pluralistic society rather than a Hindu theocracy.

"I want to tell you very frankly that you cannot ride two horses."
  Chadha, *Gandhi,* p. 448.

"Not because of pressure from outside, but of their own free will."
  Lelyveld, *Great Soul,* p. 338.

"Caste or Untouchable, Hindu or Muslim, Sikh or Christian."
  Harijan, March 3, 1946, p. 29.

"Power to melt mountains of misery."
  Young India, December 29, 1927.

"Have signed a declaration that, yes, they will vacate the Muslim homes."
Chadha, *Gandhi,* p. 453.

"Pitting all the physical strength he had left in his thin wiry body."
Bourke-White, *Halfway to Freedom,* p. 37.

"Christ gave us the goals and Mahatma Gandhi the tactics."
Shelley Tougas, *Birmingham 1963: How a Photograph Rallied Civil Rights Support* (Capstone Press, 2011), p. 12.

"The average take-home pay of its 1.2 billion people is still only $1,364 per year."
Economist, May 23, 2015, pp. 6-7.

"The light has gone out of our lives."
Rajmohan Gandhi, *Mohandas: The True Story of a Man, His People and an Empire,* p. 682.

Mother Teresa's Daily Prayer

"With a joy I cannot ascribe, we touched the soil of Bengal for the first time."
David Porter, *Mother Teresa: The Early Years* (Eerdmans, 1986), p. 38.

"It was not a vision," she said later; "it was a personal matter."
Paul Williams, *Critical Lives: Mother Teresa,* p. 20.

"I wanted to be a missionary."
Malcolm Muggeridge, *Something Beautiful for God* (HarperOne, 2003), p. 84.

"A sprawling enclave."
To visit the place in all of its colonial splendor, see the virtual tour at www.loretoentally.org.

"Our center here is very fine."
Porter, *Mother Teresa: The Early Years,* p. 52.

"These accounts are completely wrong, only a hypothesis."
Navin Chawla, *Mother Teresa,* p. 20.

"More than 90 percent of the people suffering from either dysentery or malnutrition."

These and other statistics are taken from Williams, *Critical Lives: Mother Teresa,* pp. 49-50.

"The store room was full of different kinds of vegetables and food."

Kathryn Spink, *Mother Teresa: An Authorized Biography,* p. 57.

"She knew little of art and literature."

Williams, *Critical Lives: Mother Teresa,* p. 41.

"But I have never seen her cry."

Spink, *Mother Teresa,* p. 58.

"I was sure it was God's voice."

Porter, *Mother Teresa,* p. 56.

"You say this is the will of God, just like that?"

Spink, *Mother Teresa,* p. 45.

"We had not yet been recognized as a separate congregation."

Chawla, *Mother Teresa,* p. 63.

"This is a very famous Hindu temple."

Spink, *Mother Teresa,* p. 112.

"Kill me if you want to."

Chawla, *Mother Teresa,* p. 214.

"A complete biography of Mother Teresa has yet to be written."

Gëzim Alpion, *Mother Teresa: Saint or Celebrity?,* p. 32.

"Or the disgraced British tycoon Robert Maxwell."

Christopher Hitchens, *The Missionary Position: Mother Teresa in Theory and Practice* (Verso, 1997).

"Palliative care training has been available only since 1997."

> M.R. Rajagopal, David E. Joranson, and Aaron M. Gilson, *The Lancet,* 388, July 14, 2001, p. 139.

"Many aspects of her story have yet to be explored to the fullest."

> The biographies written by Kathryn Spink and Paul Williams, cited above, do attempt to create a balanced portrait, but their narratives are short and devoid of any notes and references that a scholarly readership would expect.

Epilogue

"The things on the surface are nothing. What is deep is the Real."

> From a prayer and address delivered in Calcutta, India (October 1968), in *The Asian Journal of Thomas Merton* (1975), quoted in *Thomas Merton, Spiritual Master: The Essential Writings* (Paulist Press, 1992), p. 237.

"The different religions are beautiful flowers from the same garden."

> *Harijan,* January 30, 1937.

"What does it matter that we take different roads?"

> M. K. Gandhi, *Hind Swaraj* (Navajivan Publishing House, 1938), chap. 2, p. 16.

FURTHER READING

GENERAL HISTORY

Armstrong, Karen. *A History of God*. Ballantine Books, 1993.

Isbouts, Jean-Pierre. *The Story of Christianity: A Chronicle of Christian Civilization from Ancient Rome to Today*. National Geographic, 2014.

MacCulloch, Diarmaid. *Christianity: The First Three Thousand Years*. Penguin, 2009.

Moore, James, Jr. *One Nation Under God: The History of Prayer in America*. Broadway Books, 2007.

ABRAHAM'S PLEA

Blenkinsopp, Joseph. *Abraham: The Story of a Life*. Eerdmans, 2015.

Feiler, Bruce. *Abraham: A Journey to the Heart of the Three Faiths*. Morrow, 2005.

Isbouts, Jean-Pierre. *From Moses to Muhammad: The Shared Origins of Judaism, Christianity and Islam*. Pantheon, 2011.

Peters, F. E. *The Children of Abraham: Judaism, Christianity, Islam*. Princeton University Press, 2004.

JESUS' PRAYER TO ABBA

Chilton, Bruce. *Rabbi Jesus*. Doubleday, 2000.

Crossan, John Dominic. *Jesus: A Revolutionary Biography*. HarperCollins, 1994.

Horsley, Richard A. *Jesus and Empire: The Kingdom of God and the New World Disorder.* Fortress Press, 2003.

Isbouts, Jean-Pierre. *In the Footsteps of Jesus: A Chronicle of His Life and the Origins of Christianity.* National Geographic, 2012.

Reed, Jonathan. *Archaeology and the Galilean Jesus: A Re-Examination of the Evidence.* Trinity Press International, 2002.

THE DREAM OF CONSTANTINE

Grant, Michael. *Constantine the Great: The Man and His Times.* Scribner, 1994.

Kousoulas, D. G. *The Life and Times of Constantine the Great.* BookSurge Publishing, 2007.

Potter, David. *Constantine the Emperor.* Oxford University Press, 2013.

Stephenson, Paul. *Constantine: Roman Emperor, Christian Victor.* Overlook Press, 2010.

THE VOICES OF JOAN OF ARC

Castor, Helen. *Joan of Arc: A History.* Harper, 2015.

Goldstone, Nancy. *The Maid and the Queen: The Secret History of Joan of Arc.* Penguin, 2012.

Pernoud, Régine, and Marie-Véronique Clin. *Joan of Arc: Her Story.* Palgrave Macmillan, 1999.

Taylor, Larissa Juliet. *The Virgin Warrior: The Life and Death of Joan of Arc.* Yale University Press, 2009.

Martin Luther's Hymn

Bainton, Roland H. *Here I Stand: A Life of Martin Luther.* Abingdon Press, 2013.

Logan, Donald. *A History of the Church in the Middle Ages.* Taylor & Francis, 2012.

Lull, Timothy F., and Derek R. Nelson. *Resilient Reformer: The Life and Thought of Martin Luther.* Augsburg Fortress Publishers, 2015.

Oberman, Heiko Augustinus, and Eileen Walliser-Schwarzbart. *Luther: Man Between God and the Devil.* Yale University Press, 2006.

George Washington's Prayer

Brumwell, Stephen. *George Washington: Gentleman Warrior.* Quercus, 2012.

Buchanan, John. *The Road to Valley Forge: How Washington Built the Army That Won the Revolution.* Wiley, 2004.

Ferling, John E. *First of Men: A Life of George Washington.* Oxford University Press, 2010.

Lengel, Edward G. *General George Washington: A Military Life.* Random House, 2005.

Lillback, Peter, and Jerry Newcombe. *George Washington's Sacred Fire.* Providence Forum Press, 2006.

The Prayer of St. Francis

Boff, Leonardo. *The Prayer of St. Francis: A Message of Peace for the World Today.* Orbis Books, 2001.

Ferri, Giuliano. *The Prayer of St. Francis.* Illustrated Children's Book.

THE PRAYER FOR BASTOGNE

Atkinson, Rick. *The Guns at Last Light*. Little, Brown, 2013.

Barron, Leo, and Cygan, Don. *No Silent Night: The Christmas Battle for Bastogne*. New American Library, 2012.

Beevor, Antony. *Ardennes 1944: The Battle of the Bulge*. Viking, 2015.

Keane, Michael. *Patton: Blood, Guts, and Prayer*. Regnery, 2012.

Kershaw, Alex. *The Longest Winter: The Battle of the Bulge and the Epic Story of World War II's Most Decorated Platoon*. Da Capo Press, 2004.

GANDHI'S PRAYER FOR PEACE

Bourke-White, Margaret. *Halfway to Freedom*. Simon & Schuster, 1949.

Chadha, Yogesh. *Gandhi: A Life*. Wiley, 1997.

Gandhi, Rajmohan. *Mohandas: The True Story of a Man, His People and an Empire*. Penguin/Viking, 2006.

Gandhi, Rajmohan. *Gandhi: The Man, His People, and the Empire*. University of California Press, 2008.

Lelyveld, Joseph. *Great Soul: Mahatma Gandhi and His Struggle With India*. Knopf, 2011.

MOTHER TERESA'S DAILY PRAYER

Alpion, Gëzim. *Mother Teresa: Saint or Celebrity?* Routledge, 2006.

Chawla, Navin. *Mother Teresa: The Authorized Biography*. Element Books, 1996.

Greene, Meg. *Mother Teresa: A Biography*. Greenwood Press, 2004.

Spink, Kathryn. *Mother Teresa: An Authorized Biography*. HarperOne, 2011.

Williams, Paul. *Critical Lives: Mother Teresa*. Alpha, 2001.

ILLUSTRATIONS CREDITS

INDEX

ABOUT THE AUTHOR

Jean-Pierre Isbouts is a historian, best-selling author, and doctoral professor in the social sciences Ph.D. program at Fielding Graduate University in Santa Barbara, California. Dr. Isbouts has written a number of books on art, history, and biblical archaeology, including the best sellers *The Biblical World* (National Geographic, 2007) and *In the Footsteps of Jesus* (National Geographic, 2012). His other books include *From Moses to Muhammad: The Shared Origins of Judaism, Christianity and Islam* (Pantheon, 2010), *Who's Who in the Bible: Unforgettable People and Timeless Stories From Genesis to Revelation* (National Geographic, 2013), *The Story of Christianity: A Chronicle of Christian Civilization From Ancient Rome to Today* (National Geographic, 2014), and *Jesus: An Illustrated Life* (National Geographic, 2015). An award-winning filmmaker, Dr. Isbouts has also produced a number of historical documentaries, including *Manet in Love* (Arts, 1999) with Richard Neil; *Walt: The Man Behind the Myth* (Disney/Buena Vista, 2001), narrated by Dick Van Dyke; *Operation Valkyrie* (Koch/History Channel, 2008); and *The Mona Lisa Myth* (GRB-TV, 2014), narrated by Morgan Freeman. His website is www.jpisbouts.org.